A CRITICAL GUIDE TO
INTELLECTUAL PROPERTY

A CRITICAL GUIDE TO INTELLECTUAL PROPERTY

Edited by Mat Callahan and Jim Rogers

ZED

A Critical Guide to Intellectual Property was first published in 2017
by Zed Books Ltd, The Foundry, 17 Oval Way, London SE11 5RR, UK.

www.zedbooks.net

Editorial Copyright © Mat Callahan and Jim Rogers 2017

Copyright in this Collection © Zed Books 2017

The rights of Mat Callahan and Jim Rogers to be identified as the editors
of this work has been asserted by them in accordance with the Copyright,
Designs and Patents Act, 1988

Typeset in Plantin and Kievit by Swales & Willis Ltd, Exeter, Devon
Index by ed.emery@thefreeuniversity.net
Cover design by Andrew Brash

A catalogue record for this book is available from the British Library

ISBN 978-1-78699-114-0 (hb)
ISBN 978-1-78699-113-3 (pb)
ISBN 978-1-78699-115-7 (pdf)
ISBN 978-1-78699-116-4 (epub)
ISBN 978-1-78699-117-1 (mobi)

MIX
Paper from
responsible sources
FSC   FSC® C013604
www.fsc.org

Printed and bound by CPI Group (UK) Ltd, Croydon, CR0 4YY

CONTENTS

ACKNOWLEDGMENTS

Earlier versions of "Running Through the Jungle, My Introduction to Intellectual Property," and "The Political Economy of Intellectual Property," first appeared in *Socialism and Democracy*, #64 (Volume 28, no. 1) March, 2014. See http://sdonline.org/back-issues/#64.

ABBREVIATIONS

A2K	Access to Knowledge
A2M	Access to Medicines
A&R	Artist and Repertoire
ABS	Access and Benefit Sharing
ACTA	Anti-Counterfeiting Trade Agreement
ANC	African National Congress
ASCAP	American Society for Composers, Authors and Publishers
ASKJustice	African Scholars for Knowledge Justice
AYUSH	Ministry of Ayurveda, Yoga and Naturopathy, Unani, Siddha and Homoeopathy (India)
BABS	Bioprospecting, Access and Benefit Sharing
BIRPI	United International Bureaux for the Protection of Intellectual Property
BMI	Broadcast Music Inc.
CBD	Convention on Biological Diversity
CFAA	Computer Fraud and Abuse Act (1986)
CIPO	Canadian Intellectual Property Office
CISAC	International Confederation of Authors and Composers Societies
CISPA	Cyber Intelligence Sharing and Protection Act
CSIR	Council of Scientific and Industrial Research (India)
DEA	Department of Environment Affairs (South Africa)
DMCA	Digital Millennium Copyright Act
DRM	Digital Rights Management
EFF	Electronic Frontiers Foundation
EOP	Executive Office of the President
FFF	Fight for the Future
FOSS	Free and Open Source Software
FOSSFA	Free and Open Source Foundation for Africa
FSF	Free Software Foundation
FWF	FairWild Foundation
FWS	FairWild Standard
GATT	General Agreement on Tariffs and Trade

GDP	Gross Domestic Product
GI	Geographical Indication
GIK	Ghanaian Indigenous Knowledge
GLAM	Galleries, Libraries, Archives and Museums
GPL	General Public License
GRs	Genetic Resources
ICESCR	International Covenant on Economic, Social and Cultural Rights
IDLO	International Development Law Organization
IEK	Indigenous Ecological Knowledge
IFPI	International Federation of Phonographic Industries
IGC	Intergovernmental Committee on Intellectual Property and Genetic Resources, Traditional Knowledge and Folklore (WIPO)
IK	Indigenous Knowledge (local or traditional)
INDECOPI	National Institute for the Defence of Free Competition and Protection of Intellectual Property (Peru)
IP	Intellectual Property
IPRs	Intellectual Property Rights
ISPs	Internet Service Providers
JSTOR	Journal Storage
JTB	Justified True Belief
KBD	Kaapse Bossiedokters (Cape Bush Doctors – South Africa)
LDC	Least Developed Countries
MAPs	Medicinal and Aromatic Plants
MDGs	Millennium Development Goals (United Nations)
MIT	Massachusetts Institute of Technology
MNCs	Multinational Corporations
MPAA	Motion Picture Association of America
NBA	National Biodiversity Authority (India)
NCAB	National Commission against Biopiracy (Peru)
NGO	Non-Governmental Organization
NHP	Natural Health Product
OA	Open Access
OER	Open Educational Resources
OPL	Open Content License
OSI	Open Source Initiative
PACs	Political Action Committees
PACER	Public Access to Court Electronic Records

PCT	Patent Cooperation Treaty (WIPO)
PDO	Protected Designation of Origin
PIPA	Protect Intellectual Property Act
PPI	Pirate Parties International
PRS	Performing Rights Society (PRS for Music)
RIAA	Recording Industry Association of America
ROARMAP	Registry of Open Access Repository Mandates and Policies
RPM	Revolutions Per Minute
SASA	South African Schools Act
SCBD	Secretariat of the Convention on Biological Diversity
SDGs	Sustainable Development Goals (United Nations)
SOPA	Stop Online Piracy Act
SSB	State Sustainability Board (India)
SUISA	SUISse Auteurs (Swiss co-operative society for authors and publishers)
TCEs	Traditional Cultural Expressions
TCO	Total Cost of Ownership
TEK	Traditional Ecological Knowledge
THMP	Traditional Herbal Medicinal Product
TK	Traditional Knowledge
TKDL	Traditional Knowledge Digital Library (India)
TMK	Traditional Medical Knowledge
TPP	Trans-Pacific Partnership
TRIPS	Trade Related Aspects of Intellectual Property Rights
TTIP	Transatlantic Trade and Investment Partnership
UEBT	Union for Ethical Bio-Trade
UN	United Nations
UNCTAD	United Nations Conference on Trade and Development
UNESCO	United Nations Educational, Scientific and Cultural Organization
UNIDO	United Nations Industrial Development Organization
USPTO	United States Patent and Trademark Office
USTR	United States Trade Representative
VSS	Voluntary Sustainability Standard
WHO	World Health Organization
WIPO	World Intellectual Property Organization
WSIS	World Summit on the Information Society
WTO	World Trade Organization

1 | WHY INTELLECTUAL PROPERTY? WHY NOW?

Mat Callahan and Jim Rogers

Introduction

Considering the grave dangers facing humanity today, it might appear that intellectual property (IP), though loudly controversial, is at best a tempest in a teapot, at worst a diversionary tactic designed to focus attention away from more serious issues. Compared to environmental disaster, deepening social inequality, rampant state surveillance and war without end, dispute over copyright, patent and trademark seems trivial. Though, in recent years, media attention has increasingly focused on digital piracy, genetically modified foods, the patenting of the human genome, and other IP-related matters of obvious importance, IP remains an enigma. That capitalism is in a crisis of epic proportions is beyond doubt. What role IP plays in this crisis, however, is anything but clear.

It must first be acknowledged that a great deal of legal obfuscation has to be cut through even to begin exploring the matter. IP has been above all shrouded in a fog of mystification precisely to keep out the rabble and protect the authority of lawyers. Yet laws are made and laws can be unmade, the underlying principle is justice, and justice is determined through political struggle, which is never confined to a courtroom. Indeed, the legal aspects of IP, while certainly worthy of informed debate, are by no means the most important in figuring out IP's place in current affairs. Far more relevant are the forces deployed on battlefields throughout the world.

First among these forces are of course the major industries dependent on IP for their profits. The most important are the pharmaceutical and agricultural industries in terms of patent and trademark, the film, music and publishing industries in terms of copyright. Most of the attention paid to IP has, until recently, been a result of these industries' propaganda efforts. Only in the last two decades has such propaganda been met and superseded by opposition from two other, sometimes separate, sometimes overlapping, areas, that is, social movements and "piracy."

Regarding social movements, these have formed in two distinct sectors which are, nevertheless, inseparable due to their emergence in response to the legal and political regimes organized by IP law and international treaty. These movements, furthermore, are responsible for making IP a radically different matter than was the intention of the holders of most intellectual property and their propagandists. Instead of an unimpeded privatization of knowledge and genetic resources, IP is now a focus of struggle demanding the attention of anyone concerned with changing the world.

Social movements

In the Global South, farmers and indigenous peoples, along with some governments, are waging an ongoing battle against the biggest food and pharmaceutical corporations in the world. A primary focus is the protection of "traditional knowledge and genetic resources," including cereal grains such as potatoes, corn and rice. What were in many cases the results of thousands of years of human ingenuity are now patented and turned into the private property of corporations in the Global North. This applies equally to medicinal plants, many of which have already appeared as trademarked and patented drugs in pharmacies everywhere. Another focus is on educational materials whose exorbitant costs are solely attributable to the extortionate royalties extracted by large publishing houses in the United States or Europe. What students in Rio de Janeiro must pay for the privilege of reading a chapter from a book is often prohibitive and has led to widespread disobedience followed by the inevitable police crackdowns made in the name of fighting piracy. These movements have exposed the fact that countries which only recently threw off the yoke of imperialism have been effectively recolonized by means of IP regimes. Membership in the World Trade Organization (WTO) depends on acceptance of treaties enshrining copyright, patent and trademark as they are applied in the United States or EU. In fact, the World Intellectual Property Organization (WIPO), an agency of the UN, administers 26 treaties to which all members of the UN are bound. That these treaties are based on IP laws designed in the first place to protect the merchants, manufacturers and financiers of Europe and the United States as they conquered the world seems to have been overlooked by the independence movements that at least nominally freed most of Asia, Africa and Latin American in the wake of World War II. Only socialist Cuba abolished IP (and has recently re-instituted it) but this is nowhere seriously considered. Now, popular resistance has forced both the practical application of and the philosophical justifications for IP regimes back onto the agenda.

In the Global North, what is known as the open access movement has sprung up, involving a large number and broad spectrum of people. Software programmers, journalists, scientists, artists, academics and civil libertarians have rallied to resist attempts by government and business to surveil and privately appropriate all exchanges of information taking place anywhere. Here the battle is joined along the lines of free speech, access to knowledge, sharing as a principle in education and creativity and against the intrusions of either government or business in the free association of people. It's latest manifestations have been, as is well known, the leaking of government secrets and the violently repressive measures undertaken by the US and European governments against Chelsea Manning, Julian Assange, Edward Snowden and many others. But the roots of this movement lie in the systematic effort to criminalize file-sharing which began in the San Francisco Bay Area where the enabling technology was first developed, escalating through the arrest of the founders of the Pirate Bay file-sharing website in Sweden, which led to the founding of the first Pirate Party and eventually the massive – and successful – resistance to various legislative attempts to codify sharing as piracy (SOPA, PIPA and ACTA). The death of Aaron Swartz was thus a signal and a turning point – a signal that open access is a matter of life and death and a turning point in that Swartz's Guerilla Open Access Manifesto has now explicitly linked the two sectors outlined above. Millions worldwide heard Swartz's call to make common cause between the movements in the Global North with those in the Global South.

Lest this brief overview be viewed as hyperbole or the exaggerations of an enthusiast, it must immediately be stressed that these social movements are characterized less by sustained organizational effort, than by episodic outbursts. With a few notable exceptions, they are not organizational at all, manifesting themselves instead in particular campaigns around particular issues as they arise. Sometimes these are legislative, for example, when particular laws or treaties are proposed, some are court cases involving law suits or criminal charges. Nowhere in any of these social movements is there, at present, a single, dominant discourse other than the most general calls for "fairness," "independence," "freedom" or recognition of the UN Charter of Human Rights as that document applies to indigenous communities and whistleblowers alike. While a healthy skepticism of "prevailing wisdom" about copyright or patent can be safely assumed, there is by no means a general critique of IP as such, let alone a call for its abolition. In the enormous and growing literature concerned with IP there is only a small, obscure section devoted to how the Soviet Union, China and Cuba legislated in regard to IP. Not only is this experience forgotten, it is not even known to have existed, even by many otherwise familiar with revolutionary struggle! Beyond these disclaimers is yet another: broadly speaking these movements are only potentially revolutionary. This is somewhat ironic since the subject of IP immediately exposes the foundation of bourgeois thought regarding the self, property and the state. The entire edifice of what philosopher C.B. MacPherson called "possessive individualism" is laid bare, its origins, made abundantly clear, not only in Hobbes and Locke but in the slave trade and conquest of territory.

Property is an outmoded concept

Property is an outmoded concept. It can no longer account for the most basic components of human being, genetically or intellectually. When information encoded in genes or digital files can be transmitted almost instantly to anyone anywhere in the known universe, it is beyond the capability of laws or police to prevent its dissemination. Indeed, the only inhibition that might prove effective is one that is self-imposed, by the consciousness of people acting in what they consider to be society's best interest. As radical as this assertion might at first appear to be, it is no more than the recognition of conditions as they presently exist. From recent Supreme Court rulings about the "natural" nature of the human genome to the suicide of Aaron Swartz, it is abundantly clear that limits have been reached, at which point private property as an idea, as an organizing principle or as a measurement of human freedom simply breaks down. What was the Supreme Court to do? Say that a corporation could own the human genome? What's next, the alphabet? The periodic table? This is not a matter of argument by *reductio ad absurdum*, either. What we are seeing is the incoherence of the reasoning by which bourgeois law justified property in the first place. That is, as a "product of nature." So it is "nature" that makes private property, and "nature" that takes it away. Meanwhile, there has been a low intensity civil war going on for the last 15 years. It involves millions of people – especially the young and educated – flagrantly disobeying the law and declaring those authorities charged with enforcing it illegitimate. Simultaneously, farmers and indigenous people throughout the world have risen in defiance not only of governments and corporations but against privatization as a way of thinking. From these two sites of conflict it is readily apparent that the greatest threat to IP regimes is the intellect interrogating property and finding the latter logically inconsistent and practically inoperable.

Politics and technology

It is worth recalling that much of what we are talking about when we say copyright, patent or trademark only became headline-grabbing news since the collapse of the Soviet Union. It may also be obvious that prior to the internet most discussion was confined to the business pages of the newspaper and scientific or business journals. But taken together, political upheaval and technological development has made IP a central focus, at least of those governmental and industry departments most concerned with information. Leaving aside the important questions surrounding WikiLeaks, Chelsea Manning, Edward Snowden and whistle blowing in general, the free flow of information, in whatever form, has undoubtedly been greatly facilitated by digital, fiber-optic and satellite technologies. At the same time the reactionary wave that began sweeping the world in the aftermath of the 1960s, especially since the major capitalist crisis of 1973, led to victories for neoliberalism which in turn led to the Great Crash of 2008. Under these conditions it is not merely the case that capitalists seek profit anywhere they can find it, hence their interest in IP. It is more fundamentally a question of how a global regime is constructed, especially the trade treaties and international agreements that dictate the flow of all goods and services, be they material or intellectual. Indeed, the threat many movements pose – be they indigenous people or young internet activists – is not primarily one of piracy or "theft" of the intellectual property of one corporation or another, rather, the threat is to the foundation of private property and the ownership of ideas as a conceptual framework for law or governance of any kind. In other words, within any and every conflict revolving around IP are the core principles of capitalism: possessive individualism, private appropriation of public wealth – especially natural resources – and the despoiling or destruction of the commons. Thus, what makes IP a vital battlefront for our time is that the stakes are capitalist enslavement or human liberation.

Outline of the book to follow

In Chapter 2, Mat Callahan advances his own "personal" introduction to intellectual property. Drawing initially upon years of experience as a musician, and his own accumulated knowledge of how the music industry works, he puts forward a variety of evidence which ultimately points to the conclusion that the copyright system is not only inherently unjust but cannot be reformed if the aim is delivering fair and equitable reward for musical creativity. After discussing and critiquing a range of reform initiatives from the mid-1990s onwards, the author argues that the copyright system must be abandoned in favor of an alternative approach to providing appropriate credit and compensation to musicians. Challenging the conventional notion of the composer and that music can actually be owned by any given individual, the chapter ultimately puts forward four fundamental principles around which to build a new model which would ensure that authors, composers and inventors receive fitting recompense and acknowledgment for their creative and artistic endeavors and contributions to culture and knowledge.

Beyond this, the bulk of the remainder of this book is divided into three broad thematic strands:

Section 1 comprises three chapters that combine to consider the historical context, and theoretical and conceptual origins of intellectual property rights, crucial to understanding and interpreting their form and nature in the contemporary environment, and fundamental to addressing more orthodox conceptualizations of IPRs in earlier scholarly works.

Section 2 contains four chapters in which the focus shifts to specific terrains of conflict where tensions between the "possessive individualism" that underpins and characterizes the approach of the IPR regime and the social/common good are playing out. Here, the domains of music, education, food production and technology are each in turn brought under a critical lens.

Section 3 offers three chapters that work to unpack and examine what intellectual property law actually is. Here, we consider commonalities and points of distinction between different national and international IP regimes, including treaties and policies of various bodies and jurisdictions.

In sum, these three aforementioned sections combine to offer not only critical appraisal of how copyrights, trademarks and patents have evolved across various dominions to affect and shape our lives, they offer as well a range of alternatives and proposals for reform in terms of the management and administration of knowledge, natural resources and culture.

A brief breakdown of the chapters contained in each section follows.

Section 1: Historical context and conceptual frameworks First, in Chapter 3, we see Colin Darch interrogate the reported history (or more accurately, *histories*) of intellectual property rights and their diffusion around the world, and emphasize the necessity for a more holistic approach and subtle critique in the examination and historical appraisal of IPRs. At the outset, this chapter points to some issues and problems around how we fundamentally conceive of IPRs. Primarily, that contemporary academic discourse on the topic is dominated by economists and legal scholars who pay little or no attention to copyrights, patent or trademarks in their historical context(s). Moreover, Darch points to how those histories that do exist essentially reflect global power inequalities, privileging local narratives, particularly the history of copyright in England and subsequently its local emergence in the United States. Taking such accounts to task, Darch proceeds to deconstruct what he recognizes as "an amorphous and scarcely articulated ragbag of legal and economic relationships" which are almost always portrayed as a single, coherent, teleological narrative of IP, driven by powerful economic interests, which boxes it almost exclusively as a legal concept. Emphasizing that such "universal" discourse is hindering our understanding of IPRs, the chapter proceeds to deconstruct this "nomothetic narrative," stressing the more complex and nuanced reality by outlining and critiquing the history and trajectory of proprietary rights (or their absence) in other knowledge traditions (e.g. various religious faiths, China and the Soviet Union). Ultimately (drawing upon Woodmansee, Hesse and other scholars in the field) the chapter moves to challenge contemporary myths regarding the centrality of property rights to creativity. In essence, Chapter 3 thus works to complicate and problematize more conventional understandings of how intellectual property has evolved and is understood.

The political economy of intellectual property is unpacked in Chapter 4. Here, as Michael Perelman illustrates, fundamental contradictions in how the market operates (e.g. markets lead to monopolies and the absence of competition) mean that conventional economics does not provide the tools for an adequate analysis and understanding of IPRs. Focusing on the realm of patents, the chapter illustrates how periods of economic stagnation and intensified flux may be characterized by processes of reconfiguring and restructuring of capital which have promoted fundamental expansions in the scope of IPRs. As such, Perelman argues, we should regard IPRs as an "expression of the failure of the market." Moreover, he demonstrates how the extended arm of patent (and other IP) law carries with it significant drawbacks or costs which ultimately curb innovation in science, technology and other fields as well as carrying onerous financial costs for both private companies and the public purse arising from legal actions in the domain.

In Chapter 5, Mat Callahan critically unpacks the theoretical roots and conceptual origins of "ownership" and in doing so provides a very important analytical lens that can be applied to offer a fresh and original dimension to the history and evolution of intellectual property itself. This chapter sets out the ontology of ownership, and the moves to highlight and address the misappropriation of philosophy as a discipline in intellectual property discourse and the future of current ideas of private property. In achieving this, the chapter pursues a number of key objectives, including an informed and comprehensive unfurling of the theory of "possessive individualism" where Macpherson's dilemma is comprehensively exposed and critiqued; likewise with Locke, on the ownership of self, other people and ideas, and Hegel's "personality justification" of intellectual property. Ultimately the concept of "sharing" is explored as fundamental to the formation of human consciousness, as to emphasize how philosophy, as a discipline, *must* be opposed to the ownership of ideas, and their expressions. As such, drawing upon a vast range of sources and evidence, this chapter raises numerous fundamental questions that challenge the "common sense" conventional wisdom regarding the concept of ownership per se.

Section 2: Terrains of conflict and terms of engagement In Chapter 6, which opens this section of the book, Josef Brinckmann critiques developments around traditional knowledge, and the necessity to shield such forms of knowledge – in the case at hand, fundamental to health and food security – from the reach of the intellectual property rights regime. Here, Brinckmann examines the commercialization and globalization of traditional botanical foods and medicines in the context of traditional knowledge (TK) that informs ecological sustainability with regard to the harvesting, use and trade of medicinal and aromatic plants. Brinckmann delivers an account of the ongoing commodification of these domains, and associated detrimental implications for the sharing of specific forms of traditional knowledge which the author argues have been fundamental to enabling food and health security, new drug discoveries and preventing ecosystem collapse. His chapter is fundamentally structured around the qualitative evaluation of specific actions in the South American and Indian contexts. Drawing upon case studies from Peru (where Brinckmann details and examines the National Commission Against Biopiracy) and India (where he focuses on the Traditional Knowledge Digital Library) we are introduced to projects designed to protect traditional knowledge fundamental to health and food security. In doing so, the author advances the case for keeping such traditional knowledge outside the IP system. As such, Brinckmann shows how such initiatives are representative of particular types of property protection regimes that differ fundamentally from the orthodox Western conception of individual property ownership.

The Access to Knowledge (A2K) movement comes under the spotlight in the Chapter 7. Here, Caroline B. Ncube makes a case for a public-interest- and human-rights-based approach to copyright in the South African context. Opening with a critical discussion of the public interest in copyright and education, with reference to the rights to education, culture and science, the chapter moves to address how such an approach to copyright administration bolsters arguments and proposals that have been put forward in relation to access to knowledge for schools, libraries and archives. In doing so, Ncube critiques and unpacks the concept of knowledge in the context of A2K discourse, examining patterns and processes of production and consumption which show how most copyright-protected knowledge emanates from the Global North, with primacy afforded to specific types of knowledge. She then proceeds to offer an historical overview of the A2K movement, its activities and its discourse(s) before addressing the access concerns of schools, libraries and archives in South Africa, and examining key proposals for copyright reform in this area. As such, Chapter 7 ultimately sets out what is *actually* happening in particular domains of the education sector where intellectual property serves to regulate knowledge and hinder the rights of citizens per se to freely engage in ideas and with cultural life.

In Chapter 8 Jim Rogers deals with the recent trends in the global music industry. With innovations in the realm of digital technologies commonly perceived to be undermining the economics of the music industry and resulting in a significant decline in revenues for major labels, copyright is often considered unenforceable in this context. However, drawing upon recent empirical-level studies based out of Ireland, this chapter illustrates how the music industry is characterized by a range of different activities which allow for better control of the realization of economic value from their access and consumption by users. Copyright and trademark, the legal mechanisms that enable music texts and brands to be monetized, have assumed a more central role, and recent decades have seen the major music rights owners successfully lobby for stricter IPR protections. As such, this chapter demonstrates how, as music companies generate greater revenue opportunities through the licensing of their content (in multitudinous forms) across not only new and traditional media alike, but also by colonizing an increasing variety of spaces in our social world, they have fundamentally reconfigured their core structures as to enable them to exploit the intellectual property they control more fully. The chapter proceeds to argue that the ramifications arising from such developments are significant and multi-fold for artists and consumers alike, and the polarization of wealth that is occurring in the industry (despite the extant arguments regarding disruptive technologies) is consistent with some of the most rabid features of neoliberal policy. Moreover, these developments carry significant consequences for the social function of music per se, and how, as listeners, we use and respond to music in our everyday lives.

Chapter 9 brings us into the territory of the open source software and free software movements. Here, Paul McKimmy provides a comprehensive and critical overview of key developments across this broad area, and his chapter also serves as a useful and engaging critique of both domains. The chapter offers some historical context to both of these movements, outlining the core values and characteristics that define free software and open source, and importantly, clarifying how they differ (as they are often conflated/confused with one another). Following a comprehensive analysis of Richard Stallman's GNU project and the evolution of "copyleft," McKimmy chronicles the emergence of a number of "opposition" movements such as the Open Content Project, the Creative Commons and Free Cultural Works, and latterly a synopsis of the roles and preoccupations of the Electronic Frontiers Foundation and the Pirate Party. Subsequently, McKimmy provides an overview of the Aaron Swartz case. Considering these various voices and agendas placed against the backdrop of ongoing international trade agreements that, in privileging corporate interests, carry significant IP restrictions, the chapter highlights fundamental tensions between IP stalwarts and opposition activists and ultimately moves to offer a series of proposals for reform in terms of balancing the public good against private interests. Moreover, this chapter concludes with a coda written by Bob Jolliffe in which he briefly highlights and problematizes three core "radical" claims that can be made in relation to FOSS.

Section 3: Law, policy and jurisdiction In the opening chapter of this section, Debora J. Halbert urges a fundamental rethinking of the World Intellectual Property Organization (WIPO), revising its core functions and reforming the form and nature of its roles and practices in partnership with a range of other United Nations organizations. The chapter first takes us through an historical trajectory of the organization from the political maneuverings and interplay between UN organizations in the 1960s which saw it evolve out of the United International Bureau for the Protection of Intellectual Property (BIRPI) and become established as the foremost UN agency for dealing with intellectual property issues. Halbert then proceeds to cast a critical eye on WIPO's more recent evolution, chronicling its decreasing influence in the context of the World Trade Organization (WTO) and the Trade Related Aspects of Intellectual Property Rights (TRIPS) Agreement which came into effect in the mid-1990s. With TRIPS raising significant concerns around the impact of the global harmonization of the protection of intellectual property on developing world countries, the new millennium has, as Halbert illustrates, produced the opportunity to reconfigure and reform WIPO and its position on intellectual property. While WIPO's approach remains unchanged, the chapter ultimately and innovatively considers what the organization *could* become. It proposes an alluring vision of how WIPO could reshape itself as to fruitfully engage with its sister UN institutions (here, Halbert takes UNESCO, WHO, UNIDO and UNCTAD in turn), enhance their performance in aiding development and help them better deliver on their professed goals. As such, the chapter takes a critical lens to the evolution of WIPO, its present purpose and practices, and points to a range of possibilities for its future.

In Chapter 11, we see Blayne Haggart address the question: "what is intellectual property?" Focusing primarily on the US context, the author begins by offering the reader two guidelines for a useful discussion around the uses, scope and limitations of intellectual property law. As such, this chapter initially argues that while intellectual property law's core stated purpose (i.e. to incentivize creativity and the generation of knowledge) is easily understood, it is, in effect, difficult to achieve arising from the nature of knowledge itself, and power relations in society. Then, with the proviso that there is a dearth of evidence-based empirical research to support the contention that intellectual property law actually fulfills its professed purpose, the chapter moves to demonstrate how the field of economics provides the most useful approach to understanding the society-wide effects of IP. Haggart proceeds to demonstrate that the form and nature of the current IPR regime is, in effect, the outcome of struggles and interplay between powerful interests (e.g. pharmaceutical and other IP industries) which have served to expand and extend the reach of IP control mechanisms on a global scale. The chapter then demonstrates how a focus on intellectual property's social dimension and its effect on knowledge creation and dissemination can be used to think through controversial IP issues, using the case of Aaron Swartz's prosecution for hacking the JSTOR academic journal article database at MIT as an example. It concludes by using the two aforementioned guidelines to propose an empirical, results-focused approach to intellectual property debates that emphasizes first principles as a way for us to cut through the legal thicket and moral arguments, and to engage in a productive dialogue on how to reform the laws that govern something as fundamental as knowledge itself.

Chapter 12 serves to foreground the concept of piracy and proceeds to probe and critique it. How do we understand piracy, and why has it re-emerged to assume such significance in the politics of intellectual property? In this section, Mat Callahan suggests we examine and address this question through five critical lenses which afford us distinctive insights and combine to help us arrive at a more thorough and holistic understanding of the concept of the "pirate" in the contemporary environment. Initially, the chapter will consider the idea of moral panic to explain how the concept of piracy was introduced into the debate in the wake of the Napster case at the turn of the century. Next, Callahan will briefly reflect upon the legal definition of piracy and outline how the term has been re-conceptualized as to result in the conflation of terms (piracy) against their statutory (law of the sea) usage and the coincidence of maritime piracy and "file-sharing" as concurrent "crises." Then the section will move to question whether piracy can simply be understood in terms of a "black market" economy, characterized by unlicensed copying and distribution practices. Subsequently, Callahan suggests that we also need to consider piracy in the context of popular resistance, before, finally, moving to raise essential questions around freedom, creativity and the commons.

Finally, in Chapter 13, the editors reflect upon the various contributions and case studies from around the globe that constitute this volume, and offer some concluding thoughts.

2 | RUNNING THROUGH THE JUNGLE[1]

My introduction to intellectual property

Mat Callahan

Before beginning our investigation of Intellectual Property, some personal experience might shed light on certain perplexing questions that arise whenever the subject is broached. I am a musician, a composer and an author, a typical example of one whom the copyright system was purportedly created to serve. Indeed, I derive a small but significant portion of my annual income from royalties collected for songs I've written. This money comes mainly from fees paid by radio stations and is collected and disbursed by SUISA, the Swiss organization devoted to this task (there are similar such collection societies in most countries. In the United States two are dominant: ASCAP and BMI). Upon becoming a full-time musician, I encountered copyright more as something you had to do than as a legal concept. Songs needed to be registered, membership in a collection society secured, etc., but I accepted without question that copyright somehow helped me, even if it wasn't clear how. Until 2005, I viewed copyright in the manner one might view a driver's license: a commonsense measure accepted by everyone as necessary to sharing the road. But when I submitted what I thought was the completed manuscript of my book, *The Trouble with Music*, my publisher insisted I was not finished until I had written a chapter on internet file-sharing and its effects on music, music-makers and the listening public. Internet file-sharing had, in the five years between 1999 and 2005, become such a hot topic that no one interested in music could possibly be unaware of the controversy or not have strong opinions on one side or the other of a sharp divide.

This divide opened with the *Napster vs. Metallica* case, in which a world-renowned rock band brought a lawsuit against a trio of college students who'd written computer software that enabled the sharing of music stored in computer files. Shawn Fanning graced the cover of *Time* magazine with a tagline reading: "How Shawn Fanning, 19, upended music . . . and a whole lot more." Upon discovering that an unreleased song of theirs was circulating widely via Napster's peer-to-peer network, Metallica filed suit for copyright infringement. This was followed by drummer Lars Ulrich appearing in print and broadcast media decrying the theft of Metallica's music. The battle was on.

I was then living in the San Francisco Bay Area, home of Silicon Valley and Metallica, and the issue was impossible to avoid. Like many, I was both amused and bemused by the position a band with a vaguely anti-authoritarian reputation took toward Napster at the time. I found it strange that these guys who were by then very wealthy rock stars would position themselves as cops cracking down on their fans who were simply exchanging their favorite songs in the manner previously done with cassette tapes and vinyl records. Bootlegs have long been a staple of record collections, the mark of a dedicated fan. Bob Dylan and the Grateful Dead were famous for them. Besides, what could be more natural than sharing music? Everybody does it. It's what makes the world go round.

Knowing this, however, only made me less interested in devoting a chapter of my book to it. On the one hand, I knew it would take an enormous amount of research into law and history if I were to contribute anything useful to serious debate. On the other hand, I wasn't sure serious debate was even possible given the moral panic being spread by industry mouthpieces like the Recording Industry Association of America (RIAA). Indeed, I wasn't at first convinced there was anything novel about this hullaballoo at all. I'd already been involved in other, pre-internet, cases such as Negativland's battle with U2 and the first confrontations between music publishers and rap artists "sampling."[2] In fact, all my dealings with publishers, record companies, managers and booking agents, indicated this was just another ploy. I knew that ripping off musicians, especially songwriters, was as old as the business in music itself and that the people responsible were not the public but the publishers and record companies who made great fortunes while musicians remained poor.

But I could not ignore the fact that virtually everyone was talking about this. Moral panic or not, the RIAA had intensified its campaign of vilification and harassment, specifically targeting teenage "pirates" for prosecution and enlisting the support of musicians for Gestapo-like intrusions into private homes. The criminalization of file-sharing was an escalation more sinister than the original civil litigation brought by Metallica against Napster, as obnoxious as that was. Confronting us was nothing less than an attack on civil liberties, and to "defend" my copyright I was being asked to join a lynch mob! In this combative atmosphere I nonetheless sought to keep an open mind and learn something about law, the internet and the practical workings of copyright. What I discovered made me an abolitionist.

I did not start out with abolition in mind, yet logic and evidence convinced me that the copyright system is fundamentally unjust, cannot be reformed, and must be eliminated to make way for a new approach to the real problems confronting musicians, namely, credit and just compensation.

Now credit and just compensation are a subject in themselves to be explored later on, but from the outset a crucial distinction must be made: credit and just compensation are not equivalent to ownership. Contrary to what we have been led to believe, the conflict over copyright and IP in general is not about creativity, freedom of expression, innovation or progress; it is about ownership and collecting rent for something that ultimately belongs to everyone. It is about the "I" who privately appropriates a thought and is opposed to the "we" that shares that thought, and indeed makes thought possible. At the most basic level this clashes violently with the practices necessary to music making, a point to which we'll return.

My research began by consulting people who had experience negotiating contracts to unravel the mysteries surrounding applicable law and prevailing industry practices. I wanted to establish the extent to which contracts and court decisions conform or do not conform with the ostensible purposes of copyright, namely the protection and reward of the author or composer. Comparing, for example, the relative power of publishers, record companies and artists, one finds a structural inequality belying the claim that copyright "protects" the composer or musician. The methods for calculating royalties, recoupment costs and the burden of risk bear scant resemblance to the claim that copyright rewards creativity. Furthermore, "industry practices" were all established in the United States in the early years of the twentieth century and have remained fundamentally unchanged ever since, in spite of social and technological changes. The copyright act of 1909, supplemented by a Supreme Court decision in 1917, effectively granted state sanction to the publishers and record companies who control the music industry. Though this underwent an important modification in 1976, this modification only increased inequalities built into the original system. To better understand how this worked throughout the twentieth century and well into the twenty-first, I will summarize the information given to me by world-renowned record producer and manager, David Rubinson. With the advent of the internet some of these practices and corresponding laws have been modified but their exploitative nature remains fundamentally unchanged.

The record deal: standard industry practice in the twentieth century

1. All recording and publishing/songwriter contracts were Personal Services agreements and companies based their agreements on this model.
2. All contracts were exclusive, meaning:

   a) The company owned the exclusive rights to the services rendered by the artist.
   b) While the company could not force the artist to perform, it could prevent and enjoin the artist from performing services for others. Thus, control over the rights to the artist's works and/or performance rested with the entity (record company or publisher).

3. All contracts were based on a formula derived from the era of printed sheet music (music "publishing") and the first 78 rpm records (1900s), when recorded performance was quantified in terms of a printed sheet of music, or recorded "sides," as in one side of a shellac (later vinyl) platter or record. Records were usually packaged and sold in sets ("albums"), with a cardboard outer cover and paper sleeves for each of the platters. The definition of services was given as a minimum number of sides, and later "albums," that the performer was contracted to provide.
4. All contracts paid the artist a royalty based on the retail price of the sides or albums *minus* the packaging costs, breakage (78 rpm sides were fragile), and returns of unsold merchandise. *All recording costs* and many marketing expenses were also recouped

by the record company *prior* to the artist receiving any royalty payments on sales.

5. In record company accounting, for purposes of recoupment of all of these costs, all contracts computed an "artist" royalty rate (usually between 3 and 10 percent of retail price). It was from that "artist's" royalty alone that the artist recouped the costs of recording and packaging. This is a crucial point because 100 percent of the money received from record sales went to the record company whereas only 3–10 percent was credited to the artist for recoupment of costs.

Hypothetically, John Artist might be entitled to a 10 percent royalty rate which might amount to approximately $1.00 per record sold at $10.00 retail. Given recording costs of $100,000.00 – and 100,000 records sold – since John only recouped the costs at his $1.00 per record "artist" royalty rate – not the $10.00 per record the record company was earning – the record company would recoup all of its costs at 10,000 records sold (100,000 sales multiplied by $10.00 per record) but John would not recoup until 100,000 records were sold (100,000 sales multiplied by $1.00 per record). This meant that the record company received income on 90,000 records sold while paying John nothing. In general, a vast number of record contracts were "unearned," meaning that costs were *unrecouped* at the artists' royalty rate.

General comment: this was and remains a plantation system. Recording artists were and are equivalent to sharecroppers or slaves. Ownership of capital and control of the channels of marketing and distribution enable the record and publishing companies to compel the artist to hand over the lion's share of the goods/services he/she produces (in this case composition and performance) in order to be able to produce their work, to continue producing and to have any access to distribution. This is not fundamentally different from cotton or tobacco, gold or copper or any other industrialized crop except that in order to sell the musical composition and/or performance, notoriety has to be created for the artist (as a brand or trademark) thereby increasing demand in the marketplace. The result is that with rare exceptions, musicians have usually derived the greatest portion of their income from live performance fees, not from recordings, augmented by songwriter royalties from the licensed use of their copyrighted works (fees paid by radio, filmmakers or advertisers). Furthermore, other participants in the system such as managers, agents, accountants and attorneys derived their percentages and fees from the *gross* earnings of the artist, before expenses. The plantation analogy held for virtually every aspect of the music business until the recent breakdown of the monopoly that came with the growth of the internet, and the advent of cheap, high-quality home recording.

What's important to add to this very general summation is that this plantation system was and is particularly exploitative of black musicians and composers. Notorious examples are the treatment of Bo Diddley and Bob Marley, and such examples abound.[3] This is not to say that most white musicians were ever much better off. But the American music industry was built on slavery, Jim Crow, and the perpetuation of racism. (The term Jim Crow comes from the title of a song, "Jump Jim Crow," written and made popular by blackface performer, T.D. Rice. For over a century, minstrel shows, coon songs and degrading images of black people were indispensable elements of American popular entertainment generally, but especially music.) This was nonetheless a recognition of the profound social effect black music in its own right produced.

No one could deny the deep reservoir of emotion, virtuosity, stylistic variation and originality of the music made by slaves and their descendants. Nor could any deny the moral authority of the people making it. They didn't ask to come to America. They didn't ask to be slaves. And yet they lifted their voices and sang with an eloquence and conviction that was the envy of their masters. By the time ragtime hit, black music was by any measure the most influential and uniquely "American" of all cultural expressions emanating from the western hemisphere.

How the music business perpetuated segregation and the division of American society even as it sought to profit from black music is a story too lengthy to tell here. As regards copyright, however, the fact that countless numbers of compositions from countless numbers of composers were never "protected" or "incentivized" by copyright is impossible to overlook. This experience alone would cast doubt on any claims to fairness or balance in the practical application of copyright law. A far more relevant question to be asked is why did copyright need to be justified in terms of serving the public good and protecting the humble composer, and how did it manage to convince so many that it was effective in achieving these noble aims?

Music, technology, legislation and revenue-generation

There are complex philosophical, legal and political explanations that deserve close examination. For this introduction, however, I'll confine myself to one that bears most heavily on present disputes regarding music. That is, the relation of copyright to the phonograph and the radio, or more generally, technological evolution. What is happening now with the internet, with computers and various gadgets such as the iPod or other digital devices for storing and playing music, is based on a business model established more than 100 years ago. Indeed, what we see now, almost 20 years after the Napster case, is that much of what is called "revolutionary," "innovative," "visionary," etc. is nothing of the sort. Quite the contrary, what Apple and other gadget makers have done is to replicate – to copy – the successes of Emile Berliner and the Victor Talking Machine Company, with the phonograph, Edwin Armstrong and the Westinghouse Company, with the radio. Steve Jobs's entire strategy was "borrowed" from his predecessors, especially the deals with publishers and record companies to allow Apple to use millions of songs to sell iTunes, the iPod and all the gadgets that enable playing them. Here lies the great hypocrisy at the root of today's clamor to "protect" musicians. The real motive is twofold: to sell gadgets just as phonographs and radio sets were sold, and to dominate the internet in the same manner the airwaves were dominated before. Music is thus given away as a means of attracting customers. It is by and large paid for as an advertising cost and has nothing to do with creativity in the sense normally applied to art. Because music is an expense and one paid for by the manufacturer of a device or service, should it fail to attract paying customers it will be consigned to oblivion. Experiment is, by definition, forbidden. Only conformity is rewarded. Against this backdrop we get a glimpse of not only the ulterior motive, but the reasons the public must be led to believe that "we're all in this together," that "what's good for business is good for America" and so on. The guiding principle is mobilization of the masses to, on the one hand, support certain legislation and, on the other, consume the products sold to them, which in turn requires creating the impression that all these giant corporations do is facilitate. They don't rob and plunder; they *help*.

Some still argue that these circumstances make it even more important to defend copyright to ensure that musicians get some small share of all the revenues being generated. But this overlooks what is happening in fact and in principle. In fact, owning a copyright has no value in and of itself. If no one will pay money for your song, what difference does owning its copyright make? In fact, musicians are not being compensated proportionately to the billions in profits generated, nor could they be, since the vast majority of revenue-generating copyrights are held by a few giant corporations. Yes, I still may get a small portion of the taxpayers' money that subsidizes the broadcast of music in Switzerland (as long as the programmers choose to play my songs, that is), just as I might get a small portion of advertisers' money spent on privately owned radio in America. But the inequality is so vast as to render the comparisons ludicrous. And this, in principle, is the real purpose copyright was designed to serve.

A recent study carried out by researchers at Northwestern University School of Law confirms this, challenging common assumptions concerning the protections and incentives musicians supposedly derive from copyright.[4] The survey's author, Peter DiCola, states in his abstract:

For most musicians, copyright does not provide much of a direct financial reward for what they are producing currently. The survey findings are instead consistent with a winner-take-all or superstar model in which copyright motivates musicians through the promise of large rewards in the future in the rare event of wide popularity. This conclusion is not unfamiliar, but this article is the first to support it with empirical evidence on musicians' revenue.

Another survey result was perhaps unexpected but raises more troubling questions. Simply seeking data, the researchers confronted this anomaly:

Amazingly, given the level of attention that policy makers, scholars, and journalists give to copyright policy, the incentive theory has received little empirical study. Each side offers anecdotes but no data . . . Copyright advocates have trouble convincing the public of the need to strengthen copyright or even the whole copyright system's legitimacy. Meanwhile, copyright critics leave many commentators with sensible doubts about the wisdom of weakening or eliminating copyright. For these reasons, James Boyle has dubbed copyright policy, along with the other fields of intellectual property law, an "evidence-free zone."[5]

This observation, however, takes caution to an extreme. Considering that the copyright act dates from 1909, one has to wonder why it has taken so long to gather such data!

Attempts at reform

Perhaps answers to that question can be found by examining another dimension of the problem. At least since the mid-1990s, legal scholars have debated various measures to reform copyright in light of rapidly evolving digital technologies. Computers, the internet, the World Wide Web, and the proliferation of programs designed to use these technologies were already threatening to make copyright obsolete even before the Napster case. Lawrence Lessig at Stanford and James Boyle at Duke University penned provocative essays that commanded attention far beyond the halls of academe. Lessig's "The Architecture of Innovation" and Boyle's "The Second Enclosure Movement and the Construction of the Public Domain," pointed out the inadequacy of current copyright law and, more importantly, the inflexible attitude of the industries – namely publishing, music and film – that depended on copyright law for their profitability. Lessig's proposal was the Creative Commons license, which in no way undermines copyright but does seek to define and make legally binding the wishes of authors as to attribution and use of their works. Boyle's main effort has been directed toward a return to what he sees as the original spirit of copyright law. This meant a strictly limited monopoly, for a short time, after which copyrighted work would enter the public domain. Boyle took his argument further by attacking enclosure, making explicit the parallels with the enclosure of land that eliminated the commons in most of Europe by the mid-nineteenth century, leading to pauperization of the peasantry, and arguing that this was being repeated in the age of the internet with similarly dire effects.

Needless to say, these efforts have failed to produce the desired reforms. Their principal virtue has been to identify the logical and legal extent of the problem, revealing how the justifications made for copyright are flimsy at best, fraudulent at worst. Boyle's and Lessig's work has furthermore brought attention to the commons as both conceptual and physical space. This has undoubtedly given encouragement to organizations such as the Electronic Frontiers Foundation (EFF), Demand Progress and a host of other groups gathered loosely in occupations and institutions whose principal activity is online. Numerous campaigns have led to small but important victories which have nonetheless failed to stop the juggernaut of IP. Years of valiant effort have, in fact, led many activists to the conclusion that in order to overcome such a vast apparatus as IP, we need to get to the root of the problem. And this exposes the inherent shortcomings of reform.

Reform is, after all, meant to serve an existing system, not to substantially change it. Thus, almost 20 years after Napster, it has become abundantly clear that reform of this system is only desirable to those benefiting from it, and those benefiting from it are not the great majority of authors, composers, inventors or the public at large. The real beneficiaries are the same small group of publishers, manufacturers and financiers who established copyright (and IP generally) in the first place. Some people said so from the very beginning. John Perry Barlow, lyricist with the Grateful Dead and co-founder of EFF, published his famous "Declaration of the Independence of Cyberspace" in 1996. Barlow argued that government and industry were not only oppressive but effectively obsolete, "Your legal concepts of property, expression, identity, movement, and context do not apply to us." Instead, such concepts only serve to reveal that "increasingly obsolete information industries would perpetuate themselves by proposing laws, in America and elsewhere, that claim to own speech itself throughout the world. These laws would declare ideas to be another industrial product, no more noble than pig iron." To such tyranny one could only respond in the manner revolutionaries so often have:

> These increasingly hostile and colonial measures place us in
> the same position as those previous lovers of freedom and
> self-determination who had to reject the authorities of distant,
> uninformed powers. We must declare our virtual selves immune
> to your sovereignty . . . We will spread ourselves across the

Planet so that no one can arrest our thoughts. We will create a civilization of the Mind in Cyberspace. May it be more humane and fair than the world your governments have made before.[6]

Utopian as such rhetoric undoubtedly is, it nonetheless offers a stinging rebuke to those who seek to limit discussion to the comfortable boundaries set by none other than the copyright industry itself. Questions which have hitherto been shrouded in mystery or silenced by a *Denkverbot* – the prohibition of thought – can now be seriously posed and widely discussed.

There ain't no "I" if there ain't no "we"

Music cannot exist without a "we" to make it and experience it. Its fundamental premise is sharing and not possession. (Paradoxically, this is precisely the reason it is coveted by the privatizers. Were it not for music's social force, it would have no use as a commodity. But turned into a commodity it loses its social force – as is evident in the degradation of music and musician alike in today's neoliberal environment. What place has love in a whorehouse?) Except as a pure concept, which cannot in any case be copyrighted, actual music exists as sound transmitted by the air. Instructions for its performance may be stored in various mediums from paper to computer file, but it only becomes music when it disturbs the air in the proximity of human eardrums. (Of course, one can read music and imagine the sound it will make, but this is simply the memory replaying previously heard sounds in the mind of a trained reader/listener.) Even more fundamentally, music is an activity. It is made by people for diverse purposes, including the simple pleasure of making it, but every purpose is ultimately social in nature.

The presumption that the individual composer is the source of music, or at least our best music, has no foundation; it is a fable constructed to make copyrights generate revenue. It is no surprise that "the composer" was born with the first copyrights and patents and develops in accordance with the rise of the bourgeoisie in Europe. The composer as a revered and privileged figure (a "star") did not exist until after the French Revolution, in fact not until well into the nineteenth century. Previously, musicians were attached to aristocrats or the Church as employees or servants. There was little reverence and less privilege even for giants such as Bach (famous in his day, not for composition, but for his extraordinary ability to improvise!). Indeed, if the origin of the composer (or "author" or "artist") as a legal category and not merely a vocation is critically and comprehensively appraised, one can see that it has been a mixed blessing. For all the wonderful music that has been produced there has been a high price not only in the poverty of most composers but in the destitution of traditional or folk forms of music. The composer's rise to dominance is mirrored by the decline of popular participation in the music-making process. This is evident if one looks at how prevalent pianos, guitars, banjos and other instruments were in the homes of people – even poor people – less than 100 years ago. Music was until very recently something that most people *did* – at home, at church, at union meetings and social gatherings of all kinds. That this is no longer the case is considered progress by defenders of copyright and purveyors of "music players." (The only parties interested in people playing music are musical instrument manufacturers – a subject beyond the scope of this introduction, but analysis of which supports my argument.[7])

The point here can be summarized thus: the premises upon which legal authorship are based sharply contrast with the processes by which music physically and intellectually enters and exits the world. Indeed, I would argue that there is no composer in the abstract form we're accustomed to idolize (and which is enshrined in law). Of course, there are real composers who devote enormous energy, time and skill to produce wonderful pieces of music. But that does not mean they aren't deeply indebted and indissolubly bound to a wide range of social actors including teachers, other musicians, traditional sources as well as their audiences. Furthermore, composition of a piece of music does not make ownership of it a natural and inevitable consequence. This may be obvious given the vast number of compositions in the public domain. But even if that were not the case, there are practical obstacles to attaching the concept of "ownership" to music. Certainly I can say, "This is my song, I wrote it." But a sudden transformation takes place when I ask an audience to listen to my song. The audience, I hope, will give me its attention in hopes of gaining something in exchange. I then give the music to the audience and, in so doing, dispossess myself of exclusive knowledge or experience of this music. This is called sharing. And parents and teachers routinely socialize children precisely through sharing. It takes great feats of intellectual gymnastics to establish ownership over something everyone possesses. Once we've heard it, is it not ours? How are we to divest ourselves of the experience and the knowledge of this music? It is ours whether we like it or not. Besides, as John Perry Barlow put it in another of his famous pieces, "Napster.com and the Death of the Music Industry," "Whatever the current legalities, I personally find defining 'my' songs to be a form of property to be as philosophically audacious and as impractical as would be a claim that I own 'my' daughters, another blessing that just happened to pass into the world through me."[8]

Credit and just compensation

What happens if IP is abolished? What measures can be taken to insure that authors, composers and inventors are given the credit and compensation due them for their labor, their skill and their ingenuity? While this is a subject large enough for book-length exposition, I shall here provide a brief outline of how a different system could work.

Four principles guide my thinking:

1. The public must support the arts in general and music in particular.
2. Support must include money for musicians and composers.
3. Credit must be accurately assigned, but that must include every contributor to a musical composition or performance, not only the titular "composer."
4. Music is free.

The first two of these principles are already in use, albeit in a very limited sphere, namely, classical music (and in Europe, jazz). Public funding and the donations of rich patrons are what keep symphony halls, opera houses, orchestras and facilities for recording this music from disappearing. Certain sectors of society deem our "cultural legacy" worthy of defense from the vicissitudes of the market. This is a tacit admission that, without such subsidization, it is highly unlikely that classical music could survive, at least on the scale or with the status it now enjoys. Yet, if all music were subsidized in a similar manner it would immediately solve the problem of compensation because musicians would be compensated in a manner similar to those of symphony orchestras today. Who qualifies for compensation will undoubtedly be a bone of contention, but here again, there are many institutions that already make such decisions, from music schools to juries awarding grants and so on. Undertaking this task will, moreover, be a public responsibility shared by all and not the personal risk of isolated musicians. Impoverished as they may be under today's neoliberal regimes, public administration of education, recreation and celebration still provides alternatives to the music industry. Public libraries are exemplary in their emphasis on lending and borrowing – as opposed to stockpiling or hoarding – a public good. What is clear is that the market is not the best, let alone the only, way compensation can be made for the labor, skill and ingenuity of musicians.

As for the question of credit, everyone contributing to a composition or performance should be acknowledged. The tambourine player who comes up with a distinct pattern in the opening bars of a popular recording deserves to be credited for her/his creativity as well as the execution of his/her part in the ensemble's performance. The guitarist who comes up with a distinct lick that identifies a new version of an old folk song should be acknowledged as a contributor to a composition not only as a guitarist. An endless list could easily be compiled revealing the distortions created by copyright's insistence on there being an individual author to whom ownership can be assigned. None of this will matter much, however, when people are no longer fighting for rank in the pecking order. No doubt, some will contribute more than others to specific forms and innovations that go on to be the most influential. This should be duly noted by all concerned, and I, for one, have faith in the basic honesty of people who love music and wish to honor the outstanding contributions of certain individuals. But what matters most is that credit will be awarded freely and fairly based not on criteria of ownership but on actual effort and musical effect.

Finally, music is free. Free because it's ours. Once we recognize that the people pay for everything anyway, it is no greater burden to be, on the one hand, supporting music-makers and, on the other, freely exchanging the resulting compositions and performances. It is self-evident that as taxpayers or consumers, the "masses" or the general public pay for everything. It is only the publishers, record companies and other "middle men" who will lose in the new arrangement, since it is the share they appropriate from what the public pays that constitutes their profit. This is an enormous waste of resources and such waste will be eliminated. Imagine how much more could be devoted to supporting the arts and the artist when all the exorbitant fees and rents presently filling the coffers of non-productive parasites are instead directed to their rightful place.

Notes

1 *Run through the Jungle* is a song composed by John Fogerty, recorded and released by his group, Creedence Clearwater Revival, in 1970. Saul Zaentz and his company, Fantasy Records, owners of the song's copyright, sued John Fogerty for copyright infringement when Fogerty authored and released another song in 1984, *The Old Man Down the Road*, claiming the two songs were musically indistinguishable, though the lyrics were different. Fantasy Inc. was therefore accusing John Fogerty of plagiarizing himself. Though the jury ruled in Fogerty's favor, the suit was not considered "frivolous," the only legal basis on which a defendant can claim court costs against a plaintiff. To recover his court costs, Fogerty had to take his case to the US Supreme Court, which eventually ruled in his favor saying that, in this case, Fogerty was not required to prove that Zaentz/Fantasy had brought the original suit frivolously. Absurd? Illogical? That's copyright law, and it was not altered by two rulings favorable to Fogerty. Indeed, Fantasy's decades-long exploitation of Fogerty is among the most egregious examples in the history of copyright.

2 Negativland is a band that, in 1991, published a musical parody of a song by another band, U2. According to US copyright law, parody falls under the category of "fair use," one of several legal exceptions allowing copyrighted work to be used without the permission or compensation of the author. U2 and

their record company, Island Records, got a temporary restraining order from a federal judge that led to, among other things, confiscation and destruction of the offending records (vinyl) and the payment of penalties larger than what Negativland had earned in its entire career to that date. I was drawn into this case because I was signed to Island Records by Chris Blackwell, then Island's owner, but was also a friend of Negativland. The band approached me rather desperately asking if I would appeal directly to Blackwell to get Island to lay off. I spoke to Blackwell only to be told it was out of his hands. For the full story visit: https://en.wikipedia.org/wiki/Negativland#U2_record_incident.

3 Bo Diddley's story is both notorious and typical. Bo Diddley earned a pittance from worldwide sales worth millions. The same thing happened to Little Richard, Chuck Berry and many of the black "founding fathers" of rock and roll. Diddley, however, loudly denounced such treatment, which many of his peers, fearing reprisals, did not do. One interview, typical of many in which Diddley made his case, is available here: www.rollingstone.com/music/news/bo-diddley-the-rolling-stone-interview-19870212.

The Bob Marley case is slightly different but equally outrageous. In 2010 a New York court reaffirmed ownership of the copyright by Universal Music Group of many Bob Marley albums, declaring them "works for hire," thereby making UMG the effective "author" of the works. "Works for hire" is a stipulation in US copyright law specifically designed to ensure that a copyright owner need not be the actual composer or performer of music. See Jamaica Intellectual Property Office 09/14/2010 www.jipo.gov.jm.

4 Peter DiCola, "Money from Music: Survey Evidence on Musicians' Revenue and Lessons about Copyright Incentives," Northwestern University School of Law, January 9, 2013, http://ssrn.com/abstract=2199058.

5 Ibid. James Boyle is a professor of Law at Duke University. He is, along with Lawrence Lessig, a founder of Creative Commons and has written many essays and books on IP.

6 John Perry Barlow, "A Declaration of the Independence of Cyberspace,"

February 8, 1996, https://projects.eff.org/~barlow/Declaration-Final.html.

7 The fact that musical instruments of all kinds continue to be widely sold clearly demonstrates that people love to make music. Yet the context has changed several times over the last hundred years, especially since the 1960s when a generation made music its voice. Since the 1960s, and in direct response to the radical threat posed to the status quo, the professionalization of education and performance has tended mainly to intensify the separation between those who make and those who consume music. This is likely to change again as people rally together to fight the depredations of capitalism.

8 John Perry Barlow, "Napster.com and the Death of the Music Industry," *The Technocrat*, May 12, 2000.

SECTION ONE

HISTORICAL CONTEXT AND CONCEPTUAL FRAMEWORKS

Here, we are concerned with probing and unpacking the historical evolution and conceptual origins of intellectual property rights.

Certain concepts provide a necessary framework for understanding copyright, patent and trademark. These concepts have a history of development. They did not fall from the sky or visit human beings as revelations. These concepts furthermore concentrate contradictions arising from economic forces, such as expanding trade, technological development and competition on an increasingly global scale. Finally, these concepts were a product of their own development in the domain of philosophy, the influence of which was far greater 200 years ago than it might be today.

So, beginning with a critical analysis of intellectual property *histories* from different knowledge traditions around the world, a key aim of this section is to "correct" the misconception that IPRs can be characterized in terms of a single, "universal" narrative (which is, in essence, an Anglo-American narrative projected on to the world).

Beyond this, the politics of IPRs is deconstructed and interpreted through the lens of radical political economy so as to, among other things, demonstrate the constraints placed on creativity and innovation by IPR mechanisms.

The final task of this section sees the dissecting and exposition of the concept of ownership as to illustrate how the domain of philosophy has been misapplied and abused in arriving at conventional and orthodox conceptions of intellectual property.

In short, it is the purpose of this section to clarify both foundational elements as well as current controversies in the history, political economy and philosophy of intellectual property.

3 | INTELLECTUAL PROPERTY RIGHTS AND THEIR DIFFUSION AROUND THE WORLD

Towards a global history

Colin Darch

Introduction

In general, both academic and popular accounts of intellectual property (IP) focus much more on the contemporary legal and economic aspects of the subject than on its history. Ideally, a comprehensive global history of IP, were it to be written, would consist of two intimately intertwined but distinct narratives. One would be the story of how the relationship between "creator" and "creation" – writer and text, inventor and invention, manufacturer and product – was conceived philosophically in different ways in different societies over time. It is clear even in the absence of a comprehensive history, that this was not always or everywhere a property relationship:

> The concept of intellectual property *has not existed at all times or in all places*. Our understanding of its historical development stands at a relatively rudimentary stage.[1]

The other narrative would tell the story of how a historically contingent, post-Enlightenment, Western European and capitalist regulatory system, tightly controlling what is essentially the ownership of ideas, came to its present global hegemonic position.

However, the history of IP as it presently exists – specifically the history of copyright, patents and trademarks – is dominated by local narratives that focus on developments in Europe, and especially in England.[2] Relatively little attention is paid to the experiences of non-Western literate societies. There is also an implicit claim in our widespread current use of the term "intellectual property" that IP in fact constitutes a logically coherent umbrella category, and is therefore a legitimate object for historical inquiry. Significantly, however, most accounts treat patents, copyright and trademarks as historically distinct phenomena. Much of the historical writing on copyright, for example, is oriented towards literary questions such as the emergence of the idea of the individual "author" and the relationship of that idea to disputes over the nature of property during the Enlightenment.[3]

Current *academic* IP discourse is largely the product of analysis by lawyers and economists, with historical, literary and sociological studies very much bringing up the rear. However, the study of IP is not only fragmented in *disciplinary* terms. More importantly, several competing and irreconcilable contemporary *discourses* around IP – reaching far beyond the academy – constitute a major obstacle to a comprehensive understanding of how this set of legal and economic mechanisms came to worldwide dominance. To rely only on processes of globalization for an explanation is to mistake description for analysis, at least partly because of the fundamental contradiction between the neoliberal ideology of comprehensive *deregulation* of all aspects of economic activity, alongside an increasingly ferocious system of reification and *regulation* in the world of ideas.

Most dangerously, the popular discourse of IP is dominated by an aggressive promotion by commercial interests of the supposedly wide-ranging benefits of copyright enforcement, more and more patents, and strong protection for trademarks. Serious analysis is often drowned out by this noisy propaganda, much but by no means all of it generated by US entertainment industry associations such as the MPAA and RIAA and their various dependent bodies. These ideas are disseminated not only through the media, but also in large quantities of apparently serious glossy research reports produced by a range of industry-funded bodies. Such material should clearly be treated with the same extremely cautious skepticism with which we regard research funded by, for example, the tobacco industry on the health risks of smoking, or by food companies on the dangers of eating fast foods. Historical knowledge of IP is advancing, but the universalizing discourse driven by economic interest continues to muddy the waters.[4]

The dominant discourse generated by the "core copyright industries"[5] and their allies does not depend solely on research of doubtful reliability, however. It is supported by a wide range of other tactics, some of them implemented by government agencies such as police forces, trade ministries and parliaments. There is constant pressure on legislatures for tougher laws to protect IP rights; IP rights are expanded to cover new areas, and for longer periods; IP violations are gradually criminalized; advertising in cinemas and articles in newspapers hammer home the theme that unauthorized use is a form of theft; and selected file-sharers and others are prosecuted "pour encourager les autres."[6] The constant reiteration of doubtful statistical assertions about the economic damage that results from less than rigorous enforcement is accompanied by claims that IP piracy is a source of funds for both terrorist organizations and organized crime.[7] Ominously, critics of IP are also falsely represented as holding extreme positions that they do not in fact defend, and are accused, strangely, of being "ideologically motivated."[8]

The teleological narrative of IP development serves a particular justificatory purpose. Built into it is the ahistorical argument that first, property is a human right; second, that intellectual property in its various manifestations is an entirely unproblematic component of property in general and therefore also a human right; and last, that it has ever been so. In other words, IP is *not* an historically contingent juridical-economic regulatory system, but is rather an expression of universal human values. By cherry-picking shaky examples from the remote past, evidence for the position is gradually introduced into the public consciousness, as we shall see.

Pushing the present back into the past

Lawyers and economists do not generally think historically about IP.[9] Justin Hughes has pointed out that

> instead of researching and citing primary materials, intellectual property scholarship frequently refers *only* to other legal scholarship for evidence of non-legal data . . . the practice of citing only legal scholarship for evidence of non-legal data means that a few casual but incomplete historical claims by a few respected legal scholars can get replicated through the system – and beyond.[10]

If this is true in the academy, the situation is even worse in popular discourse. For example, an online text claims that "legal protections for intellectual property have a rich history that stretches back to ancient Greece *and before*."[11] Another asserts confidently:

> The history of intellectual property . . . begins in 500 BCE when
> Sybaris, a Greek state, made it possible for citizens to obtain
> a one year patent for "any new refinement in luxury." Patent,
> trademark and copyright laws have become more complicated in
> the ensuing centuries *but the intent remains the same.*[12]

A book on TRIPS in China begins by stating that "known references to intellectual property protection in the West can go back as early as ancient Greece and Rome."[13] These quotations are not taken from specialist historical sources, but their sweeping claims are close to becoming accepted popular wisdom.

There are good reasons why this is so. In an assessment of ideas about authorship in ancient Greece, another writer comments that "in almost every case [intellectual property] issues are addressed briefly *in the service of some other project.*"[14] It is not hard to see what the other project is: a desire to show that IP is not historically contingent but universal across cultures, stretching back to the beginnings of civilization, and hence immune to critique.

The source for the claim about Sybaris is Phylarchus of Naucratis, a minor Greek historian of mixed reputation whose books are now lost, but who is quoted in a surviving work by Athenaeus, also from Naucratis.[15] The story entered the mainstream, as far as IP is concerned, in the 1940s, when it was repeated in an article on patents.[16] However, the tale of Sybaris was dismissed by a US patent historian as "well-known, but *apocryphal*" as long ago as 1967.[17] The same author noted that "Hellenic Greece *failed to protect inventors* and the era following Alexander's death saw little improvement."[18] It is probably safe to conclude, therefore, that the often-repeated idea that the ancient Greeks had an *operational* concept of a proprietary right is hard to sustain; it boils down to a single reference of doubtful provenance about practices in one Greek city in southern Italy.

The classical historian Mary Beard cautions us in general terms, with reference to the ancients, that while it may be "tempting to imagine [them] as some version of ourselves," at the same time much of their world is "completely alien territory."[19] It makes no sense to project modern concepts of "property in ideas" backwards into the remote pre-capitalist and pre-technological European past. What seems familiar is all too often actually "completely alien."[20]

The history of IP – an amorphous and scarcely articulated ragbag of legal and economic relationships – fits uneasily into a single, nomothetic narrative in which the intent always "remains the same," and in which other cultures serve simply as illustrative points of reference. On the contrary, both the intent and the content of what appear at first glance to be analogues of modern IP always turn out to be different in significant ways. The kind of history that we need in order fully to understand contemporary *global* struggles over IP rights needs to be constructed out of a wide range of highly idiographic approaches in multiple academic disciplines before a balanced synthesis can become possible.

The excellent existing histories of copyright, patents, and trademarks, as these categories have developed in Western Europe, provide a firm foundation for an understanding of their *local* development, but run the risk of implicitly *generalizing* the history of IP from the experience of its local emergence in England and the United States. In the case of copyright the story focuses on highly specific developments subsequent to the English Statute of Anne (passed in 1710), and in the case of patents on origins within the Venetian legislation of 1474 and the subsequent English Statute of Monopolies of 1624. Account may occasionally be taken of differences in the Franco-European approach to issues such as copyright.[21] But a normative and Eurocentric (or even Anglocentric) historical narrative, valuable as it is, remains insufficient for a complete understanding of *current* circumstances.

Economists, broadly speaking, are uninterested in this perspective, and legal research is ill-equipped to help us. Comparative legal studies – in which Western norms and other traditions are uneasily brought together – have been severely criticized as suffering from "unresolved scholarly problems of a methodological and theoretical nature which too often continue to be ignored within the literature," as well as from "numerous distortions and falsifications that invalidate their scientific status"; they are deficient "in theory and method"; they do not address "important issues of cultural specificity, diversity and contingency"; and they fail to "challenge attitudes of dogmatic complacency and ethnocentricity."[22] They often appear, indeed, to believe that "the legal culture of *the Others* is not really legal at all," and may presumably be safely ignored.[23]

The impulse towards a nomothetic narrative

In a speech given in the House of Commons in February 1841, Thomas Macaulay characterized IP issues as "a subject with which political animosities have nothing to do."[24] In the twenty-first century it is hard to imagine a more mistaken perspective. We live in a world where global capitalism is well on the way to imposing a standardized, highly regulated and expansionist IP system on most of the countries of the world. Scholars, activists, commercial interests, governments and international organizations are all engaged in constant and heated debate around the topic. David and Halbert have pointed out in a recent book that "the rise of IP over the last three centuries has culminated in the last three decades with an attempt at global IP harmonization alongside radical expansion in reach, duration and depth."[25] Similarly, in an interview published in 2001, the Belgian lawyer and writer Alain Berenboom has commented:

> *s'il y a un domaine où la mondialisation a fait des progrès,*
> *c'est bien dans le domaine du droit d'auteur* [if there is one area where globalization has made progress, it is in the field of copyright].[26]

One of the most important elements in this process is ideological in nature, and involves constructing an ahistorical account of intellectual property as an unambiguously beneficial phenomenon that is both an immensely powerful force for social good and simultaneously under massive threat from criminal and terrorist organizations.[27] In this process, it can be argued, memory is erased to protect commercial interest, privilege and wealth, at the expense of both historical truth and the collective interests of the majority.

Justin Hughes has criticized the idea that the actual phrase "intellectual property" is a modern or recent coinage that marks "a massive paradigm shift in how judges think about copyright (and patent)."[28] He points out that "courts and legislatures . . . regularly discussed copyrighted works as 'property' throughout the seventeenth, eighteenth, and early nineteenth centuries."[29] The expressions "industrial property" and "literary property" were also widely used in the nineteenth century, and not just in English: the Spanish term "prop-iedad intelectual" dates back to the first half of the nineteenth century, and there are similar examples in French and Italian.[30] But these early examples of both literary and intellectual property are nearly always synonyms for copyright, and are not used as an umbrella term for every kind of IP. There was at that time some rec-ognition of the special character of IP as a form of property that has now largely disappeared. It is therefore fair to say that the history of the term IP is "complex and its use inconsistent, both between juris-dictions and within single jurisdictions."[31] None of this, however, means that current conceptual difficulties disappear.

It is not hard to discern why the popular narrative of the history of intellectual property has developed along this particular path, and what interests are served by it. I have argued elsewhere that the economic weight of the "core copyright industries," especially in the United States, makes them too big to fail, and that they have consequently largely seized control of the process of legislating IP protection, while at the same time the US government actively promotes the adoption of increasingly wide-ranging laws around the world.[32] This phenomenon includes measures for the criminalization of any unauthorized use of protected material.

In the official view, IP is seen unproblematically as a real form of property (which is in turn itself proclaimed a basic human right), with its antecedents (as we have already noted) going back to the ancient Greeks. It is thus represented as both very old and universally recognized. Although few modern-day defenders of the system would now express it quite so bluntly, this is essentially the story of a hypothetical "ancient and eternal idea of intellectual property."[33] The key word here is "property," a concept that is

> so fundamental to the way lawyers think [that they] tend to treat
> [it] as if it is *a natural way to view the world*. But the language
> of property has a history. The earliest common law writs, all of
> which had something to do with rights in land, make no mention
> of property.[34]

In other words, the concept of property as a legal relationship between a person and a thing is historically contingent. It is neither universal nor timeless: indeed, some societies believe that pretty much everything can be owned, while others – and not just the surviving hunter-gatherers of the Amazon or southern Africa – still do not.

In modern legal thought, a distinction is usually made between real and personal property (in common law systems) or between immovable and moveable property (in civil law systems); in both cases the first term refers basically to land and the second to personal items. But it is clear that the idea of absolute ownership of either form emerges in Europe only with the demise of feudal land tenure, and in some customary law systems even now it has not necessarily assumed its present Western form. The property relation is essentially a legal right over the thing owned, which may be exclusively possessed, made use of, and disposed of or alienated. Such rights are often, but not invariably legally enforceable.

In addition, the property right is often claimed to be an important *human* right. Although Article 17 of the Universal Declaration of Human Rights (1948) – a document that has no legal force – states that "Everyone has the right to own property alone as well as in association with others. No one shall be arbitrarily deprived of his property," the status of the property right as a human right has remained controversial until the present day, and it is omitted from some international instruments. This has implications for claims about IP, which as a form of property, has also been asserted as a human right and hence a universal value.[35] We see this tendency, for instance, in the International Property Rights Index (IPRI), whose website carries an unambiguous statement by Hernando de Soto that "the lack of enforced property rights is an issue of human rights." The index, he goes on to explain,

> ranks countries on three main components: Legal and Political Environment (LP), Physical Property Rights (PPR), *and Intellectual Property Rights* (IPR) . . . the IPR component features three subcomponents: Intellectual Property Protection, Patent Protection, and Copyright Piracy Level.[36]

This is, of course, only an example, but the sleight of hand is easily spotted. First of all, *property itself* is both a human right *and* one of the key characteristics that "[determines] freedom and economic prosperity for a country." Then IP and various aspects of its enforcement are quietly thrown into the mix as just another type of property, alongside the traditional categories of movable and immovable property. In this way IP becomes an ahistorical and universal value, a part of human nature, an element of *la condition humaine* which must be accepted by everybody as immutable reality. Who, after all, is against freedom or economic prosperity, except perhaps a few *mafiosi* and a handful of terrorists?

Where are property rights in other knowledge traditions?

Carla Hesse has pointed to the fact that the "great civilizations of the modern world – Chinese, Islamic, Jewish, and Christian" were characterized by "a striking absence of any notion of human ownership of ideas or their expressions."[37] But, as Hesse goes on to recognize, the mere absence of an idea of ownership does not necessarily mean that the relationship between author, text or invention, and distribution was not the subject of sophisticated reflection.[38]

Although we have already dismissed the idea of an *operational* concept of a proprietary right among the ancient Greeks, it should be noted that some scholars believe that "*some of the components* of the notion of 'intellectual property' are evident in antiquity."[39] Until the invention of printing, texts were reproduced by scribes who copied them out by hand – the books owned by wealthy Romans, for example, "would have been copied by their own slaves in their own homes."[40] Given that the process of copying itself was hardly an issue, the identifiable proto-components consist primarily of specific concerns around what are now known as moral rights, particularly the issue of textual integrity and the identification or assertion of authorship.

Of these moral rights, as distinguished from the proprietary right of economic exploitation, it does appear that a concern with the integrity of canonical texts existed in the ancient world, most especially in highly juridico-religious cultures – including "both Western (Zoroastrianism, Judaism, Christianity, and Islam) and Eastern (the Pāli canon of Theravāda Buddhism)" examples.[41] Interestingly, some modern scholarship loses sight of this concern; in a study published in 2003, Levinson criticized what he called "literary theory's infatuation with ancient Jewish *midrash*" because of the tendency to romanticize "rabbinic hermeneutics as championing radical textual indeterminacy."[42] On the contrary, Levinson argues that the essence of a canon is that it be stable, self-sufficient, and delimited . . . Moses twice admonished his addressees in Deuteronomy: "You must not add anything to what I command you nor take anything away from it" . . . The formula . . . originally sought to prevent royal inscriptions, including law collections and treaties . . . from being altered.[43]

The later Book of Revelation repeats the threat from Deuteronomy in similar terms:

> For I testify unto every man that heareth the words of the prophecy of this book, if any man shall add unto these things, God shall add unto him the plagues that are written in this book;
> And if any man shall take away from the words of the book of this prophecy, God shall take away his part out of the book of life, and out of the holy city, and from the things which are written in this book.[44]

Behind these warnings is a recognition of the special canonical status of religious and legal texts (often the same thing) and of the necessity for them to be preserved in a fixed form. The *Quran*, which is considered in Islam to be primarily a recitation rather than a text, was fixed in a similar way. Since the seventh century CE, it has been written or printed with both diacritical marks on consonants as well as vocalization, with the objective of establishing a definitive line of transmission, a fixed text and a fixed pronunciation.

Similarly, the authentic transmission of Islamic *ḥadīth*, the traditions consisting of sayings ascribed to the prophet Muhammad or descriptions of his deeds, was and remains a major focus of attention for Islamic scholars, and can be viewed as an issue of textual integrity, as well as of the attribution of authorship as a means of authentication. The level of confidence that could be attributed to specific transmitters of *ḥadīth*, especially given the known existence of falsifiers, was an important aspect of this preoccupation.[45] Indeed, in these ancient examples, the author–text relationship may be turned on its head, with the attribution of authorship "a property ascribed to a text rather than a fact about its origins" or anything like a statement of intellectual ownership.[46] From this perspective, the attribution of authorship does not function as a proprietary claim, as Beecroft has argued in a comparative study of both China and ancient Greece:

> If . . . we ignore the possible historicity of biographical anecdotes, and concentrate instead precisely on what those anecdotes say *about the ideologies of their sources*, scenes of authorship become rich sources of information on all sorts of questions concerning the production, distribution, and value of literature. The scene of authorship serves as a link between text and context, not merely claiming to tell us who "wrote" a poem, but also frequently *making a variety of claims about how and why the poem was composed, and how and where and why it should circulate.*[47]

Of all the intellectual traditions outside the Western European one, the most difficult for proponents of "the ancient and eternal idea of intellectual property" to explain is pre-modern China. We must remember that the core argument of defenders of IP expansionism is that without economic incentive, creativity and invention will dry up. "Market capitalism," in other words, is an "unparalleled innovation engine."[48] The US government believes this without reservation:

> the most important, but least understood, of the forces driving innovation [is] the complex system of institutions, laws, and practices referred to as intellectual property (IP) . . . IP laws evolved over centuries as a tool to derive public benefits from the innovation cycle. Because it is so tightly linked to innovation, intellectual property holds a key to our future.[49]

The late Jack Valenti of the Motion Picture Association of America, an aggressively pro-IP industry group, remarked that "copyright protects not just the financial interest of people who create artistic or intellectual property, *but the very existence of creative work.*"[50] This argument in its various forms persists even though it has been disproven on multiple occasions. As long ago as 1966, Hurt and Schuchman demonstrated that there are a wide range of intrinsic rewards, including "the propagation of partisan ideas; notions of altruism . . .; desire for recognition; and enhancement of one's reputation."[51] Recent research in behavioral economics has reinforced the view that monetary compensation can actually be a poor incentive.[52]

Between roughly the Tang Dynasty (618–906 CE) and the sixteenth century, Chinese science and technology was probably the most innovative in the world. This has been exhaustively documented in Joseph Needham's monumental *Science and Civilization in China* (published in 27 books organized in seven volumes), and there is no point in attempting to list all the inventions again here. But there is no trace during this period of any systemic idea of IP protection as an appropriate method of rewarding creativity. Indeed, one of the most exhaustive treatments of the phenomenon, by William P. Alford, warns that, despite the fact that there are some scattered references to

> restrictions on the unauthorized reproduction of certain books, symbols, and products . . . this should not be seen as constituting what we . . . now typically understand intellectual property law to be, for their goal was not the protection of property or other private interests.[53]

Other authors follow Alford:

> there is little if any Chinese tradition of intellectual property rights (IPRs) protection. Throughout China's millennia-long imperial history, except for some fragmentary, individual rules, or official pronouncements protecting author or editor, there has been no centralized uniform system protecting IPRs.[54]

How, then, to explain centuries of innovation in the absence of monopolistic rights of exploitation over an invention or a text? This problem has been posed most famously, if indirectly, as "Needham's Grand Question" or the "Needham Question" which asks why China was eventually overtaken by Western technologies, despite its head start over several centuries.[55] The two aspects of the same question are essentially, why did the emergence of modern scientific method *not* happen in China; and conversely, why *did* it happen in Europe? What were the determinant variables?

Some responses to these hypotheticals have included the suggestion that the absence of strong property rights in general, and IP rights in particular, was one such variable. It is certainly clear, at least, that pre-modern Chinese legal culture varied significantly from modern Western norms. A person could be punished for an offence that did not break an existing law, for example, and punishments and outcomes varied according to an offender's social standing.[56] But to privilege the absence of IP protection, with the concomitant absence of incentives for innovators seems improbable, given that Chinese innovation was sustained over such a long period, and especially since it is clear that such early Western innovators as Galileo, Boyle or Newton were not driven primarily by a desire to profit from their discoveries.[57]

Contemporary China's subsequent adoption of Western norms of IP protection has been extremely rapid, driven largely by China's need to satisfy trading standards in order to access world markets. "Harmonization" has meant for China – and many other countries – a "growing stress on IP protection, the so-called global 'minimum standards', as against the 'national treatment' principle."[58] In 1980 the China Patent Administration was established, and in the same year the country joined the World Intellectual Property Organization (WIPO). Patent legislation was passed in 1984, and China successively ratified the Patent Cooperation Treaty in 1994, and joined the World Trade Organization (WTO), agreeing to TRIPS enforcement, in 2002.[59] This process required changes that "were sweeping in nature and required the Chinese government to make changes to hundreds of laws, regulations and other measures."[60] In essence, new laws were being transplanted into the Chinese system; legislation developed in the context of one particular society and culture were inserted into a different society and culture in the hope – to stretch the metaphor to its limits – that the recipient body would not reject them. This artificial practice had started with "the introduction of intellectual property laws during the late Qing dynasty [i.e. in the late nineteenth century] and the Republican era" but accelerated sharply with "the recent laws and amendments adopted by the People's Republic."[61]

We have already noted the many difficulties with legal transplants, not the least of which is an unreflective assumption of universalism. The risks involved in basing the process on "false generalisations and universalisations of what are, in fact, little more than localised, western-liberal perspectives" is high.[62] What has been identified as an "objectivist stance" based on the illusion that a "a culturally and cognitively neutral frame of mind" is achievable, leads all too often to the imposition of a "non-transparent and taken-for-granted Western ideology of [a] value-free scientific approach."[63] It appears that the triumphalist discourse of global IP protection is not especially concerned with such subtleties and complexities, and it is consequently not especially surprising to read in a 2015 US government report that difficulties have arisen that have included

> serious problems with intellectual property rights enforcement . . . including in the area of trade secrets; the Chinese government's wide-ranging use of industrial policies favoring state-owned enterprises and domestic national champions in many sectors; troubling agricultural policies that block US market access; numerous continuing restrictions on services market access; and inadequate transparency.[64]

What is all too easily forgotten is that *"the others also have law as history and as practice, and it has never in recorded history been possible to avoid contamination."*[65]

Socialist and Marxist practice is another case in point. Space does not permit a full exploration of experience in the Soviet Union, post-1948 China or in Cuba but suffice it to say such experience does not neatly conform to norms established in the US or Western Europe. Soviet reluctance to join international copyright agreements was partly inherited from nineteenth-century Russian attitudes, as well representing an attempt to reconcile a recognition of authors' rights with the principles of Marxism-Leninism. The first Russian copyright law was adopted in 1828, but bilateral conventions, first with France and subsequently with Belgium, were both abandoned in the 1880s, and Tsarist Russia did not take part in the Berne conference of 1886.[66] In the early Soviet period works were "nationalized" but some recognition of individual author's rights gradually developed within the context of a collectivist cultural policy in which the state and party played leading roles.[67]

It is clear that Soviet IP practice was initially grounded in an attempt to theorize cultural production within a socialist problematic. Nevertheless, one of the best-known and most widely condemned features of later Soviet copyright practice was the uncompensated translation of foreign works into Russian and other Soviet languages.

One estimate puts the figures as high as one billion copies of foreign books produced between 1917 and 1950, including "seventy-seven million copies of 2700 books by some 200 United States authors."[68]

Historical contingency, or universalism plus individualism

The constituent elements of intellectual property – the proprietary component of copyright, the patent system, trademarks – arose in the specific conditions of early Western European capitalism. All serious historians of the subject agree on this. The invention of printing, the emergence of individualism and the rise of the concept of the author, new theories of knowledge and the scientific revolution, the growth of a leisured middle class, all contributed to the development of what eventually coalesced into what we now designate "IP," with its complex sets of justiciable rights.

It is this *historical* understanding of the *historical* contingency of IP that makes it impossible to accept universalizing claims that IP rights have existed around the world and throughout history, or that they are part of a generalized and accepted "property right."[69] Indeed, even to frame IP as "absent" in other traditions and societies is to implicitly *normalize* the modern Western concept and at the same time to *delegitimize* other ways of understanding the relationship between a creator, located in society, and her creation.[70]

The dominant discourse is, unsurprisingly, one that speaks of encouraging creativity, but creativity conceived of entirely as the product of individual effort – the author writes a text alone, the inventor is struck by a brilliant idea.[71] But individual authorship (and by implication other forms of creative or innovative endeavor) is, as Woodmansee had pointed out, an historically contingent idea that developed in the specific conditions of economic and technological change:

> in its modern sense . . . [authorship] is the *product of the rise in the eighteenth century of a new group of individuals*: writers who sought to earn their livelihood from the sale of their writings.[72]

But Hesse, writing a few years later, suggested that, taking the French revolutionary experience into account,

> literary historians and critics may need *a more complex view of the relationship between the law and cultural change*, one that accounts

for the political as well as the socio-economic forces at work in the reshaping of the legal world . . . [But] politics, and a concern for public life, mediated the successive negotiations between the private interests of authors and publishers and the concerns of legal authorities. As a consequence, the revolutionary legislators produced a legal conception of authorial identity that not only consecrated *but also limited the author's power of self-determination for the sake of the public good.*[73]

Hesse's writings have played an important role in expanding our understanding of possible alternatives to an Anglocentric narrative within Western Europe, by taking account of the intellectual ferment of the French Revolution from 1789 to 1799, and showing that IP as a mechanism of control may have had multiple origins, not limited only to the commercial needs of the growing bourgeoisie but also taking into account the oligarchy's desire to control and benefit from the flow of information. Hesse draws the English-speaking reader's attention to the debates for and against control involving such figures as Denis Diderot (1713–1784) and the Marquis of Condercet (1743–1794) which raged before, during and after the Revolution.[74] The opposition to propertization was both fierce and coherent:

Between 1789 and 1793, the mandate to liberate the Enlightenment from censorship and to re-found cultural life on enlightened principles translated itself into a massive deregulation of the publishing world. By 1793 anyone could own a printing press or engage in publishing and bookselling. What is more, with the abolition of privileges and prepublication censorship, it appeared that anyone could print or publish anything. Thus the first few years of the Revolution saw the corporatist literary system of the Old Regime entirely dismantled and replaced with a free market in the world of ideas.[75]

The battle – not only in France – revolved to a significant extent around what have been termed the "modern myths of creativity."[76] The "archetypal" myth of creativity has been described in the following terms: a "clever individual . . . driven by ambition and the promise of great riches, hits upon a brilliant idea in a sudden flash of insight and the world changes."[77] But Marx demolished the idea of the inspired individual genius in a couple of sentences as long ago as 1844:

> when I am active scientifically, etc., – an activity which I can seldom perform in direct community with others – then my activity is social, because I perform it as a man [*sic*]. Not only is the material of my activity given to me as a social product (as is even the language in which the thinker is active): my own existence is social activity, and therefore that which I make of myself, I make of myself for society and with the consciousness of myself as a social being.[78]

Defenders of IP expansionism have never succeeded in crushing this way of thinking completely, and academic endeavor in particular continues to be seen by many as primarily a collective, social activity in which ideas, arguments, terminologies and phrases bounce around and stick together in unexpected ways to produce new insights:

> against the dictats of the intellectual property border-guards, ideas, critical ideas in particular, can only develop in the fertile hothouse of debate, argumentation and confrontation . . . Nothing I have ever written belongs to me exclusively. Every text is always a tissue of texts and discussions, sounds and thoughts, smells and colours many of which started with others.[79]

Conclusion: towards an idiographic approach to IP history

The history of IP – or, better, the *histories* of author's rights, copyright, patents, trademarks and all the rest – is and are gradually, and in a fragmentary way, being written within sub-disciplinary silos in terms of multiple constituent elements: changing and contested theories of knowledge at various historical conjunctures; the emergence of the author as creator; a growing understanding of the collective nature of inspiration and invention; the impact of technologies of production and reproduction; and the significance of systems of distribution. Such research is essential as we move towards a political economy capable of explaining how aggressive and monopolistic IP legislation and regulation is used, all over the world, to avoid competition, limit innovation and reap "profits in excess of what a competitive market would afford."[80]

But it may be a necessary condition of historical understanding to take another, further step, and to reconfigure the concept of "intellectual property" altogether, by ceasing to grant it, as a category, acceptance as a reflex of a real phenomenon that is a legitimate object of historical inquiry. It is widely accepted that modern IP lacks intellectual coherence as an *umbrella concept*, and therefore also as a social phenomenon. An extremely wide variety of practices and socio-economic, legal and literary relations are now classified as IP. Its reach is constantly expanding in terms of law. But it is far from clear what these varieties of relationships have in common, beyond the fact that they are juridically defined rights of economic monopoly that are extremely ill-equipped to deal with the realities of rapid technological change, and are consequently widely ignored by large numbers of people in their daily lives.

Hughes has shown that the phrase "intellectual property" and its apparent cognates can be found not only in English but in (at least) several Romance languages as well, in the early nineteenth century. As this chapter has argued, the global history of the multiple elements of IP are to be found in an extraordinarily wide range of contradictory and contentious sources and disciplines, and we have only begun to scratch the surface. In 1858, Karl Marx noted in the *Grundrisse* that there are occasions when "the only possible answer [to a question] is a critique of the question and the only solution is to negate the question."[81] This, it seems to me, is precisely one of those occasions.

Notes

1 Pamela O. Long, "Invention, Authorship, 'Intellectual Property', and the Invention of Patents: Notes toward a Conceptual History," *Technology and Culture* 32, no. 4 (October 1991): 848. Emphasis added.

2 The classic studies on copyright include Lyman Ray Patterson's *Copyright in Historical Perspective* (Vanderbilt University Press, 1968); Mark Rose's *Authors and Owners: The Invention of Copyright* (Harvard University Press, 1993); and Adrian Johns' *The Nature of the Book: Print and Knowledge in the*

Making (University of Chicago Press, 1998). Also important are the writings of Martha Westmansee, especially on Germany; and on France, Carla Hesse's *Publishing and Cultural Politics in Revolutionary Paris, 1789–1810* (University of California Press, 1991) as well as the anthology edited by Jan Baetens, *Le combat du droit d'auteur: anthologie historique* (Impressions Nouvelles, 2001), which includes texts from Alain-René Lesage (1668–1747) to Victor Hugo (1802–1885), including an extract from *Les majorats littéraires*

(1862) of Joseph Proudhon (1809–1865). Hesse's article "The Rise of Intellectual Property, 700 B.C.–A.D. 2000: An Idea in the Balance," *Daedalus* 131, no. 2 (Spring 2002): 26–45, is notable for beginning by discussing several non-Western European knowledge traditions.

3 The key texts are Hobbes' *Leviathan* (1651; arguing that property rights depend on the existence of the state) and Locke's *Second Treatise of Government* (1689; arguing for a labor-based theory).

4 US entertainment industry associations such as the RIAA and the MPAA are particularly vulnerable to accusations of less-than-rigorously-researched assertions about the impact of IP piracy, for example. See Colin Darch, "Ideology, Illusion and the Global Copyright Regime," in *The IALL International Handbook of Legal Information Management*, ed. Richard A. Danner and Jules Winterton (Ashgate, 2011), 102–103.

5 "defined as [industries] wholly engaged in the creation, production, performance, exhibition, communication or distribution and sales of copyright protected subject matter. These include literature, music, theatre, film, the media, photography, software, visual arts, advertising services and collective management societies" ("Copyright-based Industries: Assessing Their Weight," *WIPO Magazine* no. 3 [May–June 2005]: 22).

6 "In order to encourage [i.e. to scare] the others" – an ironical comment by Voltaire in his novel *Candide* (1759) in reference to the execution of the British Admiral Byng in 1757 after losing a battle against the French.

7 E.g. Gregory F. Treverton and others, *Film Piracy, Organized Crime, and Terrorism* (Rand Corporation, 2009).

8 For example, activists "promote the idea that IP rights should not be recognized" (Global Intellectual Property Center, *Creating Jobs, Saving Lives, Improving the World* (US Chamber of Commerce, 2008). This report is no longer available on the GPC website but has been cited in Darch, "Ideology, Illusion and the Global Copyright Regime," 97; and Deborah J. Halbert, *The State of Copyright: The Complex Relationship of Cultural Creation in a Globalised World* (Routledge, 2014), 68–69.

9 Mainstream economists, that is, as opposed to practitioners of political economy, who have held to an essentially historical perspective since the time of Marx and Engels.

10 J. Hughes, "Copyright and Incomplete Historiographies: Of Piracy, Propertization, and Thomas Jefferson," *Southern California Law Review* 79 (2005–2006): 996.

11 Adam Moore and Ken Himma, "Intellectual Property," in *The Stanford Encyclopedia of Philosophy* (Winter 2014), ed. Edward N. Zalta, http://tinyurl.com/jl4vn2p, accessed May 2, 2016 [emphasis added].

12 Law Office of Jeff Williams, "The Evolution of Intellectual Property," November 11, 2015, http://tinyurl.com/zaqzneg, accessed May 2, 2016 [emphasis added].

13 Guan Wenwei, *Intellectual Property Theory and Practice: A Critical Examination of China's TRIPS Compliance and Beyond* (Springer, 2014), 2.

14 Timothy Donald Behme, "Norms of Authorship in Ancient Greece: Case Studies of Herodotus, Isocrates and Plato" (Ph.D. dissertation, University of Minnesota, 2007), 5.

15 See Athenaeus, *The Deipnosophists*, http://tinyurl.com/h43de55, accessed May 7, 2016 for an English translation of the original passage. Naukratis was a Greek settlement in Egypt.

16 M. Frumkin, "The Origin of Patents," *Journal of the Patent Office Society* 27, no. 3 (March 1945): 143, http://tinyurl.com/3vftfzo, accessed May 7, 2016.

17 Bruce W. Bugbee, *Genesis of American Patent and Copyright Law* (Public Affairs Press, 1967), 166.

18 Ibid., 12, emphasis added.

19 Mary Beard, "Why Ancient Rome Matters to the Modern World," *The Guardian*, October 2, 2015, http://tinyurl.com/nknogkb, accessed May 2, 2016.

20 To cite another example, Gary Richardson's argument that early markings on exported products such as swords and pottery were effectively pre-industrial branding or trademark practices (*Brand Names before the Industrial Revolution* [National Bureau of Economic Research, 2008]) was dismissed as "particularly contentious" by Ilja van Damme, not least because of the producers' lack of control over delivery to market ("From a Knowledgeable Salesman towards a Recognizable Product? Questioning Branding Strategies before Industrialization (Antwerp, Seventeenth to Nineteenth Centuries)," in *Concepts of Value in European Material Culture, 1500–1900*, ed. Bert de Munck and Dries Lyna [Routledge, 2015], 83).

21 Alain Berenboom has argued that there is an "approche différent de l'objectif du droit d'auteur et du bénèficiaire de la protection" between Franco-European and Anglo-American copyright, to the extent that the European system operates "au seul profit de l'auteur." ("Situation actuelle du droit d'auteur: entretien avec Alain Berenboom," in Baetens, *Le combat du droit d'auteur*, 171).

22 Bogumila Puchalska-Tych and Michael Salter, "Comparing Legal Cultures of Eastern Europe: The Need for Dialectical Analysis," *Legal Studies* 16, no. 2 (July 1996): 157–158.

23 Bill Bowring, *The Degradation of the International Legal Order: The Rehabilitation of Law and the Possibility of Politics* (Routledge-Cavendish, 2008), 187, emphasis added.

24 Thomas Macaulay, "A Speech Delivered in the House of Commons on the 5th of February 1841," in *Intellectual Property Rights: Critical Concepts in Law*, ed. David Vaver (Routledge, 2006), 9.

25 Matthew David and Debora Halbert, *Owning the World of Ideas: Intellectual Property and Global Network Capitalism* (Sage, 2015), 42.

26 Berenboom, "Situation actuelle du droit d'auteur," 171.

27 The Global Intellectual Property Center (GIPC) states baldly that "illicit trade is big business, providing a major source of revenue to transnational criminal organizations, including terrorist networks," which it claims was equivalent to US$461 billion in 2013 (Patrick Kilbride, "Global Counterfeiters Are Stealing Your Well-being," GIPC, April 20, 2016, http://tinyurl.com/jh38hvu, accessed May 8, 2016).

28 Hughes, "Copyright and Incomplete Historiographies," 1003.

29 Ibid., 1006.

30 Hughes, "A Short History of 'Intellectual Property' in Relation to Copyright," *Cardozo Law Review* 33, no. 4 (April 2012): 1293–1340.

31 Ibid., 1297. In both articles Hughes largely ignores pro-IP industry propaganda.

32 Darch, "Ideology, Illusion and the Global Copyright Regime," 107–109.

33 F.D. Phager, "The early growth and influence of intellectual property," *Journal of the Patent Office Society* 34, no. 2 (February 1952): 106.

34 Thomas J. McSweeney, "Property before Property: Romanizing the English Law of Land," *Buffalo Law*

Review 60 (2012): 1139–1140, emphasis added.

35 An attempt to obtain recognition of IP in the South African Bill of Rights of 1996 was rejected by the country's Constitutional Court in the mid-1990s. See Colin Darch, "Politics, Law and Discourse: Patents and Innovation in Post-Apartheid South Africa," in *The Sage Handbook of Intellectual Property*, ed. Matthew David and Debora Halbert (Sage, 2014), 634–636.

36 Hernando de Soto, "Introduction," *International Property Rights Index*, 9th ed. (2015), http://tinyurl.com/jfxtb3g, accessed May 7, 2016.

37 Hesse, "The Rise of Intellectual Property," 27.

38 A new study (that I have not seen) deals with a specifically Jewish tradition of copyright jurisprudence since the invention of printing. Written by Neil Weinstock Netanel, the book appeared while this chapter was being prepared, and apparently claims a Jewish tradition going back to a decision by a Rabbinic court in Rome in 1518. See *From Maimonides to Microsoft: The Jewish Law of Copyright since the Birth of Print* (Oxford University Press, 2016).

39 Long, "Invention, Authorship, 'Intellectual Property', and the Invention of Patents," 848, emphasis added. Long herself believes that a "fully developed concept first emerges in the medieval period around the 12th or 13th centuries" but still recognizes its historical contingency.

40 Raymond J. Starr, "The Used-Book Trade in the Roman World," *Phoenix* 44, no. 2 (1990): 156.

41 Bernard M. Levinson, "You Must Not Add Anything to What I Command You: Paradoxes of Canon and Authorship in Ancient Israel," *Numen* 50 (2003): 5–6.

42 Ibid., 2. A *midrash* (pl. *midrashim*) is an interpretative text explaining some aspect of the Hebrew Bible.

43 Ibid., 6.

44 King James Bible, Revelation 22: 18–19.

45 G.H.A. Juynboll, *Muslim Tradition: Studies in Chronology, Provenance and Authorship of Early ḥadīth* (Cambridge University Press, 1983).

46 Alexander Beecroft, *Authorship and Cultural Identity in Early Greece and China: Patterns of Literary Circulation* (Cambridge University Press, 2010), 17.

47 Ibid., 19.

48 Steven Johnson, *Where Do Good Ideas Come From? The Natural History of Innovation* (Riverhead Books, 2010), 247.

49 Michael A. Gollin, "Intellectual Property Rights," *e-Journal USA* (US Department of State) 14, no. 11 (November 2009): 32.

50 Jack Valenti, "There's No Free Hollywood," *New York Times*, June 21, 2000, http://tinyurl.com/zsgr2fj, accessed May 9, 2016.

51 Robert Hurt and Robert M. Schuchman, "The Economic Rationale of Copyright," *American Economic Review* 56, no. 1–2 (March 1966): 425–426.

52 For studies of the complex and non-linear interplay of intrinsic and extrinsic motivations in creativity, see, for example, Roland Bénabou and Jean Tirole, "Intrinsic and Extrinsic Motivation," *Review of Economic Studies* 70 (2003): 489–520; or Emir Kamenica, "Behavioral Economics and Psychology of Incentives," *Annual Review of Economics* (2012): 13.1–13.26.

53 Alford, *To Steal a Book Is an Elegant Offense: Intellectual Property Law in Chinese Civilization* (Stanford University Press, 1995), 3.

54 Nie Jian-Quiang, *The Enforcement of Intellectual Property Rights in China* (Cameron May, 2006), 177.

55 In an extensive literature, see, for example, Nathan Sivin, "Why the Scientific Revolution Did Not Take Place in China: Or Didn't It?" *Chinese Science* 5

(1982): 45–66, and more recently Patrick K. O'Brien, "The Needham Question Updated: A Historiographical Survey and Elaboration," *History of Technology* 29 (2009): 7–28.

56 Feng Yu-Jun, "Legal Culture in China: A Comparison to Western Law," *New Zealand Association for Comparative Law Yearbook* 15 (2009): 1–9. Interestingly, data appears to show that in IP cases even today "foreigners do less well on appeals and receive significantly less damage awards" (US Chamber of Commerce, *US–China IP Cooperation Dialogue 2014–2015* [USCC, n.d.), 9 of the English text.

57 Jin Deng-Jian, *The Great Knowledge Transcendence: The Rise of Western Science and Technology Reframed* (Palgrave-Macmillan, 2016), 31.

58 Sandro Sideri, *The Harmonisation of the Protection of Intellectual Property: Impact on Third World Countries*, UNU/INTECH Working Paper no. 14 (United Nations University, 1994), 26.

59 Chen Zhang-Liang and Gao Wang-Sheng, "IP Rights in China: Spurring Invention and Driving Innovation in Health and Agriculture," in *Intellectual Property Management in Health and Agricultural Innovation: A Handbook of Best Practices*, ed. Anatole Krattiger and Richard T. Mahoney (MIHR, 2007), vol. 2, 1585.

60 US Trade Representative, *2015 Report to Congress on China's WTO Compliance* (USTR, n.d.), 3.

61 Peter K. Yu, "The Transplant and Transformation of Intellectual Property Laws in China," in *Governance of Intellectual Property Rights in China and Europe*, ed. Nari Lee, Niklas Braun and Mingde Li (Edward Elgar, 2016), 20.

62 Puchalska-Tych and Salter, "Comparing Legal Cultures," 158.

63 Ibid., 160.

64 US Trade Representative, *2015 Report to Congress*, 4.

65 Bowring, *The Degradation of the International Legal Order*, 187, emphasis added.

66 Allan P. Cramer, "International Copyright and the Soviet Union," *Duke Law Journal* 14 (1965): 533–534.

67 For a detailed analysis, see Michiel Elst, *Copyright, Freedom of Speech and Cultural Policy in the Russian Federation* (Martinus Nijhoff, 2005), 71–90.

68 Cramer, "International Copyright," 532.

69 Thomas Jefferson, for one, was clear that "ideas should freely spread from one to another over the globe, for the moral and mutual instruction of man, and improvement of his condition ... Inventions ... cannot, in nature, be a subject of property." (Letter to Isaac McPherson, August 13, 1813, in *The Writings of Thomas Jefferson*, ed. Andrew A. Lipscomb and Albert Ellery Bergh [Thomas Jefferson Memorial Association, 1905], vol. 13, 333–334, http://tinyurl.com/22udzn, accessed July 6, 2016).

70 See Akalemwa Ngenda, "The Nature of the International Intellectual Property System: Universal Norms and Values or Western Chauvinism?" *Information and Communications Technology Law* 14, no. 1 (2005): 59–79 for further development of this argument in a developmental context.

71 This is precisely the language and the perspective of the Statute of Anne, the language of the copyright clause (Article 1, Section 8, Clause 8) of the US Constitution.

72 Martha Woodmansee, "The Genius and the Copyright: Economic and Legal Conditions of the Emergence of the Author," *Eighteenth-Century Studies* 17, no. 4 (Summer 1984): 426, emphasis added.

73 Carla Hesse, "Enlightenment Epistemology and the Laws of Authorship

in Revolutionary France, 1777–1793," in *Law and the Order of Culture*, ed. Robert Post (University of California Press, 1991), 131, emphasis added.

74 For extracts translated into English, see Arthur Goldhammer, "On Diderot and Condorcet," *Daedalus* 131, no. 2 (Spring 2002): 46–59; Baetens, *Le combat du droit d'auteur*, includes some extracts from Diderot (pp. 25–37) but ignores Condorcet.

75 Hesse, *Publishing and Cultural Politics in Revolutionary Paris*, 3.

76 Trevor Ross, "Copyright and the Invention of Tradition," *Eighteenth-Century Studies* 26, no. 1 (Autumn 1992): 2.

77 Johnson, *Where Do Good Ideas Come From?*, 216.

78 Karl Marx, *Economic and Philosophic Manuscripts of 1844*, 4th rev. ed. (Progress Publishers, 1974), 92.

79 Costas Douzinos, *Human Rights and Empire: The Political Philosophy of Cosmopolitanism* (Routledge-Cavendish, 2007), ix.

80 David and Halbert, *Owning the World of Ideas*, 1.

81 Karl Marx, *Grundrisse: Foundations of the Critique of Political Economy (Rough Draft)* (Penguin and New Left Review, 1973), 127.

4 | THE POLITICAL ECONOMY OF INTELLECTUAL PROPERTY

Michael Perelman

Introduction

Intellectual property is very relevant for a discussion of political economy, especially because so many people seem to regard intellectual property as the pinnacle of a modern market economy. In reality, intellectual property represents a dilemma that neither markets nor conventional economics can successfully resolve.

Economists teach that competition is what makes markets more efficient than planned economies. Competition sparks innovation and drives prices down toward marginal costs – the cost of producing one more unit of output.

The problem is that marginal costs are trivial in the case of intellectual property. If competition were allowed to take effect, producers could not stay in business. How much does the production of a new copy of Microsoft Windows cost? To prevent the price of intellectual property from falling to that level, the government grants Microsoft and other holders of intellectual property monopoly rights to stamp out competition.

Of course, monopoly is a violation of the sacred principles of free markets. For that reason, traditional laissez faire economists opposed intellectual property rights as a violation of market principles.

The contradictions continue. The cost structure of modern industry resembles that of the production of intellectual property. For that reason, the problem of market incompatibility extends to modern industry. For example, in the railroad business, the cost of producing one more unit is insignificant because that cost does not include previously sunk costs.

During the late nineteenth century, industry discovered first how to effectively harness the power of fossil fuel on a large scale, creating what might be called "The Real Industrial Revolution." These new methods depended upon heavy investments in expensive capital goods. Much as reproducing a pharmaceutical pill or a computer program costs very little, the cost of adding another ton of freight or producing another ton of steel costs very little relative to the underlying capital costs. For that reason, in the late nineteenth century, the prices of industrial products tumbled. For example, the Bessemer process reduced the price of steel rails by 88 percent from the early 1870s to the late 1880s; electrolytic refining reduced aluminum by 96 percent; synthetic blue dye production costs fell by 95 percent from the 1870s to 1886.[1] As this pricing problem spread, the economy experienced what was called "The Great Depression" until another episode acquired that label.

As waves of bankruptcies spread across the country, faith in markets quickly dissolved. Terrified business leaders took refuge from competition by consolidating industries into operations large enough to control prices. Of course, this behavior more or less eliminated the imagined workings of a market economy.

The absence of competition allowed for higher prices to redistribute wealth and income to the already well endowed. In addition, without the prodding of competition, business no longer felt pressure to develop more efficient methods of production. In effect, manufacturing was operating much like businesses today that profit from the ownership of intellectual property.

The political economy of intellectual property

According to two distinguished scholars of intellectual property, Fritz Machlup and Edith Penrose, "At the end of the 1860s the cause of patent protection seemed completely lost." But with the onset of the Depression, those principled free traders who opposed intellectual property rights as a violation of laissez faire lost ground to the protectionists. In the words of Machlup and Penrose, "The idea of patent protection regained its public appeal when, after the crisis of 1873, protectionists won out over free traders."[2] In the midst of this horrific market failure, arguments that intellectual property represented a violation of free market principles carried little weight.

Conveniently, intellectual property rights allowed major corporations to circumvent the recently enacted Sherman Antitrust Act of 1890. Before this legislation, corporations had routinely ignored the intellectual property of independent inventors. Intellectual

property rights also helped to reinforce the powers of giant corporations, which could afford their own research laboratories and then
take advantage of the protections afforded by intellectual property
rights to create monopolies that got around the Sherman Act.

For example, the faltering of the US economy at the end of the
1960s set off a panic in many corners of the economy. To make
matters worse, the longstanding surplus in the balance of trade of
the United States turned negative. US corporations were rapidly
losing ground to foreign competitors as manufactured goods poured
into the United States. Government leaders agonized about finding
ways to increase exports. This conflict between expediency and the
principles of political economy came to the fore again. Strengthening
intellectual property rights seemed to be a logical strategy for
promoting exports from the United States while transferring money
from consumers to business.

So, rather than symbolizing the pinnacle of market success, intellectual property rights are an expression of the failure of the market.
Patents and other intellectual property rights come to the fore when
markets threaten to self-destruct.

Moreover, such a crisis is not necessarily negative from the
perspective of capitalism. As Hardt and Negri explain:

> Marx claims that capitalism does indeed have a fundamental
> interest in economic crisis for its transformative power . . .
> Economic crisis can . . . destroy unprofitable sectors, restructure
> the organisation of production and renew its technologies. In
> other words, economic crisis can push forward a transformation
> that re-establishes a high general rate of profit.[3]

Harvey identifies two fundamental ways in which excess capital
is absorbed.[4] The first involves long-term capital investment – i.e.
"temporal" fix – which can either be profit-oriented (such as the
launch of a new product) or alternatively, social expenditure (such
as the provision of public services or resources). The second form of
response that Harvey identifies is spatial, and might involve attempts
at creating new markets, or re-organizing existing resources or
seeking to find new ones (e.g. land/labor/raw materials). In practice,
these "spatio-temporal" fixes combine to offer resolution to the crisis
of over-accumulation.

We can see this "fix" in operation by observing the shift in investment strategies towards service industries from the early 1970s onwards.[5]

The most powerful multinational corporations in the United States took advantage of this climate and energetically lobbied for stronger intellectual property rights.[6] A valuable journalistic study of the subject described the change in the perception of intellectual property:

[A]s a flood of imports washed away millions of domestic manufacturing jobs, attitudes toward patents and their role in the economic equation began to change. The interests of industry and labor coalesced in the search for viable weapons in the fight against foreign competition. The election of Ronald Reagan further shifted the mood toward protection of intellectual property. The major philosophical argument against patent protection – that it was inherently monopolistic – was no longer politically or, even more to the point, economically correct in an era of increasing trade competition. The policy of using antitrust laws against companies that refused to license their patent technologies was reversed by the Justice Department.[7]

The US government's first reaction to growing exports was to coerce individual countries to restrain their exports. In the words of Paul David, an economic historian who specializes in matters concerning science and technology:

[D]uring the 1980s, the U.S. government responded to the concerns of American producers – especially chemical, pharmaceutical, electronic and information technology industries – by trying to reverse the trend of the preceding two decades. Acting with some encouragement from other industrially advanced countries, the United States pursued a direct, unilateral course of action. It did not make any major effort to negotiate agreements within the framework of the Paris Convention for the Protection of Industrial Property (patents and trademarks); the Berne Convention for the Protection of Literary and Artistic Works (copyrights) or other international conventions, nor did it offer some quid pro quo to other developing nations that would agree to such conventions. Instead, by threatening within the context of bilateral trade negotiations to impose sanctions on developing and newly industrialized nations whose retaliatory leverage was quite limited, the United States achieved considerable leverage in convincing foreign governments to acquiesce to its position on the treatment of various forms of intellectual property.[8]

Then, the government reversed course, but not without prodding. In the words of Edmund J. Pratt, Chairman Emeritus of Pfizer, published on the company website:

> In 1983, Pfizer joined with other corporations such as Merck, Johnson & Johnson, Bristol-Myers, IBM, Hewlett Packard, General Motors, General Electric, Rockwell International, Du Pont, Monsanto, and Warner Communications to form the Intellectual Property Committee to advocate intellectual property protection. The committee helped convince U.S. officials that we should take a tough stance on intellectual property issues, and that led to trade-related intellectual property rights being included on the GATT agenda when negotiations began in Punta del Este, Uruguay, in 1986.[9]

Six months earlier, before the negotiations for the Uruguay Round of the General Agreement on Tariffs and Trade, the chief executive officers of 12 major corporations belonging to the committee met again. The result was profound:

> The IPC [Intellectual Property Committee], in conjunction with its counterparts in Europe and Japan, crafted a proposal based on existing industrialized country laws and presented its proposals to the GATT Secretariat. By 1994, the IPC had achieved its goal in the Trade Related Aspects of Intellectual Property (TRIPs) accord of the Uruguay trade round . . . In effect, twelve corporations made public law for the world.[10]

Domestic law also changed to enhance intellectual property rights. The history of the semiconductor industry exemplifies this trend toward changing the legal structure to help firms gain a competitive advantage from intellectual property rights rather than from developing an edge in productive capabilities.

As late as 1981, Roger S. Borovoy, vice-president and chief counsel for Intel Corporation, complained about the need to strengthen the hold of intellectual property rights because "In the electronics industry, patents are of no value whatsoever in spurring research and development."[11] A recent study published by the Philadelphia branch of the Federal Reserve System describes the dramatic transition that came soon after Mr. Borovoy's evaluation of the importance of the patent system to his industry:

Within the US semiconductor industry, reverse-engineering was a well-established practice. But by the late 1970s, American firms objected to similar behavior by Japanese firms when they began to increase their market share in the more standardized products, such as computer memory chips. The level of competition eventually became so intense that, by the mid-1980s, most American companies abandoned these segments entirely.

When it became clear they could no longer dominate Japanese firms on the basis of production technology alone, American firms attempted to consolidate their comparative advantage in research and development. To do this, they would have to find ways of reducing their competitors' ability to reverse-engineer their products. To that end, American companies began to lobby Congress to increase intellectual property protection for their semiconductor designs. In 1984, Congress created a new form of intellectual property right, called mask rights, especially tailored to address the needs articulated by the industry.[12]

During this period, Texas Instruments and National Semiconductor were both tottering on the verge of bankruptcy. Irving Rappaport, former vice-president and associate general counsel for intellectual property at National Semiconductor recalled:

I'm not exaggerating when I tell you that National Semiconductor was only weeks away from bankruptcy in late 1990 . . . All the papers had been signed before it was decided to continue the business and give licensing a more aggressive push. And without a doubt, patent fees bought us valuable time in which to complete our restructuring process. For a while there, in fact, three-quarters of our revenues came from patent licenses.[13]

Texas Instruments struck first. Typically license fees ran about 1 percent of revenues. In 1987, Texas Instruments raised its royalties on chips to 5 percent.[14] The company filed a suit against one Korean and eight Japanese semiconductor companies, accusing them of infringing on semiconductor patents. The settlements yielded the company more than US$600 million in payments, according to a 1990 report. The company became so aggressive in seeking royalties that by 1992 it earned US$391 million in royalties, compared to an operating income of only US$274 million.[15]

In effect, these companies were beginning to transform the semiconductor industry from a manufacturing industry to a service industry, just as the postindustrial utopians would have them do it. According to one industry insider, James Koford of LSI Logic, "Silicon Valley and Route 128 are worlds of intellectual property, not capital equipment and production. Most of the employees of U.S. high technology live in southeast Asia."[16] Some, like George Gilder, applaud this arrangement, arguing that these companies will rationally maximize their profits by specializing in the design of computer chips.[17] But this new legal framework allowed some of the most important high-tech enterprises to become a perverse kind of service sector. Rather than directly providing services, they merely demanded payment for their intellectual property.

Not only did the administrative arm of government become more sympathetic to the rights of intellectual property; the judicial system, with vigorous support from the legislative side, also moved to embrace intellectual property rights more warmly. In 1982, the Federal Courts Improvement Act established the Court of Appeals for the Federal Circuit as a central patent appeals court to streamline the litigation process and create a judicial body for appellate review of the patent infringement decisions of the lower courts.[18]

This court has been very sympathetic to the claims of patent holders. Previously, the percentage of court decisions that upheld patents had been increasing from roughly 60 percent in the 1950s to more than 70 percent in the 1970s, suggesting a possible weakening of standards.[19] The new court now upholds patents 80 percent of the time.[20]

Prior to 1986, federal courts frequently decided the validity of a patent based on a preponderance of the evidence standard; that is, which side presented more convincing evidence. In 1986, the Federal Circuit ruled that a patent should be presumed to be valid until proven otherwise by clear and convincing evidence, a more difficult standard, based on several legal precedents.[21]

This trend toward upholding a larger share of patents comes at a time when the scope of patents has broadened at an unprecedented rate. For example, in recent years, the patent system has begun granting claims for computer software, life forms and even business practices. When moving into such previously uncharted terrain, a growing number of questionable proposals would be expected to come up for consideration. Nonetheless, the proportion of patents approved has continued to increase.

Each year, the government of the United States moves to strengthen intellectual property rights still further. Patents now last 20 years instead of 17, despite the fact that high technology typically becomes obsolete in less time than ever before. In addition, a new law recently has transformed many types of copyright infringement into criminal offenses.

At the time of this writing, furthering the powers of domestic holders of intellectual property in the international marketplace is one of the highest priorities of US economic policy, if not the highest. The creation of the World Trade Organization (WTO) in 1995 symbolized this expanding role of intellectual property. The forerunner of the WTO, the General Agreement on Tariffs and Trade, had the mission of liberalizing trade in goods. The WTO, in contrast, vigorously enforces trade in intellectual property.

To illustrate the outcome of such processes in broad economic terms, by 2015, the value added by the total copyright industries to US GDP was estimated at almost US$2.1 trillion (11.69 percent of the US economy), with the annual growth rate of foreign sales and exports for core copyright industries continuing to rise year on year.[22] This incorporates data from across a range of sectors including chemical, aerospace, electrical, pharmaceutical and medicines, and a host of cultural industry domains including film, music, print publishing, software publishing among others.

Moreover, the Trade Related Aspects of Intellectual Property Rights (TRIPS) agreement – an international legal agreement between WTO member states – serves to open up the markets of less developed states to major Western IPR holders. Laing illustrates how the changes to national legislation regimes brought about by TRIPS are complemented by the actions of the USTR.[23] From the early years of the Reagan era, the USTR has played a significant role in the extension of intellectual property laws around the world. With responsibility for US trade policy and bilateral and multilateral level agreements, the USTR is essentially an executive branch of the American government operating within the Executive Office of the President (EOP). US trade law requires the compilation of an annual report – i.e. *Special 301* – which identifies and examines "those countries that deny adequate and effective protection for IPR or deny fair and equitable market access for persons that rely on intellectual property protection" – (we should remember here that corporations are categorized as individuals/persons for the purposes of law). "Countries . . . that have the greatest adverse impact (actual or potential) on the relevant US products must be designated as Priority Foreign Countries." Under Section 306, the USTR "monitors a country's compliance with bi-lateral intellectual property agreements . . . [and] may apply sanctions if a country fails to satisfactorily implement an agreement."[24] May's research shows how developing countries are currently receiving extensive technical support in training legislators and administrators from a variety of international, government and non-governmental organizations.[25] According to Hesmondhalgh, "this is cultural neo-liberalism, buttressed by US trade power" and it is enabled by the "geopolitical-economic" developments outlined above.[26] In many ways we may see this as the logical "next step" in the process of accumulation by dispossession. As Harvey tells us:

> Free trade and open capital markets have become primary means
> through which to advantage the monopoly powers based in
> the advanced capitalist countries that already dominate trade,
> production, services and finance within the capitalist world. The
> primary vehicle for accumulation by dispossession therefore,
> has been the forcing open of markets throughout the world by
> institutional pressures exercised by the IMF and the WTO,
> backed by the power of the United States (and to a lesser extent

Europe) to deny access to its own vast market to those countries that refuse to dismantle their protections.[27]

The costs of intellectual property

Intellectual property was intended to rescue capitalist interests. It did so to the extent that intellectual property managed to transfer considerable amounts of money from the public to a narrow swath of the corporate sector. Nonetheless, the unintended consequences of intellectual property seem to have proved counterproductive. To begin with, control of intellectual property rights put a premium on antisocial behavior. Most absurdly, patent trolls buy up bankrupt companies for their patents, which they then use to sue other companies for violations of intellectual property rights. For the most part, paying off these patent trolls is cheaper than going through a multimillion-dollar lawsuit. The resources wasted in this way are a deadweight loss to the economy. The problem was made worse by largely defunding the US Patent Office, making it dependent on the fees it charges. This policy had a twofold negative effect. First of all, patent examiners' wages are very low relative to those of a private patent attorney. Second, because of the need for fees, examiners were expected to pump out patents too quickly be able to evaluate them effectively. The result is to create a web of confusion due to overlapping patent claims, leading to wasteful legal processes.

This arrangement means that developers of intellectual property must go to great pains in order to figure out how they can navigate the complex patent thicket without being liable for violating somebody else's virtual property. Another defensive measure is to attempt to patent everything but the kitchen sink. Whoever might be tempted to sue for violations of intellectual property would then have to face a countersuit. In doing so, the patent thicket is made even thicker.

Secrecy is a major form of defending intellectual property because others would like to claim the same work as their own intellectual property. Of course, science and technology depend upon the cross fertilization of information. In fact, one of the major justifications for the patent system was to make inventors reveal their work in return for what was a relatively short period of monopoly. That the system turned out to create incentives for secrecy is further evidence of the dysfunctionality of the whole system of intellectual property. As if the damage from secrecy were not enough, a simultaneous defunding of higher education took a serious toll. As a substitute for public funds, research universities increasingly turned to seeking profits from the production of intellectual property, often under contract with major corporations. This arrangement distorted a good deal of higher education. First of all, the bulk of new developments in science and technology come from university or government research, both of which have been defunded (except that related to military needs). Universities have shifted away from the development of basic science, the economic payoffs of which are uncertain. However, a good number of breakthroughs in basic science have had revolutionary benefits for society.

The new emphasis on applied science at the expense of basic science – often done at the behest of large corporate interests – promises quick profits at the expense of the kind of science that drives breakthrough science and technology. To make matters worse, in this new effort to finance universities, excessive resources are channeled to those parts of the university most likely to generate valuable intellectual property. In addition, in order to increase the probability of intellectual property bonanzas, secrecy becomes a priority, damaging the future prospects of science and technology.

Intellectual property creates another serious form of waste. Although intellectual property is intended to block others from using a particular kind of knowledge or technology, competitors devote considerable time and energy trying to reverse engineer technology by working around pre-existing claims – in effect, reinventing wheels.

Reverse engineering, in turn, creates another form of waste; namely that corporations take competitors to court for their efforts to reverse engineer. Such court cases can routinely cost tens of millions of dollars. These costs do not include the public expenses for paying for judges and other personnel, over and above the constructing and maintenance of the physical infrastructure used for conducting the trials. One might also count the time jurors waste, hearing these trials that can last for months. Finally, highly paid lawyers and other experts spend considerable time and expense in bringing themselves up to date in the intricacies of technology and the state of intellectual property law in order to participate in the highly lucrative business of overseeing the bickering of greedy corporations. Probably even greater than all these costs is the value of the scientific and technical progress that might have occurred in the absence of intellectual property.

An international inversion

For most of the nineteenth century, the United States was notorious for its unwillingness to respect copyrights from other countries. As soon as an important publication appeared in England, representatives of American publishers rushed across the sea to pick up a copy to reprint without paying royalties.

Once the United States had matured to the point where it became more of a producer of intellectual property in the late nineteenth century, copyrights were also strengthened. Many developing countries behave similarly for the same reason as the United States did – because they were mostly consumers rather than producers of intellectual property.

While the new regime of intellectual property is corroding the US economy, other countries are seriously funding higher education in order to produce a more vibrant system for developing science and technology. As this new version takes hold, the United States, still the primary cheerleader for intellectual property, finds itself more as a customer than as a producer for new intellectual property.

Concluding remarks

The general shift from the Keynesian, welfare-state regulatory regime to neoliberalism has wrought significant shifts in the contours of societal development, in the distribution of material wealth and income as well as power since the early 1980s. While its own discourses and practices prefer to frame such developments in terms of "de-regulation" or liberalization, from this system's perspective neoliberalism comprises another mode of regulation (or re-regulation). For sure these discourses and practices have privileged and promoted private sector interests, market-based processes and logics, individualized and consumer identities and roles over those of citizenship or the public. But in place of any fundamental "rolling back of the state" we see a selective hollowing out of certain state-based administrative and distributional roles accompanied by major extensions in other domains, not least those related to the enhancement of rights and privileges attaching to intellectual and other forms of property.

The neoliberal turn has also seen a significant centralization of power and control within the state administrative systems. This has been accompanied by similar shifts in the conduct of formal political processes deemed to regulate such systems, in part facilitated by the processes of mediatization and professionalization of politics.[28]

Other features of the neoliberal turn include a propensity to import the values, norms and practices of the private sector market economy into public sector services. Notwithstanding the rhetoric of the "rolling back" of state engagement in specific industrial sectors, neoliberal policy practices and discourses have also involved an array of initiatives directed at promoting the adoption and use of new ICT-based systems and networks. These include various "information society" or "knowledge economy" policy campaigns strategies, since the early 1980s. They also include positioning all forms of knowledge production as "a new frontier" for exploitation by capitalist market forces, signaling a fundamental shift towards deepening commodification, "making a business of information."

One of Karl Marx's most interesting insights was that efforts to overcome contradictions in capitalism tend to create new contradictions that can be even more troubling than the initial problem. Intellectual property is a case in point for two reasons; first as a strategy for overcoming immediate economic difficulties of unsustainable competitive pricing in industries with a high organic composition of capital; second (and perhaps more interestingly) as evidence of contradictions in the supposed science of economics, which pretends to demonstrate how markets, left to themselves, automatically lead to ideal outcomes. In short, while competition is presumed to be the driver of a market economy, competitive pressures will cause a market economy to self-destruct unless it has external supports – such as intellectual property rights – to limit competition.

Notes

1 Michael C. Jensen, "The Modern Industrial Revolution: Exit and the Failure of Internal Control Systems," *Journal of Finance* 48, no. 3 (July 1993): 835.

2 Fritz Machlup and Edith Penrose, "The Patent Controversy in the Nineteenth Century," *Journal of Economic History* 10, no. 1 (May 1950): 5.

3 M. Hardt and A. Negri, *Empire* (Harvard University Press, 2000), 264.

4 D. Harvey, *The Condition of Postmodernity* (Blackwell, 1989).

5 See David Hesmondhalgh, *The Cultural Industries*, 3rd ed. (Sage, 2012), for a summary of scholarly works detailing this process.

6 Ove Granstrand, *The Economics and Management of Intellectual Property: Towards Intellectual Capitalism* (Edward Elgar, 2000), 39, 53; Michael P. Ryan, *Knowledge Diplomacy: Global Competition and the Politics of Intellectual Property* (Brookings Institution Press, 1998).

7 Fred Warshofsky, *The Patent Wars: The Battle to Own the World's Technology* (Wiley, 1994), 8; Robert M. Hunt, "Patent Reform: A Mixed Blessing for the U.S. Economy?" *Business Review of the Federal Reserve Bank of Philadelphia* (November–December 1999): 19.

8 Paul A. David, "Intellectual Property Institutions and the Panda's Thumb: Patents, Copyrights, and Trade Secrets in Economic Theory and History," in *Global Dimensions of Intellectual Property Rights in Science and Technology*, ed. Mitchel B. Wallerstein, Mary E. Mogee and Robin A. Schoen (National Research Council, 1993), 20, www.nap.edu/books/0309048338/html/19.html.

9 www.pfizer.com/pfizerinclpolicy/intellectualpropfrm.html.

10 Susan K. Sell, "Multinational Corporations as Agents of Change: The Globalization of Intellectual Property Rights," in *Private Authority and International Affairs*, ed. A. Claire Cutler, Virginia Haufler and Tony Porter (State University of New York Press, 1999), 169, 172.

11 Anon., "The Patent Is Expiring as a Spur to Innovation," *Business Week*, Industrial/Technology edition, May 11, 1981: 44C.

12 Hunt, "Patent Reform," 19–20.

13 Kevin G. Rivette and David Kline, *Rembrandts in the Attic: Unlocking the Hidden Value of Patents* (Harvard Business School Press, 2000), 125–126.

14 Paul Dwyer et al., "The Battle Raging Over 'Intellectual Property'," *Business Week*, May 22, 1989, 79.

15 Warshofsky, *The Patent Wars*, 111.

16 Cited in Martin Kenney and Richard Florida, *Beyond Mass Production: The Japanese System and Its Transfer to the U.S.* (Oxford University Press, 1993), 237.

17 George Gilder, *Microcosm: The Quantum Revolution in Economics and Technology* (Simon & Schuster, 1989).

18 Warshofsky, *The Patent Wars*, 9.

19 Frederick M. Scherer, *Industrial Market Structure and Economic Performance*, 2nd ed. (Rand McNally, 1980), 155, 449.

20 Warshofsky, *The Patent Wars*, 9.

21 Robert M. Hunt, "You Can Patent That? Are Patents on Computer Programs and Business Methods Good for the New Economy?" *Business Review of the Federal Reserve Bank of Philadelphia* (first quarter, 2001): 5–15, referring to: *Medtronics Inc., Intermedics Inc., and Hybritech Inc. vs. Monoclonal Antibodies Inc.*

22 S.E. Siwik, *Copyright Industries in the US Economy: The 2016 Report* (The International Intellectual Property Alliance, 2016).

23 D. Laing, "Copyright, Politics and the International Music Industry," in *Music and Copyright*, 2nd ed., ed. S. Frith and L. Marshall (Edinburgh University Press, 2004), 70–85.

24 www.ustr.gov.

25 C. May, "Capacity Building and the (Re)production of Intellectual Property Rights," *Third World Quarterly* 25, no. 5 (2004): 821–837.

26 D. Hesmondhalgh, "New Imperialisms, Cultural and Otherwise," paper presented at the Conference of the International Association for Media and Communication Research (IAMCR), American University, Cairo, Egypt, July 27, 2006, 9.

27 David Harvey, *A Brief History of Neoliberalism* (Oxford University Press, 2005), 181.

28 A. Sampson, "The Fourth Estate Under Fire," *The Guardian*, January 10, 2005, 2.

5 | I AM BECAUSE I OWN VS. I AM BECAUSE WE ARE[1]

Mat Callahan

> As no party, in the present age, can well support itself
> without a philosophical or speculative system of principles
> annexed to its political or practical one, we accordingly find,
> that each of the factions into which this nation is divided has
> reared up a fabric of the former kind, in order to protect and
> cover that scheme of actions which it pursues. (David Hume,
> *Of the Original Contract*)

Introduction

It need hardly be said that Intellectual Property (IP) is based on
the idea that ideas – or at least certain expressions of ideas – can
be owned. It is furthermore obvious that this concept derives from
another, more basic one, regarding ownership, as such. That an idea
of ownership and the ownership of ideas have a peculiar history,
and one indissolubly linked to the European Enlightenment, is not
controversial, indeed, the facts are well documented. Carla Hesse,
Ellen Meiksins Wood and Susan B. Sell[2] are among the historians
who've offered excellent accounts of the process that led to our
present circumstances, as does the chapter devoted to the subject in
the present volume. This process of course includes the great political
conflicts of the last 500 years, encompassing not only Europe but
the entire globe and not only parliamentary debate but revolutionary
seizures of power, from which both a particular idea of ownership
and the ownership of ideas emerged triumphant.

Controversy persists, however, over the content of these ideas,
their correctness or incorrectness when tested in social practice and
whether or not they have a future, regardless of being widely held in
the past or present. After all, many ideas, such as the geocentric solar
system or the existence of different "races" of humans, have been
exposed as false after long acceptance as true. Indeed, holding such

ideas today is a mark of superstition or ignorance. In the case of IP, unquestioned assumptions purported to be "self-evident," "natural" or so generally accepted as to be "common sense," obstruct serious inquiry into the merit of the ideas themselves. A striking example is the scarcity of evidence either confirming or denying the achievement of IP's stated aims. Two hundred years should be enough to answer the question: Has "the Progress of Science and useful Arts," called for by the Constitution of the United States, been promoted or has it not? Has "the Encouragement of Learning" been facilitated or hindered? The only indisputable facts are that the overwhelming majority of revenue-generating patents and copyrights are held by a few large corporations while surveys, however inconclusive, suggest that most artists and scientists are motivated by a desire to explore and do so for little or no financial reward.[3]

This has, in recent years, attracted the attention of legal scholars such as James Boyle who declared IP to be an "evidence-free zone."[4] His call for empirical testing has been echoed by others like William Patry and Jessica Silby who decry the "faith-based" policy-making of industry and government, which show, furthermore, little regard for either the original purpose IP was to serve or the lived experience of those it is supposed to "incentivize and protect."[5] If one were to consult the arguments of Thomas Jefferson and Thomas Macaulay (as Boyle and other legal scholars recommend) one discovers that the purpose of copyright, patent and trademark was not, primarily, to remunerate authors and inventors.[6] It was for the advancement of the public, *not* the private interest. The principle: "for a limited time" was explicit, specific and repeated often for a reason: to ensure the return to the public domain of all expressions, i.e. songs, novels, designs, formulas, etc. that are, ultimately, the product of human endeavor in aggregate, and which could not be held in perpetuity by anyone, lest they deny humanity its collective inheritance.[7] Jefferson went so far as to add,

it is a fact, as far as I am informed, that England was, until we copied her, the only country on earth which ever, by a general law, gave a legal right to the exclusive use of an idea. In some other countries it is sometimes done, in a great case, and by a special and personal act, but, generally speaking, other nations have thought that these monopolies produce more embarrassment than advantage to society; and it may be observed that the nations which refuse monopolies of invention, are as fruitful as England in new and useful devices.[8]

Yet, to this day, little effort has been made to find out what, if any, social benefit has been derived from IP.

Another example is the case of indigenous peoples who are the creators or inventors of a vast storehouse of artistic and scientific knowledge but who do not share Eurocentric notions of property ownership or the egoistic assumptions underlying them.[9] If anything, the plundering of this knowledge by large European and North American firms confirms the usefulness of ideas produced without the incentives purported to be necessary by defenders of IP while simultaneously demonstrating the close resemblance between the original conquest of land that created the category "indigenous peoples" in the first place, and present-day attempts to expropriate the songs, stories, clothing, textiles, dies, medicinal and nutritional plants that are the product of thousands of years of human ingenuity. For the last 40 years or more, indigenous peoples have waged a tireless battle against this new form of colonization.[10] Their resistance is not confined to a fight over money but is a challenge to the very concepts of author, inventor and proprietor that are IP's ostensible *raison d'être*. Indeed, monetization, capitalism's solution for everything, only reveals the conflict's irreconcilability, one that bears a striking resemblance to the Copernican threat to Church dogma concerning the order of the universe!

Many tribes explain that their existence consists in this: belonging to the tribe renders incoherent or nonsensical any notion of a single person privately appropriating what originates in and depends on the tribe for its being. Thus, to suggest that a song belong to one man is as meaningless as saying that the tribe can be owned by one of its members or that a skill, such as musical composition, is to be hoarded by one person and not passed down from generation to generation. Indeed, concepts such as novelty, originality or innovation – defining characteristics of authorship or invention according to IP law – are viewed with a healthy dose of skepticism by many tribal peoples. Just because something is different doesn't make it new and just because something is new doesn't make it good or better than what is old, tried and true. The much vaunted superiority of "advanced technology" has long since proved devastating to the planet Earth, displaying not a commitment to improvement but a pathological obsession with conquest and acquisition.

These examples illustrate not only the fact that there is no consensus regarding the legal or practical application of IP regimes, they show that the philosophical premises upon which IP is based are questionable, as well. Yet in the heat of legal or political debate such premises are often overlooked or simply referred to as if they were understood and accepted by all, which nonetheless begs the question posed earlier by David Hume. Because there is nothing "self-evident," i.e. universally agreed upon, about notions of ownership, authorship, the individual or "human nature," these notions bear closer scrutiny in their own right. As we shall see, even the methods of inquiry are not irreproachable. It will therefore be the purpose of this chapter to question the concepts themselves as well as the philosophical tools used to question them.

Possessive individualism

In his landmark study, *Possessive Individualism*, C.B. Macpherson examined the work of Thomas Hobbes, John Locke, James Harrington and the Levellers to discover how ideas of property were formed establishing the individual as the sole legitimate proprietor of himself (and it was exclusively a *male* self) while binding self-ownership to rights of citizenship. Henceforth the indissoluble connection between liberty and property was promulgated providing not only a rationale for a manifestly unequal regime but an article of faith which over the next 300 years would make liberty and property, capitalism and democracy, synonymous, indeed, indistinguishable.

While Hobbes, Harrington and the Levellers each contributed to the formation and propagation of possessive individualism, the most influential at the time and ever since was Locke. His basic premises are so well known they can quickly be summarized: first occupancy, self-ownership and labor. We will examine these concepts in greater detail further on but what Macpherson revealed is that within them lay contradictions, and even if one were to accept them uncritically, social reality refused to conform to their claims of justice or universality. Macpherson therefore concludes:

> The dilemma of modern liberal-democratic theory is now
> apparent: it must continue to use the assumptions of possessive

individualism, at a time when the structure of market society no longer provides the necessary conditions for deducing a valid theory of political obligation from those assumptions . . . No way out of the dilemma is to be found by rejecting those assumptions while not rejecting market society, as so many theorists from John Stuart Mill to our own time have done on the ground that the assumptions are morally offensive. If they are now morally offensive they are none the less still factually accurate for our possessive market societies. The dilemma remains. Either we reject possessive individualist assumptions, in which case our theory is unrealistic, or we retain them, in which case we cannot get a valid theory of obligation. It follows that we cannot now expect a valid theory of obligation to a liberal democratic state in a possessive market society.[11]

The recognition of an irreconcilable contradiction between possessive individualism and social obligation was Macpherson's important insight. Even if the seventeenth-century concept establishing white, male property owners as the only eligible voters, office holders or judges was expanded to include everyone, "regardless of race, creed or color," it retained intact an exclusionary premise. If my exclusive proprietorship is my citizenship, then what authority may legitimately infringe upon my property without denying my freedom? What basis other than force and fraud can compel my acquisitive self to submit to service of society, the state, much less altruistic appeals to "the common good"?

Macpherson could offer no way out other than to suggest that the threat of nuclear war might force humanity to renew its obligation to social welfare. His book ends with the suggestion that a Hobbesian fear of mutually assured destruction might force people to cooperate albeit with a nominally democratic state instead of Hobbes's Absolute Monarch.

Having exposed the dilemma, however, Macpherson remains on its horns since he won't take the necessary step: we must "reject possessive individualist assumptions" because they are false. Their facticity resides in their being widely believed, not in their correct apprehension of reality. The "cognitive dissonance" between "possessive individualism" and a "valid theory of obligation to a liberal democratic state" arises from evidence proving the concepts to be

flawed and for specific reasons. First, because the being of ownership, its ontological status, consists in antagonism between people,
arising from and reinforcing conflict. Second, ownership applied to
a person is a justification for slavery – even if it is ostensibly only
applied to oneself. If I can own myself, I am property, all of which
market society makes subject to exchange. I can therefore decide
to make myself the property of someone else (which is indeed
what wage laborers do for part of their lives). This, furthermore,
explains why ownership must be constantly policed, inculcated and
sanctified. Not only is it not "natural" in the sense that everyone,
everywhere shares the same concept and has from time immemorial
but because it constantly – literally every day – comes up against
the reality that the individual who is purported to be the owner of
him/herself is utterly dependent for his/her existence on a multitude
of other "selves" gathered in a society all faced with the same conun-
drum: *I am because I own vs. I am because we are.*

Here Mrs. Thatcher's notorious quip, "there is no such thing
as society. There are individual men and women, and there are
families,"[12] is noteworthy in its perversity. Rather, the reverse is true.
There is no such thing as the individual. There are families and there
is society. The preponderance of biological and evolutionary evidence
indicates that the individual is only a figment of our imagination
resulting from certain features of our sensory apparatus along with
the fact that, like our skin cells, we die one by one. But otherwise, we
are born, live and create in groups and for groups and without groups
our species, including all its members, would perish.

Here it is necessary to recall that the *sovereign individual* was, in
the first place, a radical idea, not connected with any concept of
property. The Protestant Reformation made the individual *conscience*
a vital weapon in the hands of religious dissenters and political
radicals. Indeed, "individualism" was conceived in opposition to
Royal Absolutism, Papal Indulgences and, increasingly, against
slavery. If original sin created the morally culpable individual, then a
corresponding authority should reside with that individual, making
every Christian, at least potentially, a priest. The sovereign – supreme
ruler – was thereby linked to the conception of the individual free to
pursue his or her own path to God. The implications were politically
revolutionary as figures, such as Thomas Münzer and Jan Huss, and
movements like the Anabaptists were to show. By the time of the

American, French and Haitian revolutions the idea of the individual as his (in rare cases, *her*) own sovereign had taken hold in Europe and its dominions, and among all classes of people, including slaves. Oscar Wilde would argue, a century later, that individualism could even be conceived in opposition to private property: "With the abolition of private property, then, we shall have true, beautiful, healthy Individualism. Nobody will waste his life in accumulating things, and the symbols for things. One will live. To live is the rarest thing in the world. Most people exist, that is all."[13] Individualism could thus be advanced as an ideal which would unite the oppressed against suffering and injustice. There were ample reasons yeoman farmers, artisans, intellectuals, women and slaves could be united under the banner of Liberté, Egalité, Fraternité. But the realization of each person's full potential was frequently invoked as the goal and justification for revolution. Indeed, that ideal would be expressed in the communist maxim: *from each according to their ability, to each according to their need.*

It was Locke's welding together of the individual with ownership that proved decisive in the long run, however – at least until now. Now the question has arisen anew: Why does belonging have two mutually exclusive definitions in the English language: ownership vs. membership? How can one speak of "owning" oneself when all humans share genealogies that make each a part of a group be that a family, tribe, nation, class or some subset thereof? Does ownership have any material being or is it merely a debatable abstraction, or worse, a deceptive illusion? What, in other words, *is* ownership to human being, the being of ideas, to the universe or the infinite? Does ownership confer life, liberty and happiness in human community or is it the source of discord, suffering and injustice?

To explore these questions is to go beyond the limits of history and law into the realm of philosophy which, in turn, requires clarifying what is meant by the term "philosophy." Not only do many books devoted to IP use philosophy in their title, e.g. *The Philosophy of Intellectual Property*,[14] but certain philosophers are so commonly cited it borders on cliché. Locke and Hegel, for example, appear in so many chapters, articles, essays and speeches that it might appear that a consensus exists among philosophers supporting premises on which IP makes its claims. What makes this odd is not only the fact that from Locke to Hegel, arguments advanced supporting private property were contested by other philosophers – Rousseau and Marx, for example – but that philosophy is invoked as if everyone shared a precise definition of the term and the methods of inquiry by which philosophy was originally constituted. Nothing could be further from the truth, however. Along with the objections to IP raised by, among others, indigenous peoples, there are within the domain of philosophy itself founding principles that conflict, categorically, with IP's most cherished notions. A brief overview of philosophy's own development may help clarify the issue.

What is philosophy?

It is customary to attribute the coining of the term philosophy to Pythagoras of fifth century BCE Greece. According to Diogenes Laertius, "Pythagoras was the first person who invented philosophy, and who called himself a philosopher . . . for he said that no man ought to be called wise, but only God."[15] Pythagoras identified himself as a "lover of wisdom" to distinguish himself, on the one hand, from the Gods – or religion – and, on the other, from the Sophists. As Kathleen Freeman writes in her *Ancilla to the Pre-Socratic Philosophers*,

> Sophistes' originally meant "skilled craftsman" or "wise man."
> The specialized meaning of "professional teacher" did not come
> into use until the end of the fifth century B.C., the period of the
> traveling teachers. The bad sense of the word developed almost
> immediately; Aristotle summed up the Sophist's art as "the
> appearance, not the reality, of wisdom," and the Sophist as one
> who makes money out of this pretense.[16]

Once set upon its course, philosophy developed in three distinct ways as Diogenes Laertius tells us: "Natural, Ethical and Dialectic. Natural philosophy occupies about the world and the things in it; Ethical philosophy about life and the things that concern us; Dialectics are conversant with the arguments by which both the others are supported." Diogenes Laertius goes further to describe what means and ends define philosophy:

> there are certain criteria of truth: first of all the faculty which
> judges, and this is the superior one; the other that which is the
> foundation of the judgement, being a most exact appearance of

objects. And the first principles of everything he calls matter, and
the agent, and the quality, and the place. For they show out of
what, and by what and how, and where anything is done. The
end is that to which everything is referred; namely, a life made
perfect with every virtue, not without the natural and external
qualities of the body.

Since philosophy can be distinguished from religion and sophistry
according to its three divisions: nature, ethics and dialectics, it is
clear why its fundamental concerns are the questions: What is? What
is not? and What should be? Furthermore, this corresponds to three
basic functions: to explain, to justify and to advocate in a quest for
the Good, the Beautiful and the True. Along these coordinates
philosophy's founding arguments were deployed. Most specifically
directed against the Sophists among whom were the three greatest
and best known, Protagoras, Gorgias and Thrasymachus, each
associated with a particular critique of philosophy against which
philosophy had to defend itself. In brief: Protagoras – relativism,
Gorgias – no truth and Thrasymachus – might makes right.[17]

The Sophists were teachers of rhetoric and public oration. In fact,
they were the first lawyers, elevating the capacity to convince above
and against the pursuit of truth. It was precisely this power and its
undisputed dominance in public affairs that laid the foundation for
casuistry, i.e. case law, legal precedent and hairsplitting, as opposed
to first principles such as justice, equality and the common good
(anyone seeking further clarification of casuistry should read Pascal's
blistering critique in his *Provincial Letters*). As with lawyers, so with
politicians – power vs. justice, hierarchy vs. equality and self-interest
vs. the common good. Certainly, among the founders of philosophy –
most notably Pythagoras and Plato – private property was anathema;
an institution the common good could well do without. As Iamblichus
wrote in his biography of Pythagoras:

The principle of justice is mutuality and equality, through which,
in a way most nearly approximating union of body and soul,
all men become cooperative, and distinguish the mine from
the thine, as is also testified by Plato, who learned this from
Pythagoras. Pythagoras effected this in the best possible manner,
by erasing from common life everything private, while increasing

everything held in common, so far as ultimate possessions, which after all are the causes of tumult and sedition.[18]

Of course, philosophy never succeeded in overcoming its rivals let alone achieving its ends. Erasmus wrote in his *Praise of Folly* (1511) words applicable today:

> To get to the point, then, Fortune loves those who are not too bright, who are headstrong and fond of that proverb "let the die be cast." But wisdom makes men into milksops and that is why you always see these wisemen living in poverty and hunger, their hopes gone up in smoke. They are neglected, inglorious, despised, whereas fools are rolling in money, hold high public office, and (in a word) live in the highest style. For if anyone thinks that happiness consists in gaining the favor of great rulers and living on familiar terms with those bejeweled and golden gods, what could be less helpful than wisdom? Indeed, among such men what could be more harmful? If money is the object, how much profit would a merchant make if, as wisdom dictates, he had scruples about perjuring himself, if he were ashamed when someone caught him lying, if he cared in the least about all those fine points laid down by wisemen about theft and usury.[19]

The Enlightenment

The decade that witnessed the publication of *The Praise of Folly* also included Cortes's conquest of Mexico, Copernicus's publication of his astronomical findings and Luther's proclamation of his *Ninety-Five Theses*. The world began a transformation from which it has yet to emerge. Amidst growing social turmoil, the great discoveries of Copernicus, Galileo, Kepler and Newton, thinkers like Erasmus and his friend Thomas More (author of *Utopia*) were crucial in laying the basis for what has come to be known as the Enlightenment. But similarly to the term philosophy, "The Enlightenment" is often applied so indiscriminately that it serves no purpose other than to obscure the very attributes that made it an event of real significance. For one thing, the Enlightenment cannot be separated from Columbus's "discovery" of the "New World," Europe's subsequent imperial conquests and the enslavement of Africans. Genocide and slavery are as much a factor in the Enlightenment as any other. For another, the Enlightenment cannot be separated from the Protestant Reformation and from revolution, first in the case of England, but more importantly in the case of the American, French and Haitian revolutions which mark the transition from the eighteenth to the nineteenth century. (while the origins of copyright no doubt lie in England's 1710 Statute of Anne, their widespread propagation rest less on that statute than on the American Constitution and the French Rights of Man and Citizen). Though Francis Bacon, Thomas Hobbes and John Locke are considered part of a broadly defined "Enlightenment," the distinctions relevant here – what some have called the Radical Enlightenment – are preponderantly French and so closely associated with philosophy as to provide at least a glimpse of what philosophy might achieve were it to take the place of religion or sophistry in governing society.

According to historian Robert Darnton, this Enlightenment was in fact a social movement inspired by public intellectuals who dubbed themselves "philosophes." With the 1743 publication of Voltaire's *Le Philosophe* the course was set. Darnton explained the impact of this book:

> Writers should conform to an ideal type: neither a scientist nor a savant, but a new phenomenon, the philosophe, part man of letters, part man of the world, and entirely engaged in using letters to rid the world of superstition. This little tract, later incorporated in the *Encyclopédie* and in Voltaire's *Evangile de la raison*, served as a declaration of independence for the intellectual and at the same time provided him with a strategy. He should work within the power structure, promoting an alliance of *gens de lettres* and *gens du monde*, in order to advance the cause of *philosophie*.[20]

Lest there be any doubt as to the purpose or aim of the movement, the great mathematician Nicolas de Condorcet wrote in his final and defining statement:

> The time will therefore come when the sun will shine only on free men who know no other master but their reason; when tyrants and slaves, priests and their stupid or hypocritical instruments will exist only in works of history and on the stage; and when we shall think of them only to pity their victims and their dupes;

to maintain ourselves in a state of vigilance by thinking on their excesses; and to learn how to recognize and so to destroy, by force of reason, the first seeds of tyranny and superstition, should they ever dare to reappear among us.[21]

This optimistic assessment not only represented a view held by revolutionaries of several generations, it was to propel the idea of *inevitable progress* into the forefront of thought for the next 200 years. Condorcet's influence is far greater than is usually acknowledged, especially by current defenders of IP, but along with Rousseau's spirited assault on inequality and the corrupting influence of civil society, Condorcet's were the ideas that were both furthest in advance of current events and most consistent with the philosophy of Pythagoras and Plato. Not surprisingly, they were highly controversial in their own time, pitting their authors against other Enlightenment figures in disputes that have scarcely subsided. Regarding the question of private property, Rousseau was unequivocal: it was a fraudulent usurpation and the source of inequality and social strife. Regarding the ownership of ideas Condorcet was equally unequivocal, affirming the social origins and ends of thought, the inapplicability of comparisons between ideas and land and the inadmissibility of property right to works of the imagination.

As recorded by historian Carla Hesse, a struggle had ensued decades prior to the French Revolution and would continue throughout the revolutionary period. Its main protagonists were Condorcet and Denis Diderot and between their two positions the lines have been drawn from that day to this. As Hesse relates,

Denis Diderot was hired by André-François LeBreton, the chief officer of the Paris Publishers' and Printers' Guild and the publisher of the *Encyclopédie*, to write a treatise to be presented to the new director of the Royal Administration of the Book Trade, Antoine-Raymond-Jean-Gaulbert-Gabriel de Sartine, defending the guild's view of their "privileges" as a form of property.[22]

Diderot wrote:

What form of wealth could belong to a man, if not a work of the mind . . . if not his own thoughts . . . the most precious part of himself, that will never perish, that will immortalize him? What comparison could there be between a man, the very substance of man, his soul, and a field, a tree, a vine, that nature has offered in the beginning equally to all, and that an individual has only appropriated through cultivating it?[23]

Precious? Immortal? Unique? Such flowery language may have rhetorical appeal but can be met with equal conviction by asserting the opposite. As Hesse tells us,

Condorcet attacked both the royal theory of literary "privileges" and the theories of authorial property rights advanced by Diderot and the lawyers for the Publishers' and Printers' Guild. He asserted that there was, formally speaking, no property in ideas. Thus he wrote: "There can be no relationship between property in ideas and that in a field, which can serve only one man. [Literary property] is not a property derived from the natural order and defended by social force, it is a property founded in society itself. It is not a true right, it is a privilege."

Hesse next summarizes Condorcet's more extensive argument,

Unlike a piece of land, an idea can be discovered, inhabited, and used by an infinite number of people at the same time. Ideas are not the creation of individual minds, be it through revelation, appropriation, or cognition. Rather, they inhere in nature, and hence are equally and simultaneously accessible through the senses to all. They therefore can belong to no single individual.[24]

Now all this talk about thoughts, trees and fields, and of appropriation and cultivation have a specific and unequivocal lineage. The terms and concepts all come from John Locke.

John Locke: ownership of self, other people and ideas

The constant reference to John Locke in the literature concerning IP is merited by the fact that to a large extent Locke's arguments have been adopted as ruling dogma, if not within the domain of philosophy, then in the realms of politics and popular opinion. The basic premise is contained in one short statement of Locke's:

Though the earth and all its inferior creatures be common to all men, yet every man has a "property" in his own "person." The "labour" of his body and the "work" of his hands, we may say, are properly his. Whatsoever, then, he removes out of the state that Nature hath provided and left it in, he hath mixed his labour with it, and joined to it something that is his own, and thereby makes it his property. It being by him removed from the common state Nature placed it in, it hath by this labour something annexed to it that excludes the common right of other men. For this "labour" being the unquestionable property of the labourer, no man but he can have a right to what that is once joined to, at least where there is enough, and as good left in common for others.[25]

This apparently "common sense" depiction of persons, labor and nature is nonetheless questionable on several counts. First, why is a concept of ownership even necessary in the case of persons? There is nothing proprietary about organisms, including human organisms unless we're using property to mean features or characteristics which in any case has no more to do with ownership than does the color of the sky. Second, what basis is there for assuming that labor is singular, confined to the work of one person alone, a process, furthermore, by which one *appropriates*? Not only do most laborers not own what they produce, but labor is more often collective, joined with that of others, and most importantly, not simply for one's personal use but for the sharing of its fruits, for example, with one's family. Where, in real life, is the line so neatly drawn between labor one person performs and that of another person? For every case of individuals working alone there is another, collective one, upon which solitary effort depends. Finally, what is this "nature" upon which Locke so lightly touches? If Nature is merely a limitless space upon which each man labors alone, why add the caveat, "at least where there is enough, and as good left in common for others"?

One reason Locke makes ownership of the self his key premise may be that he was, among other things, attempting to justify the ownership of other people, that is, slaves. The historical aspects – including Locke's notorious involvement in the slave trade – certainly point in that direction. But why ownership of one's self was even conceived of in the first place and how such a concept succeeded in overthrowing older and more widely held views is certainly pertinent today. The evolution of the human species, not to mention current social arrangements of all kinds, involve every individual human being in a network of interdependence that is as obvious as it is insurmountable. In the context of the trade in slaves, however, a perverse logic can evolve (and it obviously did) that says: I can justify my ownership of this other person because I myself can be owned, indeed, I own myself.

But if circumstances led Locke to argue in this manner it is, in part, because his views were opposed by others, including Gerrard Winstanley and his Diggers (also known as the True Levellers)[26] as well as subsequently by philosophers from Hume to Rousseau and from Proudhon to Marx. The contradictory definitions of belonging, i.e. membership vs. ownership, clash openly here. Instead of ownership of ourselves or of other people, we have the membership of each as a necessary component of a group – that is, necessary insofar as the group's existence depends on its members being part of it and vice versa. Recognizing this biological and social fact necessitates the responsibility of each to all and all to each, in other words, the sustenance of a society. Such arguments were made throughout the entire period of European Enlightenment and Conquest, as is well known. Often overlooked, however, is that from that day to this, concepts arising from and expressing the social being of humans were widely held among the very peoples being conquered and enslaved by Europeans.[27] This, moreover, has not been somehow consigned to the past but is at the heart of current argument raised by the living descendants of these peoples. Attempts to impose IP regimes invented in Europe and the United States are being met precisely on the basis of customary or traditional laws which, however different from case to case, nonetheless share the common characteristic of opposition to the private appropriation of goods or resources, material or immaterial, originating in the group (tribe, nation, society) and produced to enrich not one, but all members of the group.

In the specific case of the ownership of ideas the most eloquent arguments made by the finest minds never succeed in proving that ownership is appropriate to the products of people's minds any more than it is to people themselves. This is for at least two reasons: first, ideas cannot be said to originate solely in individual minds but are instead inherited genetically or learned culturally. The modifications made by individuals are at most a tiny fraction, an atomic particle, of the larger body of thoughts, knowledge or truth, which makes humans human. The small contribution that even the greatest artists, inventors and thinkers have made are only significant insofar as they add to the great stock of human creativity, not as singular, remote, anomalies, with no recognizable connection to what preceded or what followed their arrival in the great conversation of which we all are part. Diderot's oft-quoted arguments, for example, aimed at justifying perpetual property in an author's work, are made without biological or historical foundation. They are simply assertions that are easily refuted – and his own work refutes them. Take for example the work for which Diderot is most famous: the *Encyclopedia*. It is worthy of note Diderot was himself accused of plagiarism since his effort was clearly based on two earlier ones.[28] But more importantly, Diderot's entire enterprise was premised on the existence of a vast body of knowledge invented or discovered by humanity, the purpose of which was to be shared and built upon by literally everyone. How can ownership be an applicable concept? Where does possession, use and disposal of an object enter into the process?

The only place is after the fact. After a publisher decides to profit from the sale or a government decides to censor the content of human knowledge – not before. The only basis for the claims made by Diderot, Fichte, Mark Twain, Edgar Alan Poe – and many other great authors and thinkers – to the effect that their works were unique, novel and original to them – was the pre-existence of proprietary claims, as such. In other words, their arguments were only advanced in a context created by Locke's argument and the policies of British, French, Dutch and other European empires in conquering the world. There was no clamor for property in ideas before then.[29]

The main issues concerning author's privileges and monopolies were, in the first instance, control by absolutist states of the ideas being disseminated to their subjects, not the rights of authors at all. Indeed, the initial impetus for the invention of the author was to make the author liable or responsible for the social effects of his ideas, not to free the author to commercially exploit them. Historical circumstances notwithstanding, the conceptual apparatus that undergirds the claims of authors and inventors to the ownership of their unique, novel and original work is based on justifications for the ownership of human beings by human beings. Absent slavery, there is no reason to expect that ownership of oneself or one's ideas would even have occurred to anyone in the first place. It certainly did not occur to many other people in highly sophisticated societies such as those of Asia, Africa and the Western Hemisphere. (Even in those which practiced slavery, justification for that institution was not based on "self-ownership" but on a completely different classificatory system, beyond the scope of this discussion.[30]) It would never occur to most Europeans, either, were it not for the fact that following the Columbian event, first the Catholic Church and later all the kingdoms involved in world conquest were forced to confront the people they were conquering and displacing and the people they were enslaving. That's what Locke's project was determined to accomplish and that was its greatest success. Locke's own words, furthermore, prove the point.

> To this purpose, I think it not amiss to set down what I take to be political power. That the power of a magistrate over a subject may be distinguished from that of a father over his children, a master over his servant, a husband over his wife, and a lord over his slave. All which distinct powers happening sometimes together in the same man, if he be considered under these different relations, it may help us to distinguish these powers one from another, and show the difference betwixt a ruler of a commonwealth, a father of a family, and a captain of a galley.
> Political power, then, I take to be a right of making laws, with penalties of death, and consequently all less penalties for the regulating and preserving of property, and of employing the force of the community in the execution of such laws, and in the defence of the commonwealth from foreign injury, and all this only for the public good.[31]

No more bald-faced justification of oppression and exploitation could be imagined. Political power to preserve property shall be in the hands of a magistrate – not to be confused with a father, master, husband or lord, who nonetheless might be one and the same person – but who, in any case, represents the "public good." It is left to the reader to decide if the public good consists in the maintenance of property rights over wives and children, servants and slaves, but it is difficult to imagine any other outcome. Furthermore, Locke's own business entanglements show in practice that this is precisely what he had in mind.

"Locke's principles perfectly suited the Southern Federalists who dominated the early years of the United States," writes economist John Quiggin.[32]

> On the one hand, they justified rebellion against the British Crown. On the other hand, they rejected any interference with property rights, including slave ownership. More broadly, Locke's theory stood in opposition to the radical democratic possibilities of the American Revolution, represented by figures like Benjamin Franklin and Thomas Paine.
>
> The contradictions inherent in Locke's position were pointed out by critics at the time, and summed up by that old-fashioned Tory, Dr. Samuel Johnson, who remarked, "How is it that we hear the loudest yelps for liberty from the drivers of Negroes?"

Indeed, not only did Locke justify slavery but he upheld the expropriation of Native American land on the basis of his property theory as Quiggin elaborates:

> [W]hen used as a justification for expropriating Native Americans, on the (factually incorrect) basis that they were mere hunter-gatherers, the idea of acquiring land through agricultural labor raises a problem. Locke wasn't an agricultural laborer, and neither were his readers. How were gentlemen like Locke to acquire property if not through labor? Locke's solution, relying on the relationship between master and servant is simple. The laborers are servants; in Locke's analysis they are, in effect, human livestock. Hence, by extension, any property they acquire belongs to their masters:
>
> > We see in commons, which remain so by compact, that it is the taking any part of what is common, and removing it out of the state nature leaves it in, which begins the property; without which the common is of no use. And the taking of this or that part, does not depend on the express consent

of all the commoners. Thus the grass my horse has bit; the
turfs my servant has cut; and the ore I have digged in any
place, where I have a right to them in common with others,
become my property, without the assignation or consent of
any body. The labour that was mine, removing them out of
that common state they were in, hath fixed my property in
them.

These arguments may appear crass to readers today since
they unabashedly make what is "common" belong to no one and
therefore available to anyone to appropriate and exploit. Though
abundant evidence exposes the falsity of such claims, they can
nevertheless be asserted. When such assertion is attached to pre-
existing wealth, privilege and military force, it commands by the law
of Might makes Right. As Hobbes, Locke and all their cohort
saw it, political power served the "public good" by liberating capital
and capitalists from any constraint which might otherwise be imposed
by those unenlightened souls who, thinking themselves human
and infected with the democratic disease, seek to impose laws limiting
"free trade" and capital accumulation.

From Locke to Hegel

Locke's argument was rejected by many thinkers, most notably
David Hume and J.J. Rousseau. Hume went so far as to deny the
existence of the Self while pointing out that "there is no property in
durable objects, such as lands or houses, when carefully examined
in passing from hand to hand, but must, in some period, have been
founded on fraud and injustice."[33] This was further developed by
Rousseau in his *Discourse on Inequality* wherein he wrote:

The first man who, having enclosed a piece of ground, bethought
himself of saying "This is mine," and found people simple
enough to believe him, was the real founder of civil society. From
how many crimes, wars, and murders, from how many horrors
and misfortunes might not any one have saved mankind, by
pulling up the stakes, or filling up the ditch, and crying to his
fellows: Beware of listening to this impostor; you are undone if
you once forget that the fruits of the earth belong to us all, and
the earth itself to nobody.[34]

Following the Haitian Revolution, these questions became far more than academic. That men and women who had themselves been the property of others would, in the name of Liberty, Equality and Fraternity, rise and strike for their freedom was an earth-shaking event. It was also the necessary consequence of the previous revolutions and the claims upon which their authority was based. If Franklin and Paine could argue for the overthrow of a monarch, if St. Just and Robespierre could defend the beheading of one, then Toussaint L'Overture could take such argument to its logical and universalist conclusion – just because we are black does not mean we are not human. Indeed we are human, and liberating ourselves is what makes us so![35]

That Hegel was aware of these developments has been well established.[36] Their influence is apparent in his most radical phil-osophical interventions to be found in the *Phenomenology of Spirit* and the *Science of Logic*. The master–slave dialectic, for example, is clearly a response to an actual revolutionary crisis. In the context of debate around IP, however, the Hegel to which most scholars refer is found in the *Philosophy of Right*. In this book, Hegel retreats from his earlier advance beyond the individualist premises with which philosophy had been preoccupied since Descartes. Hegel had previously established that since humanity is a species and the consciousness of human beings is the true object of philosophical inquiry, the abstract individual was not only not real, it was not even adequate in methodological terms, a subject to which we'll return. With *Philosophy of Right*, however, Hegel falls back on individualist notions of personhood and property ownership. According to Hegel the personality of each is expressed or "externalized" in a unique relation to objects, including abstract objects (ideas) which is not determined by labor or first occupancy, as in the case of Locke, but as an expression of self-consciousness. Awareness *of* oneself as an object of consciousness is expressed in the appropriation *to* oneself of other objects.

Yet, even in a text upholding and defending the right of individual authors and inventors to the products of their unique personalities, ambiguity arises when his argument tails off into remarks about pla-giarism and the prohibition of suicide![37] This is noteworthy since plagiarism is distinguished from other forms of misappropriation as a matter of honor, not legality; of lying, not stealing.[38] Furthermore, denial of the right to suicide fundamentally undermines Locke's self-ownership premise. Even Locke's defenders acknowledge that self-ownership implies both the right to suicide and the right to self-enslavement.[39] It appears that Hegel, responding to the debates in France, England and the United States, wanted to find a solution surer than Locke's yet commensurate with both the property-owning individual, recently made sovereign by revolution, and his own vision of the state as the culmination of human history.

It is here that Hegel's philosophical breakthroughs and short-comings are most clearly summarized by none other than his most famous student, Karl Marx. Writing in 1844 (13 years after Hegel's death) Marx said:

> The outstanding achievement of Hegel's *Phänomenologie* and of its final outcome, the dialectic of negativity as the moving and generating principle, is thus first that Hegel conceives the self-creation of man as a process, conceives objectification as loss of the object, as alienation and as transcendence of this alienation; that he thus grasps the essence of labour and comprehends objective man – true, because real man – as the outcome of man's own labour. The real, active orientation of man to himself as a species-being, or his manifestation as a real species-being (i.e., as a human being), is only possible if he really brings out all his species-powers – something which in turn is only possible through the co-operative action of all of mankind, only as the result of history – and treats these powers as objects: and this, to begin with, is again only possible in the form of estrangement.[40]

Hegel had thus broken the deadlock with which philosophy had been faced from Descartes to Kant, i.e. the individual as basic unit, or indivisible particle, of human society, from which consciousness emerges and in which it resides. Descartes' "I think therefore I am" had led to Kant's Categorical Imperative neither of which could account for, much less foresee, human history. Hegel identified human history with human labor, the master–slave dialectic and the progressive movement of human society toward heaven on earth. This was, in practice, the realization of philosophy, the overcoming of the "estrangement" or alienation that was inherent in – and had driven – the historical process. Soon after, these very breakthroughs would be subject to further critique, first by Feuerbach then by Marx. Nonetheless, Hegel's great contribution was to connect – or reconnect – human consciousness with its origin in collectivity and labor.

It was, of course, Marx who used Hegel's insights to definitively separate liberty from property, distinguishing actual *work* from *alienated labor* and *private* property from *personal* property.[41] Marx, moreover, accomplished this by returning from the abstractions: *liberty*, *property*, *labor*, etc., to the concrete practices of living people, i.e. who did what and why? This move was important not only because it dispelled the mystique enshrouding liberty and property but because hidden behind that veil were what workers, artists and scientists actually *do*, all of which rests on one fundamental practice: *sharing*.

Truth cannot be owned

Sharing is explored in depth by economists and anthropologists in studies of "sharing" or "gift-economies," diverse forms of production and exchange, as well as symbolic, ritualistic practices connecting humanity to divinity or obligation to self-fulfillment.[42] But from the perspective of philosophy sharing is not only specific economic, cultural or religious practices. Sharing is crucial to the formation of human consciousness and where the being of human consciousness resides. Without sharing, the human species is not likely to have evolved, let alone human arts and sciences. This is no more evident than in the case of creativity, imagination or inspiration, which have no necessary relation to possession, exclusivity or even usefulness. These human capacities may indeed derive from a desire for recognition by others but this only further confirms that exchange, the passing from one mind to other minds, is the motive and means for an act needing no other justification than itself. Hence, freedom of thought, freedom to explore, and freedom to fail are all expressions of sharing. The acquisition of skill, discipline and the criteria of judgment are, as well. Indeed, beauty, as a delight and illumination of the infinite, is a product of and reward for sharing. None of these capacities or capabilities can be attributed to ownership in any conceivable form, nor can they be improved upon or advanced by attaching them to individuals whether they be actual persons or legal abstractions. It can therefore be said that liberty expands in inverse proportion as property contracts.

Even within the realm of philosophy, sharing plays a fundamental role and one which prohibits ownership as a condition for participation. This is the dialectic, which, as we know from Plato onward, requires the freest possible exchange of ideas. No doubt, the Hegelian dialectic differs substantially from that of Plato but in this sense it is identical: the dialectic interrogates human consciousness in order to bring human consciousness into correspondence with the infinite multiverse of which human consciousness is itself a part. The process and its goal are, by definition and in fact, open and available to all. In short, *truth cannot be owned.*

The implications for philosophy and for law are profound. For philosophy to retain any consistency as a discipline, any coherence as an instrument for exploring reality, let alone its ethical and dialectical functions, it must be opposed to the ownership of ideas and their expressions. If law is to reject its sophistical baggage and become a seeker and defender of justice, then it will have to critique its past casuistry and servitude to privilege and power. Practically speaking, this means that defense of giant corporations on the basis of "industry practices" or precedents set in cases which ignored the claims of, for example, indigenous peoples, should all be subject to comprehensive, philosophical review. Even more broadly, questions such as ownership of the human genome must be used to examine fundamental premises. Is not ownership of the human genome tantamount to the ownership of people, albeit disguised as only owning their component parts? Is this not simply slavery in a new guise? We abolish the ownership of individual people while establishing ownership of all people?

Instead, should we not be adhering to the principle of belonging as members of the human species, as participants in, or expressions of, the human genome? Which is a more accurate appraisal of reality? Which is the more likely to achieve the Good, the Beautiful and the True?

Notes

1 This is a paraphrase of a statement by Anglican priest, John S. Mbiti, the full statement reads: "I am because WE are and, since we are, therefore I am."

2 See Hesse's "Enlightenment Epistemology and the Laws of Authorship in Revolutionary France, 1777–1793," *Representations* 30 (Spring 1990): 109–137; Wood's, *Liberty and Property* (Verso, 2012); and Sell's "Intellectual Property and Public Policy in Historical Perspective: Contestation

and Settlement," *Loyola of Los Angeles Law Review* 38, no. 1 (2004): 267–321.

3 See Sarah Laskow, "Does Copyright Law Work? New and Ongoing Empirical Research Suggests: Not Always, *Columbia Journalism Review*, September 23, 2013; Peter DiCola, "Money from Music: Survey Evidence on Musicians' Revenue and Lessons about Copyright Incentives," Northwestern University School of Law, January 9, 2013, http://ssrn.com/abstract=2199058.

4 First published as *The Public Domain: Enclosing the Commons of the Mind* (Yale University Press, 2008) as Chapter 9. A version is available under a Creative Commons Attribution-Noncommercial-ShareAlike 3.0 Unported license at www.thepublicdomain.org/download/.

5 see Jessica Silby, *The Eureka Myth: Creators, Innovators, and Everyday Intellectual Property* (Stanford University Press, 2015) and William Patry, *How to Fix Copyright* (Oxford University Press, 2012).

6 Macaulay, in particular, argued that copyright might be a mechanism to remunerate authors but then was closer in effect to taxation on consumers than a title deed to a piece of property, see http://www.thepublicdomain.org/2014/07/24/macaulay-on-copyright/.

7 See Brian Winston, *Media, Technology and Society* (Routledge, 1998).

8 See http://rack1.ul.cs.cmu.edu/jefferson/.

9 See the relevant chapter in this book: "Owning up to owning traditional knowledge of medicinal plants," also see numerous works of Vandana Shiva, especially, *Biopiracy: The Plunder of Nature and Knowledge* (Natraj Publishers, 2011).

10 From the Indian Occupation of Alcatraz (1969–1971) to the Zapatista rising (1994) to the recent confrontation between the Standing Rock Sioux and the US government, a struggle has been waged by peoples considered extinct or assimilated by European colonization. In 2009 the United Nations produced a document titled: *State of the World's Indigenous Peoples*, which acknowledged:

> There has been a vigorous and dynamic interface between indigenous peoples – numbering more than 370 million in some 90 countries – and the United Nations, an interface which, difficult as it is, has produced at least three results: a) a new awareness of indigenous peoples' concerns and human rights; b) recognition of indigenous peoples' invaluable contribution to humanity's cultural diversity and heritage, not least through their traditional knowledge; and c) an awareness of the need to address the issues of indigenous peoples through policies, legislation and budgets. Along with the movements for decolonization and human rights, as well as the women's and environmental movements, the indigenous movement has been one of the most active civil society interlocutors of the United Nations since 1945. (https://web.archive.org/web/20100215113446/http://www.un.org/esa/socdev/unpfii/documents/SOWIP_web.pdf).

11 C.B. Macpherson, *The Political Theory of Possessive Individualism: Hobbes to Locke* (Oxford University Press, 1962), 274.

12 Margaret Thatcher, September 23, 1987, to *Woman's Own* magazine, published October 31, 1987.

13 Oscar Wilde, *The Soul of Man under Socialism* (1891), https://www.marxists.org/reference/archive/wilde-oscar/soul-man/index.htm.

14 Three examples: Justin Hughes, "The Philosophy of Intellectual Property,"

Georgetown Law Journal 77 (1988): 287–366; Peter Drahos, *A Philosophy of Intellectual Property* (Ashgate, 1998); and *New Frontiers in the Philosophy of Intellectual Property* edited by Annabelle Lever (Cambridge University Press, 2012).

15 Diogenes Laertius, ca. third century BCE, *The Lives and Opinions of Eminent Philosophers* (Forgotten Books edition, n.d.), 9–13.

16 Kathleen Freeman, *Ancilla to the Pre-Socratic Philosophers* (1948; Harvard University Press, 1983), 125.

17 See John Burnet, *Greek Philosophy Thales to Plato* (1914; reprint Macmillan 1961). It should be noted that the Sophists were, in many cases, brilliant and highly learned thinkers. They were challenging interlocutors of philosophers such as Plato.

18 Kenneth Sylvan Guthrie, *The Pythagorean Sourcebook and Library* (Phanes Press, 1988), 99.

19 Desiderius Erasmus, *The Praise of Folly*, 2nd ed. (Yale University Press, 2003), 116–117.

20 Robert Darnton, *George Washington's False Teeth* (W.W. Norton, 2003), 9–10.

21 Marie Jean Antoine de Condorect, *Sketch for a Historical Picture of the Progress of the Human Mind*, trans. June Barraclough (Weidenfeld & Nicolson, 1955).

22 Carla Hesse, "Enlightenment Epistemology and the Laws of Authorship in Revolutionary France, 1777–1793," *Representations* 30 (Spring 1990): 109–137.

23 Ibid.

24 Ibid.

25 John Locke, *Two Treatises of Government* (J.M. Dent, 1988), 130.

26 Whitstanley wrote the *New Law of Righteousness* wherein he said: "All who believed were together and had all things in common; they would sell their possessions and goods and distribute the proceeds to all, as any had need." And, "in the beginning of time God made the earth. Not one word was spoken at the beginning that one branch of mankind should rule over another, but selfish imaginations did set up one man to teach and rule over another" (http://www.diggers.org/diggers-ENGLISH-1649/NEW-LAW-OF-RIGHTEOUSNESS-1648-Winstanley.pdf).

27 "In the same way that indigenous peoples consider their lands and resources to be collective assets, they see their cultural values and activities – their identity – as a function of the group, not individuals. This also applies to the ownership and custody of their cultural heritage, which is collective" (UN, *State of the World's Indigenous Peoples*, 52).

28 Robert Darnton, *The Great Cat Massacre* (Vintage Books, 1985), 198.

29 Even that great defender of the *droit d'autuer*, Victor Hugo, would write: "there must be a vast public literary domain. That is why all poets, all philosophers, all thinkers, all the producers of the greatness of the mind must be translated, commented on, published, printed, reprinted, stereotyped, distributed, explained, recited, spread abroad, given to all, given cheaply, given at cost price, given for nothing" (Hugo, *The Minds and the Masses* [1864]).

30 One such explication can be found in John Reader's *Africa: Biography of a Continent* (Vintage Books, 1997), wherein Reader discusses slavery before and after the incursion of Europeans.

31 Locke, *Two Treatises of Government*, 118.

32 John Quiggin, "John Locke against Freedom," *Jacobin Magazine*, June 28, 2015, https://www.jacobinmag.com/2015/06/locke-treatise-slavery-private-property/, and "John Locke's

Road to Serfdom" *Jacobin Magazine*, October 18, 2015, https://www. jacobinmag.com/2015/10/locke-classical-liberalism-treatise-nozick-constitution/.

33 David Hume, *The Original Contract*, http://www.constitution.org/ dh/origcont.htm.

34 Jean-Jacques Rousseau, *A Discourse on Inequality* (Penguin Classics, 1981), 120–122.

35 See Toussaint L'Ouverture, *The Haitian Revolution* (Verso, 2008) for L'Ouverture's own words.

36 See Susan Buck Morss, *Hegel, Haiti, and Universal History* (University of Pittsburgh Press, 2009).

37 G.W.F. Hegel, *The Philosophy of Right* (Prometheus Books, 1996), 74–76.

38 "Because it is not, strictly speaking, a legal concept, plagiarism has mostly been ignored by legal commentators" (Stuart P. Green, "Plagiarism, Norms, and the Limits of

Theft Law: Some Observations on the Use of Criminal Sanctions in Enforcing Intellectual Property Rights," *Hastings Law Journal* 54, no. 1 [2002]: 171).

39 Robert Nozick's *Anarchy, State and Utopia* (Basic Books, 1974) makes this explicit.

40 Karl Marx, *Economic and Philosophic Manuscripts of 1844* (Lawrence & Wishart, 1981), XXIII, p. 132.

41 Ibid.

42 See M. Mauss, *The Gift: Forms and Functions of Exchange in Archaic Societies* (1922; Routledge, 1990); Lewis Hyde, *The Gift: Imagination and the Erotic Life of Property* (Random House, 1983); Yochai Benkler, "Sharing Nicely: On Shareable Goods and the Emergence of Sharing as a Modality of Economic Production," *Yale Law Journal* 114 (2004): 273–358; David Graeber, *Toward an Anthropological Theory of Value: The False Coin of Our Own Dreams* (Palgrave, 2001).

SECTION TWO

TERRAINS OF CONFLICT AND TERMS OF ENGAGEMENT

From the outset, this book premised itself, not on arcane, academic debate, but on the mass movements that have, in the last 30 or so years, arisen worldwide in opposition to IPR regimes. Having, in Section 1, critiqued and opened out key historical contexts and theoretical concepts fundamental to a more rounded understanding of intellectual property rights, in Section 2 we now switch the focus to interrogating four specific spheres or domains where tensions between "proprietary" and "common good" approaches to the application of IPRs are currently playing out. While far from exhaustive, the four key battlefronts we foreground here are agriculture, education, music/art and technological development.

First, struggles in the spheres of food production and herbal medicines are addressed, with the ongoing commodification of traditional knowledge in relation to botanical foods and medicines being met with resistance from states in the Global South. Here, specific protection mechanisms to preserve such knowledge and shield it from the globalization process are summarized and explained.

In a context where the IPR regime places significant constraints around access to knowledge and educational materials, an outline of the benefits arising from adopting a "tiered" approach to copyright protection are advanced in relation to the sphere of education with primary emphasis placed on the public interest in copyright.

Another battleground relates to recent developments in the music industry. As such, this section will proceed to illustrate how technological innovations are, in effect, much less significant that the matching policy, institutional and organizational innovations that accompany them in an environment where the biggest corporate actors have reconfigured their core structures as to enhance their scope for exploiting the copyrights, trademarks and brands under their control, with significant costs and consequences for artists and consumers alike.

Finally, this section considers the free and open source software movements and presents a detailed and important national case study from the United States, detailing the emergence and evolution of a range of opposition movements or projects.

The contours of each battlefront are specific and, in some senses, unique. Upon closer inspection they nonetheless bear striking resemblances to each other. Outstanding among these resemblances is how current conflict is really about the future, specifically the future of food, medicine, education, tools of all kinds as well as creativity and aesthetics. Another resemblance is how in all cases, the lack of evidence supporting claims made by defenders of IP can be combatted precisely by the assembling of empirical data along with ethnographic testimony that can be verified.

6 | OWNING UP TO OWNING TRADITIONAL KNOWLEDGE OF MEDICINAL PLANTS

Josef A. Brinckmann

Introduction

This chapter examines the commodification and globalization of traditional botanical foods and medicines within a context of traditional knowledge (TK). Specifically, the TK that informs local management of eco-climatic regions for the sustainable harvesting, use and trade of medicinal and aromatic plants (MAPs) that possess a quantifiably unique composition, quality and biological activity. Unique nutritional and medicinal characteristics of certain MAPs can be attributed to influences of their natural habitat coupled with traditional agricultural and collection practices including specific methods of post-harvest processing and preparation. Who holds this TK and how is it transmitted? Who else has access to the TK and who benefits from its application? – local, rural and indigenous communities, for-profit corporations, research institutions, the state, or some combination of stakeholders?

There is a growing body of literature suggesting a rapid disappearance of TK (not being transmitted to next generation) and thus an urgent call to preserve and protect such knowledge for important reasons. Reasons include the notion that TK enables local food security and health security, informs global strategies for biodiversity conservation and climate change adaptation, and provides leads for new drug discovery to cure, mitigate or treat diseases, among other uses. In October 2015, the Intergovernmental Committee on Intellectual Property and Genetic Resources, Traditional Knowledge and Folklore (IGC) decided to continue working towards reaching an agreement on an international legal instrument relating to intellectual property (IP) protection of genetic resources (GRs), TK and traditional cultural expressions (TCEs).[1] There are some national legal instruments for IP protection of TK and GRs. For example both India and Peru have agencies charged with preventing and challenging patents alleged to be based on "their" GRs and associated TK. Peruvian regulations have made illegal the export of viable planting stock of certain medicinal GRs that are considered to be a national heritage. Furthermore, certain native plant species are afforded some protection under "protected designation of origin" (PDO) rules in the IP context. To illustrate, this chapter provides a comparison of the Indian and Peruvian systems along with information on voluntary sustainability standards (VSS) that can be used to demonstrate compliance with international agreements on access and benefit sharing (ABS). It concludes with a brief case study summarizing successes and failures of efforts to "own" the GR and associated TK of the Peruvian medicinal plant known as maca (*Lepidium meyenii* WALPERS; Fam: Brassicaceae).

TEK + TMK = $$??

Throughout history, as a matter of survival, local, rural and indigenous communities developed natural resource management strategies for food security, health security and water security. A comprehensive inventory and knowledge of the whole ecosystem of which a community or tribe is itself a part was essential to long-term survival. For example, knowing what plant parts and animal parts are edible, nutritional, medicinal, poisonous or toxic, specific methods on how, when and where to harvest, post-harvest processing and preparation of traditional foods and medicines. Although, in various literature, traditional management systems are subdivided into specialized types of TK such as indigenous (local or traditional) knowledge (IK), traditional ecological knowledge (TEK) also referred to as indigenous ecological knowledge (IEK), and traditional medical knowledge (TMK), there is considerable overlap in definitions and applications of these types of TK.

TEK has been defined as "a cumulative body of knowledge, practice and belief evolving by adaptive processes and handed down through generations by cultural transmission, about the relationship of living beings (including humans) with one another and with their environment."[2] For its definition of TMK, the World Intellectual Property Organization (WIPO) incorporates the World Health Organization (WHO) definition of traditional medicine as:

the sum total of the knowledge, skills and practices based on the theories, beliefs and experiences indigenous to different cultures, whether explicable or not, used in the maintenance of health, as well as in the prevention, diagnosis, improvement or treatment of physical and mental illnesses.

WIPO further elaborates, that in this context, the term "Traditional" means "the knowledge is created in a manner that reflects community traditions; it is often intergenerational and created and held collectively."[3] Dr. Sita Reddy, cultural sociologist at the Center for Folklife and Cultural Heritage, Smithsonian Institution, has suggested that "ownership and control over TMK and biodiversity have become the new realities and tropes of medical globalization."[4] And leave it to the World Bank to provide a working definition for IK:

Indigenous knowledge is unique to every culture and society. It is the basis for local decision-making in agriculture, health, natural-resource management and other activities. Indigenous knowledge is embedded in community practices, institutions, relationships and rituals. Indigenous knowledge is part of everyday life, such as herbal medicines, acupuncture etc.[5]

These types of TK, essential for survival throughout history, are increasingly viewed as non-essential in the daily life of people today due to the phenomena of commodification and globalization of everything and mass urbanization. At the same time, significant value has been placed upon the preservation of TK which many researchers warn is at risk of not being transmitted to the next generations.[6] The reported decreasing transmission of TK may be due, in part, to an unprecedented global mass migration of young people from rural to urban centers.[7] It may also be due to modernization in rural areas with increasingly easier access to packaged products coupled with disinterest in TK by the younger generations.[8] There is, however, an emerging counter-narrative suggesting an actual increase in cultural plant knowledge associated with migration. For example a recent study found that cultural knowledge about medicinal plants was greater in Dominicans living in New York City compared to those living in the Dominican Republic.[9] Despite a general trend of TK erosion worldwide, some TK systems may be resilient to modernization, if adaptive to change (not fossilized), and could persist in communities situated in both "developing" and "developed" countries.[10]

In either case, TK may still provide solutions to big problems facing humans and the planet today. For example there is a growing body of literature suggesting that TK may be important in areas of climate change adaptation,[11] preventing ecosystem collapse and loss of biodiversity,[12] local food and health security,[13] and new drug discovery to cure, mitigate or treat diseases.[14] Gómez-Baggethun et al. assert that TEK, as a component of biocultural heritage, is intrinsic to biodiversity conservation, ecosystem services, and to building community resilience.[15] TEK helps to build resilience in social-ecological systems by promoting biocultural diversity (the interconnected links between biological, cultural and linguistic diversity). Biocultural diversity, developed over many generations of experience of dealing with disturbance, can be viewed as an asset for climate change adaptation strategies. The study carried out by Ahmad et al. showed that rapid urban development in India has been a leading cause of habitat destruction (change of land use for city development, deforestation, highway construction).[16] The result is a significant loss in the diversity of certain medicinal plant species that are widely used in the Indian systems of traditional medicine such as in Ayurveda, Unani and Siddha medicines as well as in folk and tribal medicines. As a solution they suggest a conscious move to sustainable development methods with nature conservation as a component, paying special attention to certain medicinal plant species and their long-term survival thus helping to preserve entire ecosystems. In new drug discovery research, Jantan et al. report that while prioritization of medicinal plant species based on TK serves as an initial biological activity screening step, very little time remains due to the rapid ongoing devastation of tropical rainforest ecosystems.[17] While the number of plant species screened for potential new medical uses thus far is very small (less than 5 percent), Jantan et al. state that the Nagoya Protocol on the Convention on Biological Diversity (on access to GRs and the fair and equitable sharing of benefits) "should encourage more pharmaceutical firms to venture into natural research to discover new drug leads."[18] Screening the other 95 percent of species, however, could take decades while their habitats may be destroyed in the meantime.

Somewhere in all of this there is money to be made. To determine who is allowed to gain financially from commercial use of such TK and who isn't, the concept of ownership comes into question. While TK has become the subject of IP regulations and international agreements such as the Nagoya Protocol on Access and Benefit-sharing,[19] for TK to be protected and to serve as a repository of useful information for survival of species and the planet, does an individual, entity, organization or the state really need to "own" the specified TK?

Precisely to this point, Caruso and Grace provide salient points about the problem of IP law itself being a product of "European ontologies, epistemologies and legal frameworks":

Indigenous peoples claim that their knowledge, traditions, artistic expressions, and associated practices are indivisible, and that this body of collective biocultural heritage is connected to all aspects – spiritual, intellectual, physical, emotional, cultural, social, economic, political, etc. – of their individual and collective lives. Furthermore, this intangible cultural heritage cannot be understood as "owned" or "invented" by a particular person or group, as indigenous peoples often define themselves as custodians of knowledge and resources that have been bestowed upon them through spiritual means.[20]

In the India context, there are 705 scheduled tribes comprising 8.6 percent of India's total population whilst public and common lands account for nearly one-fifth of India's total geography.[21] Nagendra pointed out that indigenous community institutions have historically served to manage and protect biodiverse forests due to their belief in sacred spirits. These indigenous institutions, however, are insufficiently recognized by the state. Thus their ability to continue protecting forest ecosystems is threatened in the wake of rapid urbanization. Concerning India, political economist Elinor Ostrom (1933–2012) believed that polycentricity would be necessary to effectively manage the commons.[22] The concept of polycentricity has been defined as a "structural feature of social systems of many decision centers having limited and autonomous prerogatives and operating under an overarching set of rules."[23]

Examples of state actors: INDECOPI / NCAB and TKDL

Some nations have established mechanisms for the "protection" of TK such as the Peruvian National Commission against Biopiracy (NCAB), an interagency coordination and technical advisory body chaired by the National Institute for the Defense of Free Competition and Protection of Intellectual Property (INDECOPI). Another example is the Government of India's Traditional Knowledge Digital Library (TKDL), a collaborative project of the Council of Scientific and Industrial Research (CSIR) and the Ministry of Ayurveda, Yoga and Naturopathy, Unani, Siddha and Homeopathy (AYUSH).

The focus of these governmental projects has been primarily to challenge patents misappropriated to "inventors" based on documented prior art of TEK and/or TMK. But there are also cases of patents being challenged based on the inventors' use of illegally obtained GRs. For example, there are Chinese patents involving Peruvian maca being cultivated in China without agreements on access and/or material transfer from Peru.[24] Here below, similarities and differences between the Peruvian and Indian systems are summarized. One apparent point of difference is that the Peruvian system includes a clear mechanism for the state to facilitate collective ownership of GRs and associated TK by indigenous peoples or rural communities. The Indian system assumes that TK attributed to the codified Indian systems of medicine (Ayurveda, Siddha, Unani, and Yoga) is owned by the state.

INDECOPI and NACB The mission of NCAB is to "develop actions to identify, prevent, and avoid potential cases of 'biopiracy' with the objective of protecting the interest of the Peruvian State."[25] NCAB membership includes governmental organizations, NGOs, research institutions and business associations, and is chaired by INDECOPI. For context, it is useful to review a timeline of significant actions taken by the Peruvian government since 1992 as they pertain to the maca root case study discussed later in this chapter:

- 1992: Through an executive order, INDECOPI was founded with one of its main functions to protect Peruvian IP from trademarks, copyrights, patents and biotechnology.

- 1997: Peruvian Law No. 26839 provided for conservation and sustainable use of biodiversity with measures for enforcement of IP laws concerning GRs and TK.[26]

- 2002: Peruvian Law No. 27811 made provisions for INDECOPI to manage a national registry for the preservation of collective knowledge of indigenous peoples related to biodiversity. Under this law, Peruvian indigenous peoples are to be protected against unfair access to their TK without informed consent. Indigenous groups can negotiate license agreements for access to and use of their TK and not less than 10 percent of sales of products based on their TK is to be earmarked for deposit into a trust fund called the Indigenous Peoples Development Fund.[27]

- 2003: Two presidential decrees were enacted, firstly Decreto Supremo No. 039-2003-AG prohibited the export of seeds or vegetative plant material of maca (*Lepidium meyenii*) as well as unprocessed maca raw materials.[28] The related Decreto Supremo No. 041-2003 provided definition to the processed, value-added forms of maca that may be exported legally.[29]

- 2004: Peruvian Law No. 28216 created a National Commission for the Protection of Access to Peruvian Biological Diversity and to the Collective Knowledge of Indigenous Peoples, also known as the National Commission against Biopiracy (NCAB), which is chaired by INDECOPI.[30]

- 2011: INDECOPI issued a "Designation of Origin" specification for Maca Junín-Pasco, i.e. maca that is cultivated and produced in specified geographic zones and altitudes within the provinces of Junín and Pasco.

- 2012: INDECOPI registered its Maca Junín-Pasco as an "Appellation of Origin" through the World Intellectual Property Organization.[31]

Peruvian Law No. 27811 is a *sui generis* law. *Sui generis*, meaning "a special kind," refers to an IP protection regime outside of the Western concept of individual property ownership. Because TEK and TMK are premised on a concept of community ownership, this special form of protection can be applied for TK associated with certain GRs.[32] As per Peruvian Law No. 27811, indigenous peoples or rural communities may submit an application to INDECOPI in order to register certain collective knowledge related to a GR (such as the TK of maca root) in the National Register of Collective Knowledge of Indigenous Peoples. Within the national register there are three traditional knowledge registers: confidential, local and public. The public register serves as an instrument to prevent biopiracy. Indigenous peoples granted TK registrations through this system include the Aguaruna, Ashaninka, Bora, Ocaina and Shipibo Conibo, among others.[33] As of 2014 there were 2,226 entries or registries of TK in Peru's national register; 844 public and 1,422 confidential.[34] Concurrently, the NCAB has examined thousands of patent documents for possible cases of biopiracy including, as of 2013, 2,800 concerning yacón (*Smallanthus sonchifolius* (Poepp.) H.Rob.; Fam.: Asteraceae), 2,229 for tara (*Caesalpinia spinosa* (Molina) Kuntze; Fam.: Fabaceae), 555 for uña de gato (*Uncaria tomentosa* (Willd. ex Schult.) DC.; Fam.: Rubiaceae), and 550 patent documents concerning maca (*Lepidium meyenii* Walpers; Fam.: Brassicaceae), among several other prioritized Peruvian GRs.[35] The NCAB has prioritized 35 economically important Peruvian GRs for biopiracy research and actions. Dossiers are being prepared on these which are provided to IP offices in third countries as well as studies outlining potential cases of biopiracy and prior art. NCAB has also provided contributions to the IGC. As of 2014 NCAB data has contributed to the rejection, abandonment or withdrawal of nine patents involving Peruvian GRs and associated TK.[36] At the time of this writing (January 2016), NCAB had made ten completed dossiers publicly available at their website, including one prepared for maca, which also includes quantifications of maca-based patents filed globally, sorted by patent office, by year of filing, by applicant, by country and by class and subclass.[37]

TKDL The government of India's establishment of the Traditional Knowledge Digital Library (TKDL) in 2001 facilitated a registry for TMK of India's codified and scholarly systems of medicine and health care, namely Ayurveda, Siddha, Unani and Yoga as prior art.[38] The TKDL database of medicinal formulations used in the Indian systems of medicine is made freely available to patent examiners; as scanned books along with translations from the original Sanskrit, Urdu, Arabic, Persian or Tamil, etc., into English, French, Spanish, German and Japanese.

At the time of this writing (January 2016), the TKDL website showed that, through the European Patent Office alone, 89 patent applications had been withdrawn, 4 refused, and 36 applicants had amended or modified claims due to TKDL prior art evidence. Thirty-seven patent applications had been declared "dead" by the Canadian Intellectual Property Office (CIPO) due to TKDL evidence. Eleven claims had been rejected by the US Patent and Trademark Office (USPTO) and another 14 claims amended or modified due to TKDL prior art evidence. Even in India, some patent applications submitted by governmental research organizations, for example by the Central Council for Research of Ayurveda and Siddha, had been refused.[39]

Then there is TMK that stems from India's non-codified folk and tribal medicines, which is largely undocumented (oral tradition) and thus falls outside the scope of the TKDL database mechanism. Such TMK therefore remains unprotected from biopiracy.[40] Furthermore, the question has been raised about TMK that is now claimed to be part of the Indian systems of medicine that may have existed prior to the advent of Ayurveda, and therefore may be the "community property" of certain tribal groups from whom the TMK was appropriated long ago into the eventually codified system of Ayurveda.

According to Deekshitha Ganesan, LLB, "TKDL remains a defensive protection of traditional knowledge that does not fully ensure that the benefits of the information reach its original holders as far as possible." Ganesan suggests that "*sui generis*" protection for TK is needed and that India should adopt a framework similar to that of Peru so that local communities can benefit from the use of their TK by third parties.[41]

With that said, India does have a framework for access to GRs for commercial utilization and sharing benefits arising out of such access. As per India's Biological Diversity Act 2002, companies may submit an application to the National Biodiversity Authority (NBA) for approval to use an Indian GR and its associated TK. The NBA may grant such approval if there is agreement from the relevant State Biodiversity Board (SBB) and only if mutually agreed terms and an equitable benefit sharing agreement has been reached between the applicant and the "resource owners."[42]

VSS that require ABS

The implementation of voluntary sustainability standards (VSS) that include economic, environmental and social criteria and indicators is an emerging market-based approach to biodiversity conservation, sustainable harvesting and commercial use of MAPs, and to demonstrate compliance with international agreements. While such standards are voluntary, in that compliance is not required by governmental regulations, independent third-party inspection and certification organizations determine if companies are operating in compliance with the standard.[43]

Some VSS contain access and benefit sharing (ABS) requirements. ABS refers to benefit sharing as per the Convention on Biological Diversity (CBD) for the use of GRs and associated TK. The objective of the Nagoya Protocol on Access and Benefit-sharing, an international instrument for the implementation of ABS provisions of the CBD, is the fair and equitable sharing of benefits arising from the sustainable use of GRs, which theoretically should contribute to biodiversity conservation.[44] ABS has become a significant point to consider for businesses in the growing international market for traditional herbal medicinal products (THMPs) and other natural health products (NHPs). That is because TMK is central to product development and for documentation of the safety and efficacy evidence requirements for companies to obtain marketing authorization from national authorities.[45] This is also a market that attorneys are paying attention to. In 2016, capacity building courses on Nagoya Protocol implementation and enforcement, aimed at lawyers and policy officials, were launched jointly by the International Development Law Organization (IDLO) and the Secretariat of the Convention on Biological Diversity (SCBD). The course emphasizes that "Genetic resources are the raw ingredients for innovation in medicine, biotechnology, cosmetics, food and beverages, and more."[46]

One way for an enterprise to demonstrate compliance with the ABS requirements of the Nagoya Protocol is to implement a relevant VSS, one that is subject to annual inspections by an accredited third-party control body. For example, VSS that include ABS requirements include the "FairWild Standard" (FWS), developed by the FairWild Foundation (FWF), and the "Ethical BioTrade Standard," developed by the Union for Ethical BioTrade (UEBT). Criterion 4.2 of the FWS, titled "Respecting Customary Rights and Benefit-Sharing," requires that agreements made with local communities and/or indigenous peoples are executed in compliance with relevant international and national laws and ABS regulations including protection of TK.[47] Written and mutually accepted fair and equitable agreements on use of GRs and associated TK must be in place to maintain FairWild certification.[48] Section 3 of the "Ethical BioTrade Standard," titled "Fair and Equitable Sharing of Benefits Derived from the Use of Biodiversity," includes comparable requirements.[49] Some of the largest processors and traders of medicinal plant ingredients in Europe and a growing number of finished herbal product brand-holders in Europe and the Americas are participating in the FairWild and Ethical BioTrade initiatives, respectively.

The case of Peruvian maca

Maca root (actually the "hypocotyl" of *Lepidium meyenii* WALPERS of the Brassicaceae family), an herbaceous perennial, was, up until recently, grown only on the Andean central sierra of Peru, in the puna agroecologic zone above 4,000 meters above sea level, for example in the regions of Junín and Pasco.[50] In presentations made (by this author) at conferences in Lima, Peru in the early 2000s, it was emphasized that if the emblematic Peruvian plant maca should become internationally famous it would only be a matter of time before agronomists would find a way to illegally obtain planting material in order to begin cultivation trials in suitable high-altitude areas of eastern Asia. Recent history has shown that if global market demand for a MAP increases significantly, regardless of its geographical origin, enterprises in China in particular will be interested to control some part of that market. This was forewarned even with the knowledge that Peru has strict regulations in place that disallow the export of viable GRs that could be planted outside of Peru. Having been contacted directly by Chinese researchers requesting assistance towards (illegally) obtaining maca planting material, which I declined, the following rhetorical question was raised in a 2007 article: "Is it just a matter of time before viable maca germplasm (seeds, cell-cultured plantlets, or tubers) is smuggled from the Andes and cultivation experiments begin in the mountains of Asia?"[51]

Despite the regulations for protection of Peruvian GRs and associated TK, experimental cultivation of maca somehow began in the mountains of Yunnan province, China about ten years ago.

In 2015, this author also observed experimental maca cultivation in neighboring Sichuan province as well as in the Garzê Tibetan Autonomous Prefecture. China has increasingly become one of the main export destinations for Peruvian grown maca. In 2014, large numbers of Chinese buyers arrived in the Peruvian Andes just prior to the start of the maca harvest. They began making advance cash payments directly with farmers in order to take ownership of the entire harvest and control the market. In violation of Peruvian law, which requires value-adding of maca prior to export, an estimated 80 percent of the 2014 harvest was smuggled out (unprocessed) to China. Viable planting stock was also allegedly smuggled out of Peru. Some buyers/smugglers seen in Peru during the 2014 harvest season were reportedly armed members of crime syndicates from Hong Kong.[52] Where there is lots of money to be made from a medicinal GR that has become a high-demand and high-value economic crop, do the traders – and does the market – care about the many protections that have been put in place to protect GRs and the associated TK?

So far, NACB has been able to facilitate the rejection of five maca-based patents, three from Japan, one from the Republic of Korea and another through the WIPO Patent Cooperation Treaty (PCT) system,[53] and NACB is challenging Chinese patents on the basis that the starting materials for Chinese-grown maca was obtained illegally, i.e. smuggled, without informed consent or written agreements on access and use.[54] Furthermore, besides making illegal the export of viable unprocessed maca genetic materials, INDECOPI established a Maca Junín-Pasco geographical indication (GI).[55] According to WIPO, GI products "have a specific geographical origin and possess qualities or a reputation that are due to that origin," and a GI right "enables those who have the right to use the indication to prevent its use by a third party whose product does not conform to the applicable standards." In practice, how can these national and international protections work if there are actors in third countries who will apparently disregard the entire notion of GRs and associated TK being IP subject to the terms of international agreements?

Concluding remarks

Depending on who you ask, there are 195 to 206 independent states in the world, of which 193 are member states of the United

Nations and two are non-member state observers. Not all member states sign and/or ratify international treaties. For example, the United States signed the Convention on Biological Diversity (CBD) in 1992 but never ratified it. This article focused on India and Peru because these are prominent examples of biodiverse-rich states that have taken the CBD seriously, have pioneered the establishment of regulatory frameworks for implementation and compliance, but have gone about it in very different ways.

Certainly other states could have been used as examples to illustrate the main points made in this article. For example, the South African "Bioprospecting, Access and Benefit Sharing (BABS) Regulations" came into effect in April 2008, whereby the National Department of Environment Affairs (DEA) was charged to "act as the clearing house and national focal point, for ABS in South Africa." The BABS Clearing House of the Republic of South Africa was set up with a mandate to manage a bioprospecting and ABS permitting system.[56] As a result, several herbal product companies have already entered into benefit-sharing agreements with designated TK owners including the South African San Council and the Cape Bush Doctors/Kaapse Bossiedokters (CBD/KBD).

TK protected as IP necessitates the identification of "owner(s)" of the property, individual or collective. There may be altruistic reasons to protect such TK for the common good and/or to help assure that local, rural and indigenous communities benefit from the commercialization of products based on their collective TK. But where there is lots of money to be made, the reasons and mechanisms for protection of TK may vary from state to state. Peru and India, in particular, have forged ahead with innovative schemes that have relevance to the commercial development, use and trade of herbal medicinal products that are based on traditional ecological and medical knowledge. Other countries are learning from these initiatives and some are establishing similar set-ups. For example, in September 2016, similar to the Indian TKDL model, Ghana launched its online database of Ghanaian indigenous knowledge (GIK) on forest foods and medicinal plants.[57]

While there are some good actors, i.e. enterprises that voluntarily implement sustainability standards that require compliance with the Nagoya Protocol and would enter into ABS agreements with indigenous communities, there are also plenty of bad actors who will try to control and dominate access to certain GRs and knowingly misappropriate TK for their own financial gain.

Over the past 25 years, Peru has developed a comprehensive national strategy to protect its GRs and associated TK. Nonetheless, the several regulations enacted by Peru to protect its GRs and associated TK have not prevented certain actors from China from accessing and using Peruvian GRs and TK in ways that appear to violate Peruvian regulations and international agreements. Peru, although rich in biological and cultural diversity, is a relatively small country with limited capacity and resources. While Peru invests significantly towards investigating the thousands of patents filed globally involving Peruvian plant species, promoting global awareness of emblematic products of Peruvian biodiversity with specified geographical indications such as Maca Junín-Pasco, and implementing an internal control system designed to prevent the illegal export of viable maca planting stock, 玛咖 (Chinese Maca) is now a reality and has hit the market.

The approaches taken by India and Peru thus far are very public. Their initiatives are in the news, relatively often. Enough information is publically available to enable monitoring and evaluation over time. Yet, it is far too early to conclude which model will satisfactorily resolve the questions of whether an indigenous community or the state (or a company) own certain TK; whether the traditional resource managers in rural areas will ever be equitably compensated for their role in biodiversity conservation, sustainable resource management, use and trade of GRs; and whether the living heirs to the intellectual property that is a tribe's TK will retain such intellectual property rights into the future and transmit that TK to each next generation.

At this point, we can observe and opine on the actions of pioneering states like India and Peru and some others including the aforementioned South Africa and Ghana. In a generation, it may be possible to quantitatively evaluate the efficacy of the various newly emerging national models. We do not yet know how most nations in the world (especially the largest and most influential like China and the United States) will actually address the matter of indigenous TK and ABS pertaining to medicinal GRs, if at all.

Notes

1 WIPO, Assemblies of Member States of WIPO Fifty-Fifth Session October 5–14, 2015, Agenda Item 17, www.wipo.int/export/sites/www/tk/en/igc/pdf/igc_mandate_1617.pdf.

2 F. Berkes, J. Colding and C. Folke, "Rediscovery of Traditional Ecological Knowledge as Adaptive Management," *Ecological Applications* 10, no. 5 (2000): 1252.

3 WIPO, *Intellectual Property and Traditional Medical Knowledge*, Background Brief No. 6 (World Intellectual Property Organization Traditional Knowledge Division, 2013).

4 S. Reddy, "Making Heritage Legible: Who Owns Traditional Medical Knowledge?," *International Journal of Cultural Property* 13 (2006): 166.

5 World Bank, *Indigenous Knowledge for Development* (The World Bank, 2004).

6 J. McCarter, M.C. Gavin, S. Baereleo and M. Love, "The Challenges of Maintaining Indigenous Ecological Knowledge," *Ecology and Society* 19, no. 3 (2014): 39.

7 J.A. Brinckmann, H. Huggins and Z.E. Gardner, "Managing Natural Resources for Sustainable Livelihoods: Threats to the Future of Sustainable Wild Collection and Field Experience with Implementation of the FairWild Standard for Medicinal Plants," *International Journal on Biodiversity Watch* 3 (2014): 15.

8 A. Kumar, M. Mitra, B.S. Adhikari and G.S. Rawat, "Depleting Indigenous Knowledge of Medicinal Plants in Cold-Arid Region of Nanda Devi Biosphere Reserve, Western Himalaya," *Medicinal and Aromatic Plants* 4, no. 3 (2015): 2. doi:10.4172/2167-0412.1000195.

9 I. Vandebroek and M.J. Balick, "Globalization and Loss of Plant Knowledge: Challenging the Paradigm," *PLoS ONE* 7, no. 5 (2012): e37643. doi:10.1371/journal.pone.0037643.

10 E. Gómez-Baggethun, E. Corbera and V. Reyes-García, "Traditional Ecological Knowledge and Global Environmental Change: Research Findings and Policy Implications," *Ecology and Society* 18, no. 4 (2013): 72.

11 Ibid.

12 J. Ahmad, A.A. Malik and L. Shakya "Urban Development: A Threat to Wild Species of Medicinal and Aromatic Plants," *Middle-East Journal of Scientific Research* 13, no. 7 (2013): 947; E. Gómez-Baggethun, V. Reyes-García, P. Olsson and C. Montes "Traditional Ecological Knowledge and Community Resilience to Environmental Extremes: A Case Study in Doñana, SW Spain," *Global Environmental Change* 22, no. 3 (2012): 640.

13 Commission on Intellectual Property Rights, *Integrating Intellectual Property Rights and Development Policy* (Commission on Intellectual Property Rights, 2002), www.iprcommission.org/papers/pdfs/final_report/CIPRfullfinal.pdf.

14 I. Jantan, S.N.A. Bukhari, M.A.S. Mohamed, L.K. Wai and M.A. Mesaik, "The Evolving Role of Natural Products from the Tropical Rainforests as a Replenishable Source of New Drug Leads," in *Drug Discovery and Development: From Molecules to Medicine*, ed. O. Vallisuta (InTech, 2015), 3–38; S. Pande and G. Bagler, "A Data and Informatics Driven Drug Discovery Framework to Bridge Traditional and Modern Medicine," *Advanced Techniques in Biology and Medicine* 3 (2015): 141. doi:10.4172/2379-1764.1000141.

15 Gómez-Baggethun et al., "Traditional Ecological Knowledge."

16 Ahmad et al., "Urban Development."

17 Jantan et al., "The Evolving Role of Natural Products."

18 Ibid.

19 Secretariat of the Convention on Biological Diversity, *Nagoya Protocol on Access to Genetic Resources and the Fair and Equitable Sharing of Benefits Arising from Their Utilization to the Convention on Biological Diversity* (Convention on Biological Diversity, United Nations Environmental Programme, 2011).

20 E. Caruso and O. Grace, "Ethics in Ethnobotanical Research: Intellectual Property Rights, International Agreements, and Best Practice," in *Conducting and Communicating Ethnobotanical Research: A Methods Manual*, ed. E. Caruso (Global Diversity Foundation, 2016), 12.

21 C. Chandramouli, *Scheduled Tribes in India as revealed in Census 2011* (Ministry of Tribal Affairs, Government of India, 2013), http://tribal.nic.in/WriteReadData/CMS/Documents/201410210416023592674201306100104316683175RGI1ojune(1).pdf; H. Nagendra, R. Ghate and J. Rao "Governing India's Commons: The Influence of Elinor Ostrom's Ideas," in *Remembering Elinor Ostrom: Her Work and Its Contribution to the Theory and Practice of Conservation and Sustainable Natural Resource Management*, ed. J.P. Robson, I.J. Davidson-Hunt, A. Delaney, G. Lichtenstein, L. Magole and A.T. Pareake, Mead Policy Matters, Issue 19 (CEESP and IUCN, 2014), chapter 12.

22 Nagendra et al., "Governing India's Commons," 19.

23 P.D. Aligica and V. Tarko, "Polycentricity: From Polanyi to Ostrom, and Beyond," *Governance: An International Journal of Policy, Administration, and Institutions* 25, no. 2 (2012): 237.

24 Z. Portillo, "Perú denuncia a China por biopiratería de maca," *SciDev.Net*, July 4, 2014, www.scidev.net/america-latina/agropecuaria/noticias/per-denuncia-a-china-por-biopirateria-de-maca.html#.

25 UNCTAD, *The Convention on Biological Diversity and the Nagoya Protocol: Intellectual Property Implications. A Handbook on the Interface between Global Access and Benefit Sharing Rules and Intellectual Property* (United Nations Conference on Trade and Development, 2014).

26 Congress of the Republic of Peru, Ley sobre la Conservación y Aprovechamiento Sostenible de la Diversidad Biológica (Ley No. 26839 del 8 de Julio de 1997), www.wipo.int/edocs/lexdocs/laws/es/pe/pe044es.pdf.

27 M. Ruiz Muller, *Experiences in the Protection of Traditional Knowledge: The Case of Peru (Law 27811)* (Sociedad Peruana de Derecho Ambiental, 2015).

28 President of the Republic of Peru, "Decreto Supremo No. 039-2003: Prohíben exportación de semillas botánicas, vegetativas, especímenes, productos y subproductos de la maca al estado natural o con proceso de transformación primaria," *El Peruana Diario Oficial* 21, no. 8569 (2003): 256756.

29 President of the Republic of Peru, "Decreto Supremo No. 041-2003: Precisan el concepto de proceso de transformación primaria de la maca, establecido en el D.S. No. 039-2003-AG," *El Peruana Diario Oficial* 21, no. 8580 (2003): 257671.

30 Congress of the Republic of Peru, Ley No. 28216 de Protección al Acceso a la Diversidad Biológica Peruana y los Conocimientos Colectivos de los Pueblos Indígenas, 2004, www.wipo.int/edocs/lexdocs/laws/es/pe/pe013es.pdf.

31 WIPO, INDECOPI Registration No. 903: MACA JUNÍN-PASCO, *Les appellations d'origine* 41 (2013): 19–21, www.wipo.int/export/sites/www/lisbon/en/docs/bulletin_2013_41.pdf.

32 M. Wekesa, *What Is Sui Generis System of Intellectual Property*

Protection? (African Technology Policy Studies Network, 2006), 3.

33 AIPPI (Association Internationale pour la Protection de la Propriété Intellectuelle), *The Relevance of Traditional Knowledge to Intellectual Property Law*, Q232 Group Report (Peru), 43rd World Intellectual Property Congress, 2012, http://aippi.org/wp-content/uploads/committees/232/GR232peru.pdf.

34 Ruiz Muller, *Experiences in the Protection of Traditional Knowledge*.

35 A. Valladolid Cavero, "The Peruvian Experience," Workshop on Traditional Knowledge Documentation in Africa, Cape Town, South Africa, December 11–14, 2013.

36 UNCTAD, *The Convention on Biological Diversity and the Nagoya Protocol*.

37 NCAB, *BIOPAT-PERÚ: Tema: Maca* (Comisión Nacional contra la Biopiratería, 2015), www.biopirateria.org/download/Tema-Maca.pdf.

38 V.K. Gupta, "Protecting India's Traditional Knowledge," *WIPO Magazine* 3 (2011): 5–8.

39 TKDL, "TKDL Outcomes against Bio-piracy," 2016, www.tkdl.res.in/tkdl/langdefault/common/Outcome.asp.

40 V. Upadhya, H.V. Hegde, S. Bhat and S.D. Kholkute, "Non-codified Traditional Medicine Practices from Belgaum Region in Southern India: Present Scenario," *Journal of Ethnobiology and Ethnomedicine* 10 (2014): 49.

41 D. Ganesan, 'Sui generis Is the Answer: Positive Protection of Traditional Knowledge in India," *Journal of Intellectual Property Law and Practice* 11, no. 1 (2016): 49–55.

42 J.P. Sarnaik, "FAIRWILD Certification: An Enabling Framework for Building Capacity of Local Communities, Implementation of ABS and Truly Sustainable Livelihoods,"

The Sixth IPSI Global Conference (IPSI-6), Siem Reap, Cambodia, 2016, https://satoyama-initiative.org/wp/wp-content/uploads/2016/01/3-5_IPSI-6-AERFpresentation.compressed.pdf.

43 K. Komives and A. Jackson, "Introduction to Voluntary Sustainability Standard Systems," in *Voluntary Standard Systems: A Contribution to Sustainable Development*, ed. C. Schmitz-Hoffmann, M. Schmidt, B. Hansmann and D. Palekhov (Springer-Verlag, 2014), 3–20.

44 UEBT, *Nagoya Protocol on Access and Benefit Sharing: Technical Brief* (Union for Ethical BioTrade, 2010), http://ethicalbiotrade.org/dl/benefit-sharing/UEBT-ABS-Nagoya-Protocol.pdf.

45 S. Laird and R. Wynberg, *Bioscience at a Crossroads: Access and Benefit Sharing in a Time of Scientific, Technological and Industry Change: Botanicals* (Secretariat of the Convention on Biological Diversity, 2013).

46 IDLO-SCBD, "Course: Legal Frameworks to Implement Nagoya Protocol," 2016, https://absch.cbd.int/partners/idlo/events?platform=hotsuite.

47 FairWild Foundation, *FairWild Standard* (Version 2.0) (FairWild Foundation, 2010), www.fairwild.org/documents/.

48 FairWild Foundation, *Guidance Manual for Implementation of Social and Fair Trade Aspects in FairWild Operations* (Version 1.1 – December 2013) (FairWild Foundation, 2013), www.fairwild.org/publication-downloads/other-documents/FairWild-Social-Fair-Trade-Guidance-Manual-v1.1.pdf.

49 UEBT, *STD01 – Ethical BioTrade Standard – 2012-04-11* (Union for Ethical BioTrade, 2012), http://ethicalbiotrade.org/dl/public-and-outreach/Ethical-BioTrade-Standard_2012.pdf.

50 J.A. Brinckmann and E. Smith, "Maca Culture of the Junín Plateau," *The*

Journal of Alternative and Complementary Medicine 10, no. 3 (2004): 427.

51 J.A. Brinckmann, "Peruvian Maca and Allegations of Biopiracy," *HerbalGram* 75 (2007): 52.

52 T. Smith, "Maca Madness: Chinese Herb Smugglers Create Chaos in the Peruvian Andes. Consequences for the Market, Consumers, and Local Farming Communities," *HerbalGram* 105 (2015): 48.

53 UNCTAD, *The Convention on Biological Diversity and the Nagoya Protocol.*

54 Portillo, "Perú denuncia a China por biopiratería de maca."

55 WIPO, INDECOPI Registration No. 903: MACA JUNÍN-PASCO.

56 DEA, *South Africa's Bioprospecting, Access and Benefit-Sharing Regulatory Framework: Guidelines for Providers, Users and Regulators* (2012), www.environment. gov.za/sites/default/files/legislations/ bioprospecting_regulatory_framework_ guideline.pdf.

57 J.A. Brinckmann, "Online Database Launched for Ghanaian Indigenous Knowledge of Medicinal Plants," *Market Insider for Medicinal Plants and Natural Ingredients* (December 2016): 13.

7 | USING HUMAN RIGHTS TO MOVE BEYOND REFORMISM TO RADICALISM

A2K for schools, libraries and archives

Caroline B. Ncube

Introduction

This chapter makes a case for a public-interest-and-human-rights-based approach to copyright. It argues that this approach enhances arguments and proposals that have been put forward in relation to access to knowledge (A2K) for schools, libraries and archives. It also considers some of the A2K movement's history, activities and discourse. Other chapters have discussed copyright from various vantage points, e.g. those of the entertainment (primarily music) and software industries. They have presented arguments for openness and access and proposals for more equitable approaches to creation, innovation and dissemination. This chapter follows in that vein but does so from the perspective of the public sector of the education industry. In particular, it focuses on basic or pre-higher education ("schools"). It is necessary to draw the distinction between the public and private sectors of the education industry because of the human-rights-based educational obligations that bind states. These obli-gations buttress public interest arguments that call for openness and access to copyright protected materials for educational purposes. Another relevant human right, which is briefly discussed, is the right to science and culture.

The openness case for schools is primarily that they are best served by a rich catalogue of educational materials that comprises copyright protected works, open educational resources (OER) and other open access (OA) resources. Libraries and archives have a significant role to play in ensuring that school communities have access to their holdings. These holdings generally consist of hard copy and digitized versions of both copyright and public domain materials. The challenges that beset libraries and archives usually relate to the reproduction and digitization of copyright protected materials. It is important to highlight, at the outset, that libraries and archives do not only serve schools. They serve a wider public purpose, supplying a diverse group of subscribers' educational, entertainment and cultural needs. They form part of what is popularly known as the GLAM (galleries, libraries, archives and museums) aspect of A2K. However, this chapter focuses on the narrow function of libraries and archives with respect to schools.

This chapter commences with a discussion of the public interest in copyright and education, with reference to the rights to education, culture and science. Thereafter it canvasses the concept of "knowledge" and access thereto in the copyright context. Here, the significance of global production and consumption patterns of educational materials is highlighted together with the consequent calls for decolonization of curricula and, by extension, learning materials. These calls translate into initiatives to support the production and distribution of open access context-sensitive learning materials in the Global South. The following section contains a brief historical background of the A2K movement and a short commentary on its discourse, its activities and the pragmatic licensing solutions it has developed. The penultimate section focuses on the access concerns of schools, libraries and archives with a brief comment on proposals for reform. Finally, the chapter concludes with some thoughts on how a radical approach to copyright is required to break the stalemate in which the current copyright system finds itself.

The public interest and user human rights

This public interest is the lens through which this chapter accesses the status quo and evaluates proposals for copyright reform and suggestions for alternatives. The notion of the public interest is a well-worn discursive concept,[1] which in this context, signifies normative aspirations for distributive justice. Its value and usefulness as a rhetorical and normative device has been questioned because of its indiscriminate and vague use in the past.[2] It has been deployed in various contexts to support points of view of opposing sides of the copyright policy debate. In such instances, it is argued from the two primary binaries through which copyright policy is usually debated, that is from the position of the copyright holder or from that of the user. So, it may be argued that copyright is in the public interest because it "promote[s] creativity and learning and provide[s] a framework for investment by the creative industries."[3] In contrast, crafting a system that fully facilitates user access to copyright protected works is also in the public interest as access to knowledge allows specific users, and by extension society in general, to achieve their full economic and developmental potential.[4] As will be discussed later, this false bifurcation of the debate has the negative consequence of overlooking the fact that many creators are also users and that most copyright holders are in fact not the creators of the work in which they hold rights.

Despite its checkered past and fraught current usage, as illustrated above, the public interest continues to serve a useful and fundamental evaluative function in democratic systems' public policies.[5] The fundamental measure of any public policy is whether it serves the public interest.[6] Consequently, most copyright debates hinge on whether the aspect under discussion is within the public interest or not. It is thus crucial to articulate the meaning of this concept prior to making any normative assertions.

There are various categorizations of the public interest. For example Downs set out a threefold typology of a majoritarian "will of the people" approach, "an absolute standard value" approach and a "realist" approach.[7] Another example is provided by Held's preponderance, common interest and unitary theories.[8] There are some commonalities between these two approaches but there are also divergences. A preponderance or majoritarian public interest approach furthers the interests of the majority and is, as such, an "aggregative concept."[9] The determination of the majority's preferred position has to be in accordance with a specific, equitable, transparent and accepted process.[10] A common interest approach furthers "individual interests which are shared by all members of the polity."[11] It thus seeks a unanimously held stakeholder position. Held's common interest conception has some resonance with Downs's realist approach.[12] A unitary public interest or absolute standard value advances an "absolute normative principle"[13] which the polity is determined to hold based on shared moral or societal values. Each of these approaches is vulnerable to critique. For example, preponderance theories are viewed as artificial because of their underlying undemocratic "assumptions about . . . aggregated individual interests and the arbitrary rejection of other subjective legitimate preferences."[14] This shortcoming can be ameliorated by the use of open and equitable processes to determine the majoritarian position.[15]

A more contemporary conceptualization of the public interest is Ho's "*ex ante* welfare of the representative individual" approach.[16] This approach makes policy choices based on the perspective of an individual without vested interests.[17] This approach strips normative discussions of privilege and self-interest and thus gives ear to more diverse views including from under-privileged and non-conventional quarters.[18] In global debates, it is likely to go some way towards reducing the dominance of Global North concerns and preferences. On the domestic front, it would provide a platform for minority views.

However, one would have to be clear about the goals that copyright is pursuing before donning the cloak of the representative individual to make policy choices.[19] One would have to consider the relevant state's legal obligations, its socio-economic context and its national priorities. These will be found in binding international and regional agreements; domestic legislation and policies as well as other significant documents which contain aspirational statements. For instance, some of the African National Congress (ANC)-led South African government's policy aspirations can be traced back to the Freedom Charter adopted in 1955 by the Congress of the People.[20] The Charter boldly declared:

The Doors of Learning and Culture Shall be Opened!
The government shall discover, develop and encourage national talent for the enhancement of our cultural life;

All the cultural treasures of mankind shall be open to all, by free exchange of books, ideas and contact with other lands;

The aim of education shall be to teach the youth to love their people and their culture, to honour human brotherhood, liberty and peace;

Education shall be free, compulsory, universal and equal for all children;

Higher education and technical training shall be opened to all by means of state allowances and scholarships awarded on the basis of merit;

Adult illiteracy shall be ended by a mass state education plan;

Teachers shall have all the rights of other citizens;
The colour bar in cultural life, in sport and in education shall be abolished.

The Freedom Charter was probably informed by Article 26 of the Universal Declaration of Human Rights, 1948, which contained several important norms but was of a non-binding nature. The right to education was articulated in a binding international instrument, 11 years after the adoption of the Freedom Charter in Article 13 of the International Covenant on Economic, Social and Cultural Rights of 1966 (ICESCR) which provides that:

1. The States Parties to the present Covenant recognize the right of everyone to education . . .
2. The States Parties to the present Covenant recognize that, with a view to achieving the full realization of this right:

   (a) Primary education shall be compulsory and available free to all;
   (b) Secondary education in its different forms, including technical and vocational secondary education, shall be made generally available and accessible to all by every appropriate means, and in particular by the progressive introduction of free education;
   (c) Higher education shall be made equally accessible to all, on the basis of capacity, by every appropriate means, and in particular by the progressive introduction of free education;
   (d) Fundamental education shall be encouraged or intensified as far as possible for those persons who have not received or completed the whole period of their primary education;
   (e) The development of a system of schools at all levels shall be actively pursued, an adequate fellowship system shall be established, and the material conditions of teaching staff shall be continuously improved.

The normative content of this article has been the subject of extensive commentary emanating from the UN[21] and other quarters.[22] Its essence is that states are obliged to respect, protect and fulfill the right to education. This entails that they must make education "available, accessible, acceptable and adaptable."[23] In addition, Article 14 of the ICESCR provides for compulsory free education. The ICESCR's foundational provisions on the right to education were then restated in other international agreements,[24] regional instruments, most countries' constitutions, other legislation and relevant policies. They were also later reaffirmed by the United Nations' Millennium Development Goals and Sustainable Development Goals.

To return to the South African example, the Freedom Charter's educational aspirations are now encapsulated in national policy to promote literacy and a constitutional obligation[25] for the state to provide access to a basic education.[26]

The Constitutional Court has held the following:[27]

> Section 29(1)(a) has no internal limitation requiring that the right be "progressively realised" within "available resources" subject to "reasonable legislative measures" . . . [it] is "immediately realisable" and may only . . . be limited in terms of a law of general application that is reasonable and justifiable in an open and democratic society based on human dignity, equality and freedom

This would mean that, for South Africa, the public interest in relation to copyright protected works, which are used in educational contexts, takes a particular hue. Therefore, it would have to be distinguished from the public interest in other copyright protected works, such as those primarily for commercial purposes.

Helfer and Austin provide the following compelling examples of how other jurisdictions have placed a premium on the linkages between copyright and education and sought to ensure meaningful compatibility between them:

> Conceptually and textually, there exist venerable connections between education and intellectual property. These connections are particularly clear in the copyright context . . . The first copyright statute, the English Statute of Anne of 1709, was entitled "An Act for the Encouragement of Learning." Similarly, the Copyright Clause of the U.S. Constitution empowers

the U.S. Congress "to promote the progress of science" (or, in modern parlance, "knowledge") by creating a national copyright system. In the early years of the French Revolution, responsibility for the development of copyright law passed to the "Committee for Public Instruction," and by 1793, it was accepted that "enacting a copyright law formed part of a grander scheme of public education."[28]

In addition to the right to education, the right to science and culture serves as a basis to further A2K. Article 27 of the Universal Declaration of Human Rights provides:

> Everyone has the right freely to participate in the cultural life of the community, to enjoy the arts and to share in scientific advancement and its benefits.
> Everyone has the right to the protection of the moral and material interests resulting from any scientific, literary or artistic production of which he is the author.

Shaver argues that this provision "must be understood as a call for culture and science to be governed as global public goods, rather than as private property."[29] This argument has gained traction and it has been put forward by the Special Rapporteur in the field of cultural rights in a report on copyright policy issued in 2015 after a series of stakeholder and expert meetings to interrogate the content of the right.[30] The rights to cultural participation and protection of authorship are reiterated in Article 15.1 of the ICESCR. The Committee on Economic, Social and Cultural Rights' General comment on the meaning of the protection of authorship right references the economic needs of authors.[31] The current copyright system now often furthers the economic benefit of third parties, such as commercial production and distribution intermediaries, at the expense of authors. The ICESCR provision directs copyright law back to the welfare of authors. In this sense, it can be said that it reveals tension between copyright law and the human rights of authors. The committee has also commented on cultural participation[32] but not yet on the right to enjoy the benefits of scientific progress.[33]

Knowledge, A2K and copyright

The concept of knowledge often goes unexplored in treatises on A2K.[34] Giving content to the concept is important, as it then would more robustly animate calls for access. It has been suggested that to give meaning to the concept it is necessary to define it, highlight the privileging of some types of knowledge and identify patterns, sites and means of production, distribution and consumption of knowledge.[35]

There are various typologies of knowledge, ranging from Ryle's "Knowing How and Knowing That"[36] categorization to the threefold typology of procedural (also known as competence or know-how), personal (or acquaintance) and propositional (or knowing-that or declarative) knowledge.[37] Procedural knowledge relates to a person's competence to perform an act, such as being literate.[38] Personal knowledge is acquired through personal experience, such as being acquainted with another person.[39] Propositional knowledge pertains to the knowing of certain facts or information.[40] It is under this rubric that various bodies of subject matter knowledge fall and with which the A2K movement is concerned.

In view of its significance, it is important to provide a detailed definition of propositional knowledge. The most well known epistemological definition of propositional knowledge is the Cartesian conception, which is named after its originator Rene Descartes.[41] Under this conception a person would have knowledge of something (x), if he believes it without any doubt, if it is true and he has a reason that guarantees the veracity of x.[42]

Another definition is the standard or accepted definition of knowledge which posits that a person knows x if three conditions are met, namely that he accepts or believes x is true, x is in fact true and he has a reason or justification for his belief.[43] This *justified true belief* (JTB) approach is accepted by many philosophers but there are other definitions that differ from it.[44] These alternatives were necessitated by Gettier,[45] who demonstrated that the JTB approach could encompass situations where the three conditions were met, but a person would not really have knowledge of proposition x.[46] To eliminate such outcomes, various solutions have been offered by philosophers over the years. One such proposal is the introduction of a fourth condition to the JTB approach, namely that the reason or justification for the belief in the veracity of x must not be an accident or coincidence. In other words, it must not be by mere chance of circumstances that a person's reasoning turns out to be true. A discussion of the various solutions that have been put forward falls beyond the ambit of this work and the competence of this author. Suffice it to say that a universally accepted solution is yet to be found.

Beyond the field of philosophy, other disciplines also primarily concern themselves with propositional knowledge. For instance, Bell defines knowledge as:

> a set of organized statements of facts or ideas, presenting
> a reasoned judgment or an experimental result, which is
> transmitted to others through some communication medium in
> some systematic form.[47]

Similar definitions have been put forward by A2K theorists, such as Benkler who defines knowledge as:

> the set of cultural practices and capacities necessary for
> processing the information into either new statements into the
> information exchange, or more important in our context, for
> practical use of the information in appropriate ways to produce
> more desirable actions or outcomes from action.[48]

It is clear from these definitions that facts or information are required to generate knowledge. Therefore, in some instances calls for A2K are calls for access to information.[49] However, the A2K movement deliberately mobilizes around the concept of knowledge because it evokes the sense of competencies that have the potential to generate economic, cultural or technological progress.[50]

It is trite that there are various kinds of knowledge such as technical, scientific and ethical knowledge.[51] Such classifications of knowledge are based on its subject matter content. It is also possible to classify knowledge according to who produces it. For instance knowledge created by traditional or indigenous communities is known as traditional knowledge (TK). Copyright law protects expressions of knowledge that meet the protection criteria of originality and reduction to material form provided that the creator of the knowledge is a citizen or resident of a Berne Convention country.

Production, distribution and consumption patterns show that most copyright protected knowledge originates in the Global North.[52] The

Global South largely receives knowledge produced in the North. This proposition is true for most types of knowledge with the exception of traditional knowledge which currently largely emanates from the Global South. The provenance of knowledge in the North causes problems of cost and access in the Global South and one of the main rallying points of the A2K movement has been to call for better and more equitable access. It also raises questions about the relevance of learning materials to the Global South. Hence calls for the decolonization of curricula at all levels of education[53] and concerted efforts to promote the production of locally authored educational materials that are context sensitive.[54]

It is important to end this section with an acknowledgement that "to access is not to know"[55] and that the work done in pursuit of A2K has to be supplemented with others' efforts to reform curricula and teaching environments and practices. However, a discussion of these elements falls beyond the scope of this paper.

The A2K movement

The A2K movement is a grouping of a wide range of actors that include academics, civil society, digital rights groups, consumer rights groups, open source and open content communities, libraries and archives.[56] Each of these actors has a set of concerns that are its primary focus and in some instances these focal points do not permeate the entire movement.[57] It is not possible in a chapter of this nature to do justice to all the concerns of this broad range of actors, consequently the chapter focuses on schools, libraries and archives.

It is difficult to precisely pinpoint the exact moment when any social movement emerged because there are always several incidents that work together and finally coalesce in the movement. There are also frequently many role players who all contribute to its creation, albeit some more visibly than others. Some accounts of the nascent stages of the A2K have been published[58] but an authoritative account of its emergence and development is yet to be published.[59] From Latif's comprehensive account it is clear that the first steps were taken by civil society, some academics and developing country Geneva-based diplomatic staff in the early 2000s.[60] Impetus grew around several key events at which these and other interested individuals continued to share and crystalize their ideas. These events included the World Summit on the Information Society (WSIS) held in Geneva in 2003, the second UNCTAD-ICTSD Bellagio Dialogue on Development and Intellectual Property Policy held in Bellagio, Italy in 2003 and a side meeting at the Global Access to Essential Learning Tools conference held in New York in April 2004. It was at the last of these that the choice was made to coin the movement's agenda in the "access to knowledge" slogan and within a short while thereafter the abbreviation A2K was adopted.[61]

Generally, the A2K movement "aims to create more equitable public access to the products of human culture and learning."[62] These issues are not confined to copyright law but extend to other types of IP such as patents. In relation to patents, a prominent strand of the movement focuses on access to medicines (A2M).[63] A2M gained much traction in the Global South in the wake of the HIV/AIDS pandemic. For instance, in South Africa several campaigns have been run with the most recent being the Fix the Patent Laws campaign that was launched in 2011.[64] Usually, the different branches of the movement pursue core issues separately, but in some instances they purposefully work on disparate issues simultaneously. For example, the African Scholars for Knowledge Justice (ASKJustice) project considers both A2M and A2K matters concurrently.[65]

Members of the A2K movement are involved in a variety of norm-setting initiatives at international, regional and national levels. In particular, they have a credible presence at the inter-governmental institutional level.[66] It is beyond the scope of this chapter to enumerate all, or even most, of their activities. Suffice it to say, the movement has a decidedly activist nature to it.[67] However, this is just one aspect of this multi-faceted movement. The A2K movement's other contributions to copyright reform have comprised draft legislative text, in the form of complete drafts (for example the Draft A2K Treaty),[68] compilations of existing and suggested legislative provisions for inclusion in domestic statutes.[69] It has also produced tools to facilitate easier copyright licensing in creative commons licenses and free and open source licenses for software. These licenses are premised on the current copyright system.

The A2K movement's activism and scholarly output is powered by the discourse of "commons," "public domain," "openness," "access" and "sharing."[70] In contrast, descriptions of the current IP-centric position are painted in the starkly contrasting language of enclosure.[71] As a counter-point to the primacy given to rights holders' private property rights, the movement highlights the human rights of other creators, users and society at large.[72]

Another powerful discursive device is the intentional shattering of the popular bifurcation or false binary of IP stakeholders into the rights holder vs. the user camps. Many A2K scholars and activists have been at pains to show that most stakeholders are both rights holders and users. If that is the case, then it would be prudent to make IP policy choices that are equitable. This would give effect to Ho's *ex ante* representative individual approach. In order to enable this, several studies that seek to provide empirical evidence to illuminate policy making have emanated from the A2K movement. For example, country studies of Brazil,[73] India,[74] Egypt,[75] South Africa[76] and several other African countries[77] have been published. In addition to jurisdiction-specific studies, there is also scholarly consideration of the international position.[78]

Generally, the A2K movement is not perceived as being radical, either by participants in the movement or by observers. Krikorian, an example of the former, writes:

Not only does A2K not look like a mass movement, but many of its advocates are not very radical, and, as a whole, the movement is rather utilitarian. Finally, A2K is not as confrontational as many other social mobilizations. Most A2K advocates so far seem interested in withdrawing from the dialectal logic of direct power struggles, either with the state or with industry.[79]

This view is shared by others.[80] It is perhaps primarily due to the movement's provision of open licensing solutions. These open licenses are used by a wide range of creators. In the education context they are used to license learning materials (open educational resources). They support the activities of those who publish for altruistic purposes (social publishing innovators). Examples of such innovators abound. In the context of the production of children's fiction literature in African languages, they include Book Dash[81] and the African Storybook Project.[82] The usual mode of creation is to set a date for teams of volunteers to converge at a venue and to write books together in a single sitting. Teams often consist of a writer, an illustrator and a designer. Once complete the book is licensed using creative commons and posted on the project website.

Schools, libraries and archives

Schools are not usually the drivers of copyright policy debates; instead their needs are the focus of policy debates. However, in some instances teachers and learners have become quite active in debates and participate in protest action. A prime example is South Africa's Equal Education, a non-profit organization, which comprises school communities and other stakeholders.[83] Equal Education has been party (as amicus) to several significant cases pertaining to access to education and protecting the rights of learners.[84] Another organization that has played a prominent role is Basic Education for All which was involved in the delivery of school textbooks matter.[85] This decision (*Minister of Basic Education vs. Basic Education for All*) is the most recent articulation of the content of the right to basic education in South Africa. As stated above, it emphasized that this right is immediately realizable. The matter pertained to the Basic Education Department's failure to provide each learner in Limpopo province with a text book for each subject prior to the commencement of the school year. The Constitutional Court found that this failure constituted "a violation of the rights to basic education, equality, dignity, SASA [South African Schools Act] and s 195 of the Constitution."[86] None of these cases have directly addressed copyright but the linkage is patently clear: copyright affects the right to education to the extent that it impacts access to learning materials.

Librarians and archivists have historically been more activist than school communities.[87] Typically, they act collectively through associations to which they belong such as the International Federation of Library Associations and Institutions. Libraries and archives have a broad mandate and serve different sections of society. Copyright is a primary concern for them because their holdings are usually copyright protected and they face significant challenges in their quest to bring reading materials to the world. For purposes of this chapter, their educational mandate is of primary concern and the focal concern is their role in providing access to learning materials.

The access needs of schools are quite simply put: in order to meaningfully realize the right to education, learners need adequate supplies of up-to-date, subject and contextually relevant learning materials. In the Global South, where internet and device availability is high but usually too expensive for disadvantaged portions of society, bulk hard copies are required.[88] Most schools purchase text books for classroom use but libraries and archives serve a key role in providing other learning materials such as reference texts, general reading materials for use in researching assignments and enrichment reading. To meet some of these needs, multiple copies are required. Some legislation permits the making of multiple copies and the copying of a work for preservation, inter-library or inter-archive loans, amongst other purposes. However, the conditions under which these copies may be made are frequently unnecessarily restrictive.

In order to critique the position of libraries and archives, it is necessary to have recourse to specific statutory provisions. To this end a brief analysis s. 13 of the South African Copyright Act and its accompanying regulations follows. Section 3 of the regulations[89] specifies that libraries and archives can only copy a work and distribute those copies if:

a) it is for non-commercial purposes;
b) its collections or holdings are open to the public or available to researchers; and
c) the reproduction of the work incorporates a copyright warning.

Further, Section 2 requires that the copy must be limited to a "reasonable portion" and "not conflict with the normal exploitation of the work." Inter-library or inter-archive loans are permitted subject to limitations on the amount of the work copied and usage is restricted to private study or personal or private use of the person to whom the material is provided. Where an unused copy of the work is unavailable at a fair price libraries or archives may, upon request, copy the whole work or a substantial portion of it. The copy may only be used for private study or personal or private use. These provisions have several shortcomings. Their reference to the qualitative concept of a reasonable portion is problematic; it fails to address the making of multiple copies, digitization, translation, adaptation and conversion to accessible formats for persons with sensory impairments.[90]

In relation to A2K for schools, the dominant discourse draws extensively on human rights and developmental justifications. The starting point is to emphasize state obligations to provide education and the right to science and culture found in Articles 13 and 15 of the ICESCR respectively. As noted above, these foundational provisions find expression in most countries' constitutions, other legislation and relevant policies. They were also reaffirmed by the United Nations' Millennium Development Goals and Sustainable Development Goals. The core argument built on this foundation is that the current copyright system results in inadequate access to the learning materials needed to acquire an education or to participate in science and cultural life. Therefore reform is needed to rectify this.

Reform proposals for greater access to learning materials have largely been confined to finding solutions within the current copyright system. These span suggestions for the reform of exceptions and limitations;[91] a limited translation right for copyright protected works accompanied by local language limitations;[92] assignment of rights; licenses and remedies. Exceptions to this non-radical approach include proposals for the introduction of constitutive copyright registration[93] and the shortening of the duration of copyright to much less than the default life plus 50 rule.[94] Suggestions for a two-tier copyright system[95] could also be included in this radical category, to the extent that one or both of the tiers could be impermissible under the existing copyright framework. These proposals are radical to the extent that they would require re-writing or "burning"[96] Berne.

All these proposals will not be outlined here in detail as they have been comprehensively set out elsewhere.[97] Suffice it to say that they seek to meet the pervasive concern – if the current copyright system was completely jettisoned, or fundamentally altered, how would the provision of learning materials be guaranteed, or at the very least stimulated? For instance having constitutive registration coupled with different tiers or classes of copyright would enable authors to choose which type of copyright suits them. One tier could be of very short non-renewable duration, say seven to fourteen years. Another could be of an initial term of one year that is renewable indefinitely if the work meets certain criteria such as grossing a set revenue threshold. Such a tier would suit the needs of commercial works. Finally, authors may simply choose to opt out of the system and allow their works to enter the public domain from inception. Government procurement systems can be used to stimulate the production of certain types of educational materials if it appears that the new copyright system is failing to do so. However, considering the rich body of OER and other OA materials suitable for learning contexts, it is unlikely that such a measure would be required.

The following sub-sections set out why a tiered system is necessary and then sketch a proposal for tiered copyright. This is followed by an evaluation of the proposal under the current international copyright system to illustrate why radical changes are required rather than trying to fix the current system.

Why we need to tier copyright protection

Arguments for nuancing copyright are frequently made from the perspective of users. For example, currently it is obvious that there is a huge disparity between copyright law and social norms.[98] Studies such as "Infringement Nation"[99] and "Copy Culture in the US and Germany"[100] show that the majority of people routinely infringe copyright when they engage in activities they consider to be morally and socially acceptable. Therefore, it would make sense to create a copyright system that does not criminalize or prohibit activities that users routinely engage in without any sense of moral blameworthiness.

Arguments for nuancing copyright are equally persuasive from a creator's perspective. Current copyright law does not consider creators' motivation in creating protected works. Using US copyright law as an example, Loren notes that "works created by accident, without thought or with no consideration of the material rewards that might result"[101] are protected by copyright as long as they are original, reduced to material form and the author is a qualified person (one eligible by citizenry or domicile of that jurisdiction or another Berne Convention state). This approach, which is applied globally, leads to the protection of all works that meet the above criteria. In some instances, such protection hinders the creator's intended distribution of the work. Therefore, creators would also benefit from a system that is sensitive to their motivations and needs. Such a system would not grant the same rights in the same way to all creators.

Examples of existing tiers of copyright protection

Tehranian[102] notes that in the United States copyright protection is already hierarchal and that tiers are de facto created by the unique[103] provisions relating to statutory damages.[104] He notes:

Through formalities, the 1976 Copyright Act actually created two distinct tiers of effective protection for copyrighted works.

Sophisticated, routine creators – generally corporations in content-creation industries – timely register their works and therefore enjoy generous remedies against infringers. These remedies include the recovery of reasonable attorneys' fees and the assessment of statutory damages – which can rise to the draconian level of up to $150,000 per willful act of infringement. Absent any proof of actual damages, such plaintiffs can elect statutory damages that quickly create the possibility of a multi-million dollar judgment in their favor. By sharp contrast, unsophisticated creators, like individual artists, typically do not timely register their works and are often left with little except moral force and the uncertain threat of injunctive relief to enforce their intellectual property rights. The dichotomy between sophisticated and unsophisticated creators thereby determines the relative sanctity of copyrighted works.[105]

Loren notes that the US Copyright Act's limitation of rights in nondramatic musical works[106] is another example of tailoring copyright. The following section sets out one of the proposals for tiering copyright.

Skladany's revenue-based tiers

Skladany[107] suggests a two-tier system of copyright protection based on the protected works' revenue generation. Protection through either tier would be conditional upon registration, preferably online, of the relevant work by the person who seeks protection. Such a person would have to be legitimately entitled to procure protection, for example through being the creator of the work. Before discussing how the tiers would work, it is important to consider the validity, under Berne, of registration requirements.

Would the registration requirement be permissible under Berne?

Registration requirements raise concerns about compliance with Article 5(2) of the Berne Convention which requires that copyright protection must subsist automatically and not be subject to any formalities.[108] The only way such a registration requirement can pass muster under Berne is if it is voluntary and the subsistence of copyright is not dependent upon its fulfillment.[109] For example, the registration could be used to serve other purposes such as the creation of "a rebuttable presumption that the facts registered are valid."[110]

Another example is the United States' use of timely registration as a prerequisite for seeking statutory damages. To implement Skladany's proposal, a new copyright order would have to be created.

The tiers

Tier 1 works would get copyright protection for a non-renewable prescribed period of time. Skladany is not prescriptive about this period but suggests 10, 14 or 20-year terms. Tier 2 works would obtain initial protection for one year that would be renewable indefinitely upon the payment of renewal fees provided that the work meets a set revenue threshold. Skladany nuances this tier in the following five ways:

1. the renewal revenue threshold should be high;
2. this threshold should be raised annually at above-inflation levels;
3. the renewal fees should be high;
4. these renewal fees should be raised annually at above-inflation rates; and
5. only a certain portion or percentage of tier 2 eligible works should have their copyright protection renewed each year.

Skladany further points out that his proposal could be nuanced in other ways. For instance, the terms of protection in either tier could be adjusted; other tiers could be introduced; the revenue benchmarks could be raised or reduced; and registration could be required for only tier 2.

Evaluation

The main feature of this system would be its radical shortening of the duration of copyright for tier 1 works and the introduction of indefinite protection for eligible tier 2 works. Tier 2 works would initially be protected for a year, but could be protected further after the completion of the renewal process described above. Both tiers are a far cry from Berne's prescribed duration for copyright. Similar proposals for the shortening of copyright's duration have been made by other scholars such as Patry.[111] As noted by Samuelson, such a radical reconfiguration would not be possible under the current provisions of the Berne Convention and TRIPS.[112]

However, if the necessary Berne amendments were to be passed, or an entirely new copyright order created, several benefits would follow the implementation of this proposal. First, non-commercial works could immediately enter the public domain if an author chooses not to register for copyright protection. Conceivably, some learning materials would fall into this tier, particularly those that are openly licensed under the current system. Second, non-commercial tier 1 works would enter the public domain earlier than is currently possible because the proposed tier 1 protection's duration is a fraction of current copyright terms. Third, commercial works that are protected in tier 2 would also enter the public domain in a relatively shorter time than is currently possible as their continued protection would be subject to their meeting revenue thresholds. Some learning materials would also fall into this tier, namely those produced by commercial publishers. Fourth, this proposal would eliminate orphan works due to the constitutive registration aspect which would provide records of the creator or copyright holder of protected works. This would mean that under this system, there would be no copyright protected orphan works. This would be a huge improvement as under the current system schools are unable to fully use orphan works in those jurisdictions that do not have a statutory orphan works licensing scheme in place.

Conclusion

Current copyright reform suggestions are largely constrained by the existing framework. Several proposals have emanated from the scholarly quarters of the A2K movement which advance the powerful discourse of "commons," "public domain," "openness," "access" and "sharing" matched, in some instances, with protest action and public interest litigation from aligned civic society. For example, in South Africa civic organizations are very active in obtaining court clarification of the content of the right to education and in holding the executive to account regarding the country's system of education. Other contributions from the movement include involvement in international and domestic norm-setting and the provision of practical mechanisms such as open licenses that enable copyright holders to disseminate their works more openly. These licenses have given flight to very successful OER projects which have had significant impact on education.

The second part of this chapter focused on proposals to reform the current copyright system with a particular emphasis on educational materials relevant to basic education. It found that only a few proposals venture beyond the confines of TRIPS and Berne. Suggestions for constitutive registration and tiering copyright are some of the more radical proposals that have been offered. Donning the mantle of a disinterested representative individual to consider copyright policy options *ex ante* may free minds to be truly radical in seeking solutions. Setting aside self-interest, forgetting past and current privileging of certain kinds of knowledge and jettisoning entrenched business models and aligned interests could enable the creation of a new copyright system that assures access to knowledge and allows schools to meet their educational mandate and facilitates their necessary support by libraries and archives. Such efforts would be greatly enhanced by grounding them in a public interest and human rights framework. The foundational premise then becomes: how can copyright law be crafted to be supportive of state obligations to respect, protect and fulfill the right to education, in view of the immediately realizable right to basic education? This obligation entails that they must make education available, accessible, acceptable and adaptable. Whilst a large portion of this obligation pertains to infrastructural and human resources, a very important aspect of it is the availability of, and access to, appropriate learning materials.

It has been established that in the Global South, the most pressing need is for bulk copies of print materials. Enter copyright and its restrictions on reproduction, translation and adaptation. Several studies have shown that existing exceptions and limitations are simply not equal to the task of ensuring the required access to learning materials. Efforts continue to conceive of ways to improve or better balance the system, but as persuasively argued by Story:

> It is both illusory and delusory to think that a so-called balanced or re-balanced Berne and/or global copyright system can be constructed; it is not only wishful, but also wistful, thinking and is based on a naive understanding of how this system operates, as well as its ideology and power relationships within it.[113]

In view of this, this chapter argued that a reformist approach is inadequate and radical changes are required to the current international copyright system in order to garner real results in the availability of, and access to learning materials. In particular, the chapter considers whether copyright protection should be tiered according to commerciality by predicating long terms of protection on revenue thresholds and the payment of renewal fees. Tiering protection in this way would enable the creation of a different model for public interest works (such as learning materials) as compared to commercially oriented works (such as blockbuster movies). The construction of tiers into the copyright system would require the establishment of factors to be used to categorize or screen works into the tiers. To this end, the author's intention (exercised through the decision to register the work for protection) and revenue thresholds (giving voice to the market's value of the work) would work together to marshal works into the proposed tiers. Further, the legislature can further the public interest through statutory provisions for renewal fees which would be structured in a way that is supportive of socially valuable works such as learning materials. For instance such fees could be substantially reduced or waived for certain works.

Notes

1 Geoffrey Edwards, "Defining the Public Interest" (Ph.D. thesis, Griffith University, 2007), 1.

2 Rebecca Giblin and Kimberlee Weatherall, "If We Redesigned Copyright from Scratch, What Might It Look Like?" in *What If We Could Reimagine Copyright?*, ed. Rebecca Giblin and Kimberlee Weatherall (ANU Press, 2017), 3–7; Caroline B. Ncube, *Intellectual Property Policy, Law and Administration in Africa: Exploring Continental and Sub-regional Co-operation* (Routledge, 2016), 5; Isabella Alexander, *Copyright Law and the Public Interest in the Nineteenth Century* (Hart Publishing, 2010), 16; R.C. Box, "Redescribing the Public Interest," *The Social Science Journal* 44, no. 4 (2007): 586; V. Held, *The Public Interest and Individual Interests* (Basic Books, 1970), 1; H.J. Storing, "Review: The Crucial Link: Public Administration, Responsibility, and the Public Interest," *Public Administration Review* 24, no. 1 (1964): 39–46; C.J. Friedrich (ed.), *Nomos V: The Public Interest. Yearbook of the*

American Society for Political and Legal Philosophy (Atherton Press, 1962); G.A. Schubert, *The Public Interest: A Critique of the Theory of a Political Concept* (The Free Press, 1960), 224; F. Sorauf, "The Public Interest Reconsidered," *Journal of Politics* 19 (1957): 616.

3 Guan H. Tang, *Copyright and the Public Interest in China* (Edward Elgar, 2010), 50.

4 Ibid.

5 Giblin and Weatherall, "If We Redesigned Copyright from Scratch," 8.

6 Ncube, *Intellectual Property Policy*, 5.

7 Denis McQuail, *Media Performance: Mass Communication and the Public Interest* (Sage, 1992), 22; Anthony Downs, "The Public Interest: Its Meaning in a Democracy," *Social Research* 29, no. 1 (1962): 1–36.

8 Giblin and Weatherall, "If We Redesigned Copyright from Scratch," 10; McQuail, *Media Performance*, 22; Virginia Held, *The Public Interest and Individual Interests* (Basic Books, 1970), 42–46.

9 P.M.S. Hacker, "New Books: The Public Interest and Individual Interests by Virginia Held," *Mind* 81, no. 322 (1972): 311–312. doi:10.1093/mind/LXXXI.322.311, 311.

10 W. Lippman, *The Public Philosophy* (Hamish Hamilton, 1955), 44, quoted in J. Morison and G. Anthony, "The Place of Public Interest," in *Values in Global Administrative Law*, ed. G. Anthony, J.-B. Auby, J. Morison and T. Zwart (Hart Publishing, 2011), 215, 217; Downs, "The Public Interest," 1, 5.

11 Mile Saks *Professions and the Public Interest: Medical Power, Altruism and Alternative Medicine* (Routledge, 2005), 43.

12 McQuail, *Media Performance*, 23.

13 Ibid., 23; Mike Feintuck and Mike Varney, *Media Regulation, Public Interest and the Law* (Edinburgh University Press, 2006), 108.

14 Morison and Anthony, "The Place of Public Interest," 218. Also see William Fisher, "Theories of IP," in *New Essays in the Legal and Political Theory of Property*, ed. Stephen Munzer (Cambridge University Press, 2001), 168.

15 Caroline B. Ncube, "Harnessing Intellectual Property for Development: Some Thoughts on an Appropriate Theoretical Framework," *Potchefstroom Electronic Law Journal/Potchefstroomse Elektroniese Regsblad (PER/PELJ)* 16, no. 4 (2013): 375; Anupam Chander and Madhavi Sunder, "Is Nozick Kicking Rawl's Ass? Intellectual Property and Social Justice," *UC Davis Law Review* 40 (2007): 577.

16 Giblin and Weatherall, "If We Redesigned Copyright from Scratch," 13; Lok-sang Ho, *Public Policy and the Public Interest* (Routledge, 2013).

17 Ho, *Public Policy and the Public Interest*, 7.

18 Giblin and Weatherall, "If We Redesigned Copyright from Scratch," 14–15.

19 Ibid.

20 Available at www.anc.org.za/show.php?id=72. The Charter expresses the principles pf the ANC, the South African Indian Congress, the South African Congress of Democrats and the Coloured People's Congress.

21 For example UN Committee on Economic, Social and Cultural Rights (CESCR), "General Comment No. 13: The Right to Education (Art. 13 of the Covenant)," E/C.12/1999/10, December 8, 1999, adopted at the Twenty-first Session of the Committee; *Report of the Special Rapporteur in the Field of Cultural Rights, Farida Shaheed, Copyright Policy and the Right to Science and Culture*, A/HRC/28/57, December 24, 2014; United Nations Educational, Scientific and Cultural Organization (UNESCO), *The Right to Education: Law and Policy Review Guidelines* (2014); see generally the work of the Special Rapporteur on the right to education.

22 Andrew Rens, "The Right to Education and the Internet: Case Study on the Role of the Internet in Provision and Accessibility of Educational Resources in South Africa," Association for Progressive Communications (APC), May 2016; Klaus Dieter Beiter, *The Protection of the Right to Education by International Law: Including a Systematic Analysis of Article 13 of the International Covenant on Economic, Social and Cultural Rights* (Martinus Nijhoff, 2005); Joel Spring, *The Universal Right to Education: Justification, Definition, and Guidelines* (Lawrence Erlbaum, 2000); Douglas Hodgson, *The Human Right to Education* (Ashgate, 2008).

23 UNCESCR, General Comment 1999, para. 6.

24 Articles 28, 29 and 40 of the Convention on the Rights of the Child; Article 5 of the Convention on the Elimination of All Forms of Racial Discrimination; Articles 10 and 14 of the Convention on the Elimination of

All Forms of Discrimination Against Women; Article 4(a) of the UNESCO Convention against Discrimination in Education (CDE).

25 s. 29(1) of the Constitution provides: "Everyone has the right –

    (a) to basic education, including adult basic education; and
    (b) to further education, which the state through reasonable measures, must make progressively available and accessible."

26 See, for example, Enynna S. Nwauche, "The Public Interest in Namibian Copyright Law," *Namibia Law Journal* 1 (2009): 66; L. Arendse, "The Obligation to Provide Free Basic Education in South Africa: An International Law Perspective," *PER/PELJ* 14, no. 6 (2011): 97; Shireen Motala, "Educational Access in South Africa," *Journal of Educational Studies Special Issue Social Justice* (2011): 84.

27 Minister of Basic Education vs. Basic Education for All (20793/2014) [2015] ZASCA 198 (December 2, 2015), para. 36, citing.

28 Laurence R. Helfer and Graeme W. Austin, *Human Rights and Intellectual Property: Mapping the Global Interface* (Cambridge University Press, 2011), 316.

29 Lea Shaver, "The Right to Science and Culture," *Wisconsin Law Review* 1 (2010): 128.

30 Special Rapporteur to UN OHCHR, *Report of the Special Rapporteur in the Field of Cultural Rights Farida Shaheed: Copyright Policy and the Right to Science and Culture*, Office of the High Commissioner for Human Rights (OHCHR), Human Rights Council, 28th Session, March 14, 2015, UN General Assembly, New York, 4.

31 The Committee on Economic, Social and Cultural Rights, General Comment 17 (2005).

32 The Committee on Economic, Social and Cultural Rights, General Comment 21 (2009).

33 Special Rapporteur to UN OHCHR, *Report of the Special Rapporteur*, 4.

34 Alan Story, Colin Darch and Debora Halbert (eds), *The Copy/South Dossier: Issues in the Economics, Politics, and Ideology of Copyright in the Global South* (Copy/South Research Group, 2006), 164.

35 Ibid., 164.

36 Gilbert Ryle, "Knowing How and Knowing That: The Presidential Address," *Proceedings of the Aristotelian Society, New Series* 46 (1945–1946): 1–16.

37 Jeremy Fantl, "Knowledge How," in *The Stanford Encyclopedia of Philosophy* (Spring 2016), ed. Edward N. Zalta, http://plato.stanford.edu/archives/spr2016/entries/knowledge-how/; Stephen Hetherington, "Knowledge," *The Internet Encyclopedia of Philosophy*, www.iep.utm.edu/knowledg/.

38 Fantl, "Knowledge How."

39 Originated in Bertrand Russell, "Knowledge by Acquaintance and Knowledge by Description," *Proceedings of the Aristotelian Society* 11 (1910): 108–128; Bertrand Russell, *Problems of Philosophy* (Oxford University Press, 1912), 46. For contemporary overviews see Ali Hasan and Richard Fumerton, "Knowledge by Acquaintance vs. Description," in *The Stanford Encyclopedia of Philosophy* (Spring 2014), ed. Edward N. Zalta, http://plato.stanford.edu/archives/spr2014/entries/knowledge-acquaindescrip/ and John M. DePoe "Knowledge by Acquaintance and Knowledge by Description," *The Internet Encyclopedia of Philosophy*, www.iep.utm.edu/knowacq/.

40 Fantl, "Knowledge How."

41 Rene Descartes, *Discourse on Method and Meditations on First*

Philosophy, 3rd ed., trans. Donald A. Cress (Hackett, 1993).

42 Lauren BonJour, *Epistemology: Classic Problems and Contemporary Responses*, 2nd ed. (Rowman & Littlefield, 2009).

43 Ibid., 24.

44 Ibid., 24.

45 Edmund Gettier, "Is Justified True Belief Knowledge?" *Analysis* 23 (1963): 121–123.

46 BonJour, *Epistemology*, 40; Stephen Hetherington, "Gettier Problems," *The Internet Encyclopedia of Philosophy*, www.iep.utm.edu/gettier/.

47 Daniel Bell, *The Coming of Post-industrial Society* (Basic Books, 1976), 175.

48 Yochai Benkler, *The Wealth of Networks*, 313 quoted in Amy Kapczynski, "Access to Knowledge: A Conceptual Genealogy," in *Access to Knowledge in the Age of Intellectual Property*, ed. Gaëlle Krikorian and Amy Kapczynski (Zone Books, 2010), 45.

49 Kapczynski, "Access to Knowledge," 20.

50 Ibid., 45. See also Ahmed Abdel Latif, "The Emergence of the A2K Movement: Reminiscences and Reflections of a Developing-Country Delegate," in Krikorian and Kapczynski, *Access to Knowledge*, 110–112; Yochai Benkler, "The Idea of Access to Knowledge and the Information Commons: Long-Term Trends and Basic Elements," in Krikorian and Kapczynski, *Access to knowledge*, 217.

51 Kapczynski, "Access to Knowledge," 17, 20.

52 Story, Darch and Halbert, *Copy/South Dossier*; Eve Gray and Mark Burke "African Universities in the Knowledge Economy: A Collaborative Approach to Researching and Promoting Open Communications in Higher Education," *Proceedings ELPUB 2008 Conference on Electronic Publishing – Toronto, Canada – June 2008*, 255; Leslie Chan and Sely

Costa, "Participation in the Global Knowledge Commons: Challenges and Opportunities for Research Dissemination in Developing Countries," *New Library World* 106, no. 1210/1211 (2005): 141–163; E. Ondari-Okemwa and M.K. Minishi-Majanja, "Knowledge Management Education in the Departments of Library / Information Science in South Africa," *South African Journal of Libraries and Information Science* 73, no. 2 (2007): 136–146.

53 Binaya Subedi, "Decolonizing the Curriculum for Global Perspectives," *Educational Theory* 63, no. 6 (2013): 621–638; Suellen Shay, "Advice to the Minister: Decolonize the Curriculum" (2015) www.academia.edu/12764118/Advice_to_the_Minister_Decolonize_the_Curriculum; Sid N. Pandey and Fazlur R. Moorad, "The Decolonization of Curriculum in Botswana," in *International Handbook of Curriculum Research*, ed. William F. Pinar (Routledge, 2003), 143.

54 Gray and Burke, "African Universities in the Knowledge Economy," discuss four recent projects in Southern Africa that had this goal.

55 Peter Johan Lor and Johannes Britz, "To Access Is Not to Know: A Critical Reflection on A2K and the Role of Libraries with Special Reference to Sub-Saharan Africa," *Journal of Information Science* 20, no. 10 (2010): 1–13.

56 Frederick Noronha and Jeremy Malcolm (eds), *Access to Knowledge: A Guide for Everyone* (Consumers International, 2010), 3 describes it as "a network of social movements" and Gaëlle Krikorian, "Access to Knowledge as a Field of Activism," in Krikorian and Kapczynski, *Access to Knowledge*, 70 describes it as "a movement of movements."

57 Noronha and Malcolm, *Access to Knowledge*, 5.

58 For example Latif, "The Emergence of the A2K Movement," 99.

59 Kapczynski, "Access to Knowledge," 17.

60 Latif, "The Emergence of the A2K Movement," 105–112.

61 Ibid.

62 Noronha and Malcolm, *Access to Knowledge*, 2.

63 For overviews and discussions see Ellen 't Hoen "The Revised Drug Strategy: Access to Essential Medicines, Intellectual Property, and the World Health Organization," in Krikorian and Kapczynski, *Access to Knowledge*, 127; Sangeeta Shashikant "The Doha Declaration on TRIPS and Public Health: An Impetus for Access to Medicines," in Krikorian and Kapczynski, *Access to Knowledge*, 141; Spring Gombe and James Love, "New Medicines and Vaccines: Access, Incentives to Investment, and Freedom to Innovate," in Krikorian and Kapczynski, *Access to Knowledge*, 531.

64 Fix the Patent Laws, "Timeline of Intellectual Property Reform in South Africa 1994–2015," October 29, 2015, www.fixthepatentlaws.org/?p=1037 (accessed March 3, 2016).

65 For a project overview see http://ip-unit.org/askjustice/.

66 Krikorian, "Access to Knowledge as a Field of Activism," 74; J. Carlos Fernández-Molina and J. Augusto Chaves Guimarães, "The WIPO Development Agenda and the Contribution of the International Library Community," *The Electronic Library* 27, no. 6 (2009): 1010–1025, http://dx.doi.org/10.1108/02640470911004093.

67 For a discussion of the movement's activist character see Krikorian "Access to Knowledge as a Field of Activism," 57.

68 Abbe E.L. Brown, "Access to Essential Technologies: The Role of the Interface between Intellectual Property,

Competition and Human Rights," *International Review of Law, Computers and Technology* 24, no. 1 (2010): 51–61. doi:10.1080/13600860903570178.

69 For example see the Global Network on Copyright User Rights' Masterlist: Excerpts of Representative Copyright Limitations and Exceptions (2012) and Model Flexible Copyright Exception, available at http://infojustice.org/flexible-use.

70 Krikorian, "Access to Knowledge as a Field of Activism," 65, 78.

71 Ibid., 79. For example see James Boyle, "The Second Enclosure Movement and the Construction of the Public Domain," *Law and Contemporary Problems* 66 (2003): 33.

73 For example see Shaver, "The Right to Science and Culture," 121–184.

73 Lea Shaver (ed.), *Access to Knowledge in Brazil: New Research on Intellectual Property, Innovation and Development* (Information Society Project, 2008).

74 Ramesh Subramanian and Lea Shaver (eds), *Access to Knowledge in India: New Research on Intellectual Property, Innovation and Development* (Bloomsbury Academic, 2011).

75 Nagla Rizk and Lea Shaver (eds), *Access to Knowledge in Egypt: New Research on Intellectual Property, Innovation and Development* (Bloomsbury Academic, 2010).

76 A. Rens and R. Khan (eds), *Access to Knowledge in South Africa* (Information Society Project, 2009).

77 C. Armstrong, J. De Beer, D. Kawooya, A. Prabhala, T. Schonwetter (eds), *Access to Knowledge in Africa: The Role of Copyright* (UCT Press, 2010).

78 For example see Sara Bannerman, *International Copyright and Access to Knowledge* (Cambridge University Press, 2016).

79 Krikorian, "Access to Knowledge as a Field of Activism," 72.

80 Story, Darch and Halbert, *The Copy/South Dossier*, 162.

81 www.bookdash.org.

82 www.africanstorybookproject.org.

83 For this organization's activities and agenda see www.equaleducation.org.za/.

84 See, for example, *Federation of Governing Bodies for South African Schools (FEDSAS) vs. Member of the Executive Council for Education, Gauteng and Another* (CCT 209/15) [2016] ZACC 14 (May 20, 2016) (public schools admissions policy in Gauteng province); *MEC for Education in Gauteng Province and Other vs. Governing Body of Rivonia Primary School and Others* (CCT 135/12) [2013] ZACC 34 (public schools admissions policy and implementation); *Head of Department, Department of Education, Free State Province vs. Welkom High School and Another; Head of Department, Department of Education, Free State Province vs. Harmony High School and Another* (CCT 103/12) [2013] ZACC 25 (suspension of pregnant learners); *Radebe and Others vs. Principal of Leseding Technical School and Others* (1821/2013) [2013] ZAFSHC 111 (May 30, 2013) (suspension of Rastafarian learner); *Equal Education and Others vs. Minister of Basic Education and Others* case number 81/2012 Eastern Cape High Court, Bhisho (public school infrastructure).

85 *Minister of Basic Education vs. Basic Education for All* (20793/2014) [2015] ZASCA 198 (December 2, 2015).

86 Paragraph 45.

87 For commentary on their activism see Guimarães, "The WIPO Development Agenda"; Lor and Britz, "To Access Is Not to Know"; Guy Pessach, "The Role of Libraries in A2K: Taking Stock and Looking Ahead," *Mich. St. L. Rev.* no. 1 (2007): 257.

88 Susan Isiko Štrba, *International Copyright Law and Access to Education in Developing Countries: Exploring Multilateral Legal and Quasi-Legal Solutions* (Brill, 2012); Ruth L. Okediji, "Sustainable Access to Copyright Digital Information Works in Developing Countries," in *International Public Goods and Transfer of Technology under a Globalized Intellectual Property Regime*, ed. Keith E. Maskus and Jerome H. Reichman (Cambridge University Press, 2008), 143–187.

89 Copyright Regulations, 1978, as published in GN R1211 in GG 9775 of June 7, 1985 as amended by GN 1375 in GG 9807 of June 28, 1985.

90 T. Schonwetter, C. Ncube and P. Chetty "South Africa," in Armstrong et al. *Access to Knowledge in Africa*, 240.

91 For example the A2K country studies of Brazil, India, Egypt, South Africa and several other African countries referred to earlier in this chapter.

92 Lea Shaver, "Local Language Limitations: Copyright and the Commons" (2014) unpublished paper on file with the author.

93 For example see Dev S. Gangjee, "Copyright Formalities: A Return to Registration?" in Giblin and Weatherall, *What If We Could Reimagine Copyright?*, 213–252; Christopher Sprigman, "Reform(aliz)ing Copyright," *Stanford Law Reform* 57 (2004): 485.

94 Rebecca Giblin, "Rethinking Duration: Disaggregating Copyright's Rewards and Incentives," in Giblin and Weatherall, *What If We Could Reimagine Copyright?*, 177–212; Rufus Pollock, "Forever Minus a Day? Calculating Optimal Copyright Term," *Review of Economic Research on Copyright Issues* 6, no. 1 (2009): 35; William M. Landes and Richard A. Posner, "Indefinitely Renewable Copyright," *University of Chicago Law Review* 70 (2003): 499–500.

95 Caroline B. Ncube "Calibrating Copyright for Creators and Consumers:

Promoting Distributive Justice and Ubuntu," in Giblin and Weatherall, *What If We Could Reimagine Copyright?*, 253–280; Martin Skladany, "Unchaining Richelieu's Monster: A Tiered Revenue-Based Copyright Regime," *Stanford Technology Law Review* 16, no. 1 (2012): 131–159.

96 Alan Story, "Burn Berne: Why the Leading International Copyright Convention Must Be Repealed," *Houston Law Review* 40, no. 3 (2003): 763.

97 For example see Giblin and Weatherall, *What If We Could Reimagine Copyright?*; William F. Patry, *How to Fix Copyright* (Oxford University Press, 2011); Jessica Litman, *Digital Copyright* (Prometheus Books, 1998).

98 Lydia Pallas Loren, "The Pope's Copyright? Aligning Incentives with Reality by Using Creative Motivation to Shape Copyright Protection," *Louisiana Law Review* 69 (2008): 15.

99 John Tehranian, "Infringement Nation: Copyright Reform and the Law/Norm Gap," *Utah Law Review* (2007): 537.

100 Joe Karaganis and Lennart Renkema, "Copy Culture in the US and Germany" (2013), http://piracy.americanassembly.org/wp-content/uploads/2013/01/Copy-Culture.pdf.

101 Loren, "The Pope's Copyright?" 34.

102 John Tehranian, "The Emperor Has No Copyright: Registration, Cultural Hierarchy, and the Myth of American Copyright Militancy," *Berkeley Technology Law Journal* 24, no. 4 (2009): 1399.

103 At ibid., 1409 Tehranian notes that "the United States is the only major country in the world with a timely registration prerequisite for the recovery of certain forms of damages and attorneys' fees. In other countries, full legal vindication of one's exclusive rights does not require the added

procedure of registration, let alone timely registration."

104 17 U.S.C. § 412: "[N]o award of statutory damages or of attorney's fees . . . shall be made for . . . any infringement of copyright commenced after first publication of the work and before the effective date of its registration, unless such registration is made within three months after the first publication of the work."

105 Tehranian, "The Emperor Has No Copyright," 1407.

106 17 USC §§ 110(6)–(8).

107 Martin Skladany, "Unchaining Richelieu's Monster," 141.

108 Article 5(2) provides: "The enjoyment and the exercise of these rights shall not be subject to any formality; such enjoyment and such exercise shall be independent of the existence of protection in the country of origin of the work. Consequently, apart from the provisions of this Convention, the extent of protection, as well as the means of redress afforded to the author to protect his rights, shall be governed exclusively by the laws of the country where protection is claimed."

109 WIPO SCCR Survey of National Legislation on Voluntary Registration Systems for Copyright and Related Rights (2005) (SCCR/13/2) 3.

110 Mihaly Ficsor, *Guide to Copyright and Related Rights Treaties Administered by WIPO, Geneva*, WIPO Publication no. 891 (E), 2003, 41.

111 Patry, *How to Fix Copyright*, 189–201.

112 Pamela Samuelson, "Book Review: Is Copyright Reform Possible?" *Harvard Law Review* 126 (2013): 747.

113 Alan Story, "'Balanced' Copyright: Not a Magic Solving Word," *Intellectual Property Watch*, February 27, 2012, www.ip-watch.org/2012/02/27/%E2%80%98balanced%E2%80%99-copyright-not-a-magic-solving-word/.

8 | MEET THE NEW BOSS, SAME AS THE OLD BOSS

Copyright and continuity in the contemporary music economy[1]

Jim Rogers

Introduction

Stories of the decline or even demise of the music business at the hands of online peer-to-peer file-sharing networks have been regularly relayed via news media since the advent of sites such as MP3.com and Napster in the latter half of the 1990s. The proliferation of "free" online music, plummeting record sales revenues and routine closures of physical record stores are commonly combined in journalistic and academic accounts alike to paint a picture of a digital media Armageddon.

However, such a reductionist view of developments in the music industry is far too simplistic. While digital technologies have visited various transformations upon the spheres of music production, distribution and consumption over recent years, the fundamental power structures underpinning the music industry itself remain largely unaltered. In fact, as the chapter below will illustrate, it is the continuities at the core of how the music industry performs and functions that ultimately tell the more crucial story of its unfolding in the digital era. Recent and new internet and mobile technologies may carry the "potential" to radically disrupt the interests and roles of established players in the music business, but the industry has mutated and reconfigured to sustain itself.

The music industry has been the first of the established creative or cultural industries to deal with digitalization, and in particular the challenges arising from the evolution of the internet as a medium for distribution and promotion of content. In this respect, the music industry is very much the "cultural" canary down the "digital" mine. Understanding this canary's journey and outcome to date impels us to recognize music as an industry that evolves around the utilization of property rights. Music colonizes the breadth and depth of our environment. Increasingly, it is through the ownership and exploitation of copyrights and trademarks across a widening range of spaces and places in our physical and virtual worlds that music is commodified and wealth is generated.

The music industry has traditionally been characterized by highly concentrated ownership and this continues to be the case despite the promises and potential of the internet for disintermediation. By recognizing the music industry as an interconnected set of sub-sectors that extends beyond the record industry to encompass a range of other revenue-generating possibilities for its major players, we can see how the utilization of music and recording copyrights not only bolsters the industry in a period of technological change, but also enables it to grow despite the advent of a rare and deep financial crisis across the globe.

So, as the above indicates, this chapter challenges orthodox accounts of the evolution of the music industry in recent decades. Far from conceding that internet "piracy" is "killing" the music industry, it points to the major music copyright owners using copyright law to wrestle an increasing level of control over (and revenue from) cyberspace. Moreover, this article illustrates how major music companies and artists are increasingly shifting the emphasis onto the licensing potential of the recording and music publishing copyrights across both new and traditional media formats as a means of negating the potentially harmful effects of online copyright infringement. Furthermore, it points to how trademarks are also increasingly used to bolster the revenues of major actors in the music sector in a context where music brands are becoming increasingly pervasive. Overall, in an era where the internet is widely assumed (both celebrated and bemoaned) for producing the death of copyright, the empirical studies drawn upon here demonstrate how it actually has become increasingly central to reinforcing the music industry's long-established oligopolistic power structures.

The remainder of the chapter below initially summarizes, and offers a theoretical context to conventional wisdom around the music industry and its relationship with the internet. It then proceeds to examine and discuss two of the core strategies adopted by the major music industry in their response to the evolving technological environment. First, the recourse of the major music copyright holders to the courts in an ongoing attempt to curb illicit file-sharing and extend and expand the reach of "realspace" copyright control mechanisms into cyberspace. Second, to maximize the revenue-generating potential of music copyrights across the broadest spectrum of platforms and spaces possible.

This chapter draws significantly upon earlier empirical studies conducted by the current author – initially in the form of doctoral research carried out between 2007 and 2010, and a subsequent postdoctoral project across 2013–2014. These studies each examined particular processes of change and continuity in the music industry across the digital era. The modus operandi employed in executing those projects comprised a literature review of all relevant fields of inquiry, desk research and, more significantly, the critical perspectives arising from an extensive series of in-depth ethnographic interviews conducted with a range of music industry personnel and informants at different points across those time periods. In total, more than 60 individuals were interviewed spanning the spheres of recording, music publishing, music management services, live music promotion, record production, manufacturing, music retailing and music journalism, as well as a number of musicians and recording artists. The results of this research, parts of which are summarized for the purpose of this current chapter, have earlier been published in a series of academic journal articles and a book.[2] While only highly select quotes or accounts from specific interviews are detailed in this chapter (given word-count limitations), the perspectives arrived at courtesy of analyzing and critiquing these recorded interviews and discussions informs everything that follows below.

Digitalization, crisis and the "death of copyright"?

Since the dawn of the new millennium, music industry discourse has been dominated by crisis rhetoric. A plethora of journalistic and media commentaries, industry reports and academic accounts has evolved over the years to convey a picture of fundamental crisis being visited upon this particular cultural industry sector resulting from the transition to a digital milieu. In particular, the evolution and large-scale diffusion of peer-to-peer file-sharing technologies is widely blamed for inducing a significant downturn in revenues for the established music industry companies and actors and radically disrupting their relationship with their final consumers. Headlines and commentary detailing the decline and in some cases demise of the music industry as a result of digital "piracy" have been commonly and widely circulated by national and international news publications since the late 1990s.[3] By late 2009, at the end of what *The Economist* described as a "brutal decade" where "music was the first media business to be seriously affected by piracy and has suffered most severely,"[4] the music industry had become "the poster child of failed digital opportunities."[5]

Moreover, when asked to consider the most significant changes that have occurred in the music industry in the twenty-first century, the initial responses from almost all interviewees who participated in the empirical-level studies drawn upon in this chapter relate to what they perceive as severe consequences for the music industry emanating from the widespread diffusion of internet technologies. For example, for one independent record label owner:

> People aren't paying for music anymore. That's the problem.
> I think the majors have collapsed and it is over for them.
> (Personal interview)

For other music industry executives, access to illicit file-sharing technologies has generated irrational behaviors of consumption among fans that ultimately serve to devalue music. For example:

> It is very hard to quantify the effects of file-sharing in a dollars and cents way, but what Napster did was effectively make all of the world's music available to all of the world for free. All of a sudden, everybody could be a music consumer without paying for it. So people went on an acquisition binge, literally downloading everything they could, even if they would end up never listening to it. Virtually overnight we saw music being depreciated in ways that had never occurred before because the basic market mechanism that was in place to make sure that the industry could invest and artists could get paid suddenly shifted. (Record industry trade body executive, personal interview)

Another major label marketing executive puts it thusly:

> If people are taking music for free, where does the money come
> from? Who will pay the artist? And where is the money going to
> come from for us to re-invest? When you consider the amount
> of money, in a global sense, that we need to spend on A&R,
> marketing and promoting our acts, but piracy means that at the
> end of that process, somebody just takes the music for free. That
> doesn't make any economic sense. In any industry that wouldn't
> make sense.

Others take a more fatalistic approach, not just to the viability of
music as an industry, but towards its very survival as a cultural form.
One music publisher advances:

> This is *the* problem. The culture has seeped in whereby people
> are beginning to think that music is *free*. If you take that to its
> logical conclusion, well when the music runs out there'll be no
> more music. (Personal interview)

Evidence purporting to support such dystopian perspectives is presented in yearly International Federation of Phonographic Industries
(IFPI) reports that show how the global recorded music market has
diminished since the late 1990s. For the IFPI, digital "piracy" continues to radically undermine investment in artists as the record industry
suffers the consequences of severe revenue losses in an environment
where "20 per cent of internet users worldwide regularly access unlicensed services."[6] Moreover, the Recording Industry Association of
America (RIAA) point to the US economy losing $12.5bn in total
output annually as a result of online music piracy, with some 71,000
related job losses.[7] In this context, commentators such as Scholes
argue that the illicit sharing of music online has generated a "ripple
effect" across related sectors with the broader entertainment industries losing approximately $80bn in the United States alone.[8]

While the CD boom years across the final decade-and-a-half of
the twentieth century saw music labels enjoy record revenues, the
trade value of global record industry revenues subsequently fell by
approximately 43 percent from $26.6bn in 1999 to $15.0bn by 2015.[9]
Within this, the value of the digital music market demonstrated year-
on-year growth across more than a decade to reach approximately

$7bn by 2015,[10] but, on the surface, this falls far short of off-setting the losses from an apparently impoverished physical sector.

Equally, for Kelly, running concurrently with what he perceives as the decline of the major music company is the enhanced freedom of the individual music artist.[11] Empowered by new digital technologies, those "musicians with the highest status are those who have a 24-hour net channel devoted to streaming their music."[12] Other prior accounts also celebrate the liberative possibilities arising from digital technological innovations, and point to a future where not only music production, but also distribution, promotion and consumption evolve along much more "democratic" lines, where artist and audience would no longer depend on the intervention of major media corporations in mediating their relationship with each other. Nicholas Negroponte, a professor at MIT (and celebrated *guru* of the information age) argued that: "Copyright law . . . is a Gutenberg artefact"[13] and thus rendered redundant in the internet age where it will "disintegrate," with everything capable of being digitized being potentially "up for grabs."[14] Moreover, digitalization will serve to "flatten organisations . . . decentralise control" and effectively level the mass media playing field.[15]

Indeed for Kelly, the form and extent of the changes induced across society from digital innovations would ultimately oversee the demise of the "old" economic laws that have characterized the modern capitalist era.[16]

In the music industry, control over the channels of distribution is crucial, and they have long since been monopolized by a small handful of very powerful major players who grew to dominate the global industry.[17] For example, at present, just three major multinational companies dominate the record industry – Universal, Warner and Sony.

Authors such as Théberge and Bakker have outlined how innovations in the digital realm emerged to threaten the power and control of those major music companies and visit radical disruption on the established music industry order.[18] Many authors have addressed the potential of developments in the digital domain to enable artists to pursue a "do-it-yourself" approach to the production, promotion and distribution of their music. While acknowledging that the digital distribution of music held the potential to serve the interests of the major companies, Burnett also makes the point that it "could open a Pandora's box that could ultimately destroy their own control of popular music."[19] By the turn of the millennium, much commentary and analysis pointed to the advent of the internet inducing a process of disintermediation – removing the corporate "middlemen" from the music industry chain. Costs associated with distribution and retailing would be eliminated. Rather, the rapid and widespread diffusion of the internet would mean that the music market would be exposed to the broadest and most diverse range of artists and recordings. These, in turn, could be accessed by anyone and everyone connected to the World Wide Web at the click of a mouse button.

Indeed, all of the above serves to reflect the prevalence of technological determinist thinking in society and resonates with the earlier (highly influential, if hyperbolic) claims of such theorists as McLuhan and Toffler.[20] Such digital futures were celebrated and mourned in equal measure in numerous techno-centric accounts.

However, while the transformative potential of apparently new and emerging technologies is frequently touted by many, others argue that it is impossible to separate technology from the social environment within which it emerges, and that the reification of the technological is flawed.[21] While Williams stresses the role of "real decision-making groups" such as political and economic elites in shaping the outcome of technological innovation,[22] Winston's detailed studies illuminate the complex set of social needs, political expedience and economic forces that are behind the creation and dissemination of new media technologies.[23] At the core of Winston's approach lies what he terms "the law of the suppression of radical potential."[24] This refers to the pressure and actions of established societal institutions to combat the disruptive potential of technology on existing social formations and power structures, with "the great corporation as the primary institution of our society."[25] This is highly pertinent to examining processes of change and continuity in the music industry.

Like other radical technological innovations in the mass media sphere, the internet (and related developments) carries with it the *potential* to fundamentally transform industrial structures and the "rules of the economic game," especially between different players within the cultural and media industries. This includes the *potential* to disrupt the power or role of media firms and their established industrial practices and interests, not least in the case of the music industry.[26] However, the widespread adoption and appropriation of radical technological innovations must also be accompanied and facilitated by a diverse set of "matching" innovations. The precise outcome of any radical technological innovation is always the product of conflicts and struggles between different interest groups in domains that are often far removed from any predominantly "technological" logic or trajectory. In the contemporary "knowledge economy" (of which music features as a key element), this means that we must pay special attention to one particular area of conflict and struggle over "matching" policy innovation – that related to the intellectual property rights regime, and more specifically for the case at hand, copyright. Thus, to borrow and bend Winston's phrasing, copyright forms one of the key suppressants of the radical potential associated with the internet and other digital technologies in the context of the music industries.

Copyright and the courts: enclosing musical cyberspace

The strategy of the record industry regarding using the courts as a mechanism through which to address the unauthorized use of their copyrights has been three-pronged, with waves of lawsuits being issued against the producers and suppliers of file-sharing technologies, individual music fans and internet service providers (ISPs).

In the latter half of the 1990s, the popularity of the mp3 format led to the start-up of a variety of websites that held fast to the proposition that online music possessed the potential to diminish the power of the conglomerates that controlled the record industry by offering alternative forms of music distribution. The most notable of these early sites were MP3.com and Napster. In the case of the Napster software program, it had as its basis a decentralized, distributed model that enabled individual users to access audio files located on the computers of other users. The case of Napster needs to be reviewed:

> as a clash between radically different value systems – between a particular notion of what constitutes a legitimate form of social interaction between fans, on one hand, and the commercial needs of the industry on the other.[27]

However, as Gillespie notes, faced with such threats, "those in power turn to the stability and authority of existing law; using the law they tame the new technology into submission."[28] The rise and subsequent fall of "illicit" sites such as MP3.com, Napster and a range of subsequent platforms that followed in their wake – most notably Grokster, Kazaa, Limewire and others – demonstrate how the Recorded Industry Association of America (RIAA) and other national phonographic industry trade bodies around the world have used copyright law as the club with which to beat the suppliers of file-sharing technologies since the late 1990s. For evidence of this we can visit the "news" page on the IFPI's website, the contents of which, the major labels argue, highlight the scale of the problem facing the music industry. This site publishes a litany of accounts outlining the pursuit of such sites through the courts in different countries around the world.

Here, it is also worth questioning the precise motivations of the established recording sector in pursuing such legal cases. McCourt and Burkart illustrate how the Record Industry Association of American (RIAA) used their lawsuit against Napster at the turn of the century as "a legal and public relations foil," primarily designed to deflect attention away from "lawsuits against the Big Five (record labels) for price fixing by US federal and state agencies," while "legally securing a claim to the Internet as an alternative delivery system to retail outlets."[29]

In many cases, a familiar trend has evolved whereby the record industry first issues legal proceedings against the infringing website or platform; the site subsequently agrees a settlement with the record industry; there follows a licensing agreement between both parties which has the effect of making the infringing site a legitimate operator with the potential to generate revenue for the record industry; and, in some cases, key stakeholders in the record industry subsequently a stake in the once-illicit service.

The record industry's representative trade bodies in various countries around the globe have also used copyright infringement as the basis to pursue tens of thousands of individual network users through the courts in their efforts to curb illicit file-sharing. In an initial sweep between 2003 and 2005, the RIAA issued some 9,000 lawsuits against individuals across the United States for unauthorized file-sharing offences.[30] Sterk states that this figure subsequently rose to more than 35,000 individual infringement lawsuits.[31] Again, copious amounts of space on the IFPI website's news pages have been devoted to detailing such cases. While on one hand, such accounts reinforce the message that the problems posed by digitalization to copyright owners are many and widespread, they equally celebrate a significant level of success for the same copyright owners against "infringers" in the courts. Thus, they advance another reality – the continued, successful and sometimes lucrative pursuit of individual "pirates" by the record industry's various national trade bodies across the world.

Here, it is worth noting that the fines meted out to individuals by courts for copyright offences have increased in severity over the years. For example, one such case that generated widespread media coverage in 2009 related to Minnesota woman Jammie Thomas-Rasset. At her initial trial she was directed to pay the RIAA total compensation amounting to $1.92m in reparation for sharing 24 songs on the Kazaa file-sharing network. In instigating proceedings against Ms. Thomas-Rasset, the RIAA had placed a value of $150,000 in lost revenues on each of these individual music files and thus sought an overall penalty of $3.6m. However, the court determined an award of $80,000 per track as a more appropriate estimation of the losses incurred by the respective record labels. In a subsequent series of retrials and appeals, this amount was reduced to $54,000, then increased to $1.5 million before subsequently being reduced again to $54,000. At the time of writing, another appeal by the music companies against the last reduction is ongoing. As Lessig has earlier argued, all of this illustrates how the penalty for sharing music in cyberspace is excessively punitive compared to penalties issued for traditional forms of theft in the "physical" world.[32]

The music industry has also turned its attention to the pursuit of ISPs. In recent years, the websites of various national record industry trade bodies around the world, as well as the IFPI, indicate ongoing developments in a host of countries between ISPs, governments and the record industry aimed at addressing copyright violations and making provisions for terminating the accounts of network users who are found to be repeat infringers. As these stories indicate, cooperation from ISPs is what the industry has been actively pursuing and in many cases achieving in recent years.

While in some cases, ISPs such as Sky in the UK forged partnerships with the major labels at a relatively early stage in order to provide additional platforms for the sale and licensing of recorded music, in other instances the record industry has also been successful in obtaining legal judgements that hold ISPs responsible for activities that result in copyright infringement on their networks. Developments in many territories have seen ISPs become increasingly involved in acting in the interests of major music copyright holders. For example, the publication of the Gowers Report (2006) in the UK recommended that appropriate legislation be drafted by the then UK government in order to encourage the cooperation of ISPs regarding the protection of creative industry copyrights in cyberspace.[33] This ultimately led to the drafting of the Digital Economy Act that was enacted in 2010. Under this act, "graduated response" actions are provided for, which require the ISP to impose a series of increasingly punitive sanctions against users that persist in the sharing of music files on their respective networks.

In France, November 2007 saw French ISPs and copyright owners enter an agreement forged by the French government that approved the adoption and implementation of a "three strikes and you're out" approach to combating the online sharing of copyrighted music files. Network users would, in effect, receive a warning from the ISP for each instance of detected infringement. Three violations would see individuals risk losing their internet access. Related legislation came in 2009 in the form of the HADOPI law.

A recent cursory examination of the IFPI website indicates that many such developments, aimed at enhancing the cooperation of ISPs in the protection of music copyrights, are ongoing in many other countries including Ireland, Belgium, France, Japan, the Netherlands, New Zealand, Denmark, Spain and more.

Here, it is also worth remembering that intellectual property is enshrined in the Charter of Fundamental Rights of the European Union.

Exploiting music IPRs in the digital age

Understanding how music operates as a copyright industry also demands that we must consider how music possesses key characteristics and features that distinguish it from other forms of content.

As previous authors have indicated, music has become ubiquitous, and its ubiquity makes music distinct as a media and cultural form.[34] Music is everywhere. It colonizes our private worlds and public environments. It possesses the ability to access places and spaces that other forms of media cannot reach. We find music not only on our personal portable media player, our laptop, our home stereo system and our car, we also find it in our workplace, shopping malls, restaurants, hair salons and filling stations. In fact, music meets and greets us in almost every conceivable space we inhabit. Moreover, aside from existing as a stand-alone media form, music also forms a core constituent element of almost all other forms of audio-visual media, both traditional and new. We find it on radio, television, films, advertising, digital games and a plethora of mobile and online platforms (such as social networks, streaming services, etc.). As such, music's value as a commodity to be licensed to such an array of spaces and sites offers the owners of the most popular and well-established music copyrights immense potential for revenue generation.

As the market for recorded music sales has declined since 1999, the major labels have intensified their focus on, among other things, licensing platforms. Here it must be emphasized that every space or site that music can access acts not only as a site of promotion for the recording itself, but also as a potential (or more likely probable) site of revenue generation for the recording and publishing copyright owner(s).

In cyberspace, ad-supported streaming services, subscription-based sites and social networks offer a wealth of online platforms (Spotify, Deezer and We7 offer some of the most notable examples here, with video streaming outlets such as YouTube and Vevo becoming more and more significant in terms of both promotion and revenue). Since the mid-noughties, the global market for digital music has climbed year-on-year to a (trade) value of $6.7bn by 2015, representing approximately 45 percent of overall global recording revenues.[35] While this represented an increase of more than 10 percent on the previous year, the contribution of streaming within this revenue sector rose by more than 45 percent across 2014–2015.

And offline too, the spaces for music to occupy have burgeoned with the revenues from licensing music to film, TV and radio becoming more important to the music industry's economic wellbeing. Not just in terms of the promotional value they bring to music and artists, but in terms of the direct revenues generated through licensing across these platforms. With the rapid deregulation and privatization of the broadcasting sector that occurred across Europe since the early 1990s, radio and television outlets have proliferated, and in turn driven a vast increase in music licensing revenues from these sectors. Likewise, digital games and advertising have offered other useful avenues for the exploitation of music catalogues. In short, synchronization has evolved as a major aspect of the music business. As one artist manager advances:

> Syncs are now a huge part of the business, huge. They can provide that real adrenaline shot . . . It's the one thing that managers, record companies, publishers are desperate for. (Personal interview)

A music industry lawyer puts it more crudely:

> Synchronization is a much more valuable tool in terms of getting a serious wedge of cash . . . If you get placed on an advert or in a TV programme, that can be it. (Personal interview)

Another interviewee elaborates on this point:

> It's become so much more sophisticated in recent years . . . Music to sell a film. Music to sell television. Advertising. Music to sell a brand. You have advertisers migrating to link with bands and music brands more and more . . . Music revenues are more and more generated by the application of music in other things. It's music as a secondary factor. Music used as an emotional hook to attach you to other brands. (Personal interview)

That major music copyright owners have increased their focus on licensing their copyrights to advertising is evidenced through the growing range of major label-controlled repertoire used in commercials in recent years.[36] Moreover, songs by folk and rock artists that even in relatively recent history would not have been conceived in such a context, now find themselves used in national or global advertising campaigns for a range of products and services. For many, his "Car Song," which was recently to be found promoting the Audi Q5 in a TV commercial in recent years, is their main, if not only experience of Woody Guthrie. He might have once sung about the plight of migrant laborers and social inequalities, but now Woody Guthrie sells cars. Guthrie's arrival in the world of automobile advertising mirrors excursions into similar terrain by a few other notable troubadours. The music of Bob Dylan now sells lingerie (Victoria's Secret). The songs of Lennon and McCartney sell hardware and electronic products (Target) and banking services (The Halifax). Perhaps with the Beatles repertoire we should be less surprised, as such a context is less new. It is now approximately a quarter of a century since "Revolution" (penned by Lennon as a critique of the various political protests that occurred across Europe in 1968) was adopted by Nike.

However, when we consider the range of artists and music that is used in advertising campaigns, and how aggressively they are promoted to advertising executives by the major labels, this trend effectively goes against time honored standards for authenticity in folk and rock music culture.

And as Guthrie and Lennon both prove, being dead is no barrier to a musician carving a new career as an ad man. Copyright takes care of that. While recording copyright has a duration of 70 years, music publishing copyright lasts for 70 years beyond the death of the songwriter. Here, we must remember that the principal owners and exploiters of music copyrights are not necessarily the creative artists themselves, but rather cultural industry intermediaries who can exercise control over, and exploit these rights for decades.

The exploitation of music copyrights in such contexts is proving highly lucrative. When we take the above factors into account and place them alongside the thriving live music industry, the overall economic health of the music sector is in a very good state indeed, and quite far from the picture of radical decline painted by viewing record sales data in isolation. And there is indeed significant data and research to support such an argument. For example, the International Confederation of Authors and Composers Societies (CISAC) point to global royalty revenues (which include performing rights, mechanical rights and other) demonstrating strong and consistent growth, reaching an overall value of $7.9bn by 2014, with music repertoire accounting for close to 90 percent of this total.[37] Moreover, the Performing Rights Society indicated that overall music industry revenues have been steadily increasing in the UK throughout the twenty-first century, despite the downturn in the recording sector. They point to an annual growth rate of 4.7 percent across the industry with total combined revenues from recording, publishing and live streams rising from £3.2bn in 2007 to £3.6bn in 2008.[38]

Here, it is worth noting that historically, the music publishing sector in particular has proven itself to be recession resilient. While, as Harker notes, Britain experienced a lengthy period of economic stagnation throughout the 1970s and 1980s, the music publishing sector thrived in this environment.[39] The final years of the 1970s saw revenues generated through performing rights treble in value and continued to grow throughout the 1980s.

Beyond copyright, music trademarks also offer themselves as potentially lucrative sources of income for their owners. Trademark can plug many of the gaps left open by copyright. As such, band names, song titles, album titles can all be trademarked and exploited in their own right. Alderman's account of developments at Elvis Presley Enterprises provides a useful example here. The word's "Elvis Presley" and "Graceland" have been trademarked since the mid-1980s. Many of the titles of Presley's hit songs have also been trademarked. For example, "Heartbreak Hotel" was trademarked for a licensed restaurant chain and subsequently for use on "pants, shorts, shirts, sweatshirts, jackets, hats, and socks . . . shot glasses, martini glasses, goblets and tumblers."[40] Equally, "All Shook Up," "Love Me Tender," "Don't Be Cruel," "Hound Dog" and "Jailhouse Rock" are used to brand a range of products encompassing key chains, spoons, bumper stickers, pens, golf balls, snow globes and cigarette lighters. As Alderman bemoans, "alas, *Blue Suede Shoes* may eventually be used to brand everything except navy leather footwear."[41]

Perhaps the best example of trademark revenues in operation for the major music industry relates to Lyric Culture, a company founded in 2006 that produces clothes and jewelry lines "branded" with song titles. The company has secured licensing rights from the publishing arms of all of the major labels to reproduce the titles of 92 different songs on items including jackets, T-shirts, jeans, scarves, rings and bracelets.

As an increasingly important site of revenue generation, the music merchandising sector has witnessed an accelerated level of takeovers, mergers and joint ventures in recent years involving established music labels, independent merchandising companies, and players in the e-commerce market.[42]

So, to put the overall global music industry revenue picture in some context: on one hand, some reports show that the global music industry has remained quite stable across the twenty-first century, contracting by just 3 percent between 2000 and 2013.[43] Elsewhere, other commentators (albeit using a different set of evaluation criteria) point to a much more lucrative "digital era" for the music industry with overall global revenues rising from $51.2bn to $71.1bn between 1998 and 2010.[44] This represents an overall growth of 40 percent across those sectors over that 12-year period, and, this positive trend does not seem to have been affected by the economic crisis.

In terms of the three major music labels that dominate the global landscape (Universal, Warner and Sony), while media accounts have consistently painted a picture of crisis, their overall revenue reports indicate stability. Over the 11 years to 2014, full-year revenues for the Universal Music Group fluctuated mildly year-on-year, dropping overall from $4.8bn in 2004 to $4.6bn in 2014.[45] Over the same period, the Warner Music Group saw its overall revenues drop from $3.4bn to just in excess of $3bn,[46] while Sony Music Entertainment saw its overall revenues marginally dip from ¥523bn to ¥520 between 2009 and 2014.[47] Such statistics illustrate how declines in the value of record sales are largely offset by gains made in other areas.

This all serves to illustrate how music has an economic relevance that extends far beyond the scope of record sales and how revenue from licensing agreements (both recording and publishing) that legally facilitate the use of music across such an array of spaces has been fundamental to the music industry's sustenance and indeed its overall growth in recent years. To this end, the major music labels have proved extremely successful at lobbying at both national and international levels for the extension and expansion of copyright control mechanisms both in real space and cyberspace.

Moreover, the above strategies and developments all combine to demonstrate that the figure of the recording artist has undergone a fundamental re-conceptualization in recent years. No longer does the recording artist sell records and perform concerts, nowadays the figure of the music artist represents an all-encompassing bundle of IPRs that can be simultaneously exploited across a range of platforms. As one former major label executive bluntly attests:

> You used to make a fortune out of one or two columns, records being the obvious one, and publishing, whereas now you can make money from everything. Everywhere you look, everywhere you walk, everything you do seems to have music behind it . . . and people are making money from that. (Personal interview)

Often, the music artist is positioned as a universal source of revenue for one central rights holder who controls and administers all rights on behalf of that artist. This is best exemplified through the evolution of 360-degree deals whereby all revenues generated through the exploitation of artist copyrights, trademarks, patents and other are funneled back to the same corporate entity. These 360-degree deals, thus, see artists sign contracts with one company, assigning to them the handling of all facets of the artist's career including recording, publishing, live performance, primary and secondary ticketing for tours, merchandising, endorsements, all aspects of image rights and all other artist-related rights. As one interviewee (the manager of an internationally successful singer-songwriter) explains:

> The labels are obviously very keen to get their share of every aspect of an artist's income, from recording to publishing to merchandising to live to whatever. That's very much one way that they look at the future, one sort of big umbrella organization with everything under the same roof. (Personal interview)

Elsewhere, a London-based music industry lawyer advances that for the majority of artists, "[Y]ou are dealing with Goliath, so I am not sure that you are ever going to have much bargaining power, especially at entry level" (personal interview).

In this context, we should also note the continued polarization that characterizes the distribution of wealth in this sector. As Mulligan illustrates, 77 percent of record industry revenue was accounted for by just 1 percent of recording artists in 2013.[48]

All of these developments also mean that, on one level, power and wealth within individual music sectors (e.g. recording, publishing, live, merchandising) remains concentrated, but equally, as record labels have morphed into fully rounded "music" companies, power across the broader music industries per se has become increasingly concentrated with mergers, take-overs and alliances continuing to characterize its evolution, despite the potential associated with digital innovations for more decentralized control.[49]

Summary

Undoubtedly the music industry has experienced significant change since the advent of the internet as a medium for the mass circulation and distribution of music. The spheres of production, distribution and consumption of music have all evolved through a period of significant technological turmoil. The extent and form of digital platforms for music presents both established and aspiring recording artists with a wealth of possibilities for promoting and administering their music and brands in a manner that would have been inconceivable to earlier generations. For consumers and music fans, the spaces and opportunities through which we can experience music in our lives have increased multi-fold over the past few decades to a point where recorded music colonizes so much of our private and public environments. Additionally, there exists an expanding range of new media technologies invading our lives to facilitate the flow of music to our ears.

In the context of all this, the recording industry has apparently endured a mammoth decline with sales of recordings radically falling throughout the early years of the twenty-first century.

However, despite such changes, it would be wrong to assume that the popular music industry has undergone fundamental structural upheaval in the wake of digitalization. As we have seen, the radical innovations that have occurred in the realm of technology have been countered by a set of matching innovations in other areas, none more prevalent than the realm of intellectual property. The strategies adopted by the major music copyright owners have seen them extend and expand the reach of copyright control mechanisms and grow the revenue-generating potential of the copyrights under their ownership and administration. As such, they have not only negated many of the potentially harmful effects of technological change to their oligopolistic dominance, this period has seen power in the music industry remain as concentrated as ever. The major music labels' ownership of the most lucrative and popular copyrights in terms of both publishing and recording has served as a bulwark against the effects of "limitless substitution" of music files in cyberspace. As such, forces of change have been significantly tempered by forces of continuity.

There is little doubt that revenues from record sales have gone south (and with that, the major labels have experienced significant job cuts), but equally, opportunities for licensing music have proliferated. Music's value as a "licensable" commodity for synchronization use and other is rarely acknowledged in the numerous media accounts that address the music industry's ongoing struggles with file-sharing technologies and other perceived "horrors" of the "internet revolution." Yet, the exploitation of music copyrights and brands across a proliferating range of platforms and the nature of music's "embedding" in other media forms offers the major music industry economic sustainability and continuity.

The more things change, the more things stay the same, or, to quote The Who: "Meet the new boss, same as the old boss."

Notes

1 An earlier version of this chapter appeared under the title "Canary Down the Mine: Music and Copyright at the Digital Coalface" in *Socialism and Democracy* 28, no. 1 (2014).

2 J. Rogers and S. Sparviero, "Understanding Innovation in Communication Industries through Alternative Economic Theories: The Case of the Music Industry," *International Communications Gazette* 73, no. 7 (2011): 610–629; J. Rogers and S. Sparviero, "Same Tune, Different Words: The Creative Destruction of the Music Industry," *Observatorio* (OBS*) 5, no. 4 (2011): 1–30; P. Preston and J. Rogers, "The Three Cs of Key Music Sector Trends Today: Convergence, Concentration and Commodification," in *Global Media Convergence and Cultural Transformation: Emerging Social Patterns and Characteristics*, ed. Dal Yong Jin (IGI Global, 2010), 373–396; P. Preston and J. Rogers, "Social Networks, Legal Innovations and the New Music Industry," *Info* 13, no. 6 (2011): 8–19; P. Preston and J. Rogers, "Crisis, Digitalisation and the Future of the Internet," *Info* 14, no. 6 (2012): 72–83; P. Preston and J.

Rogers, "Convergence, Crisis and the Digital Music Economy," in *Media and Convergence Management*, ed. S. Diehl and M. Karmasin (Springer, 2013); J. Rogers, *The Death and Life of the Music Industry in the Digital Age* (Bloomsbury Academic, 2013).

3 See, for example, Rogers, *The Death and Life of the Music Industry in the Digital Age*, 5–8.

4 "Singing to a Different Tune," *The Economist*, November 12, 2009, www. economist.com/node/14845087.

5 D. Tapscott, "Business Models for Five Industries in Crisis," *The Huffington Post*, July 11, 2011, www.huffingtonpost. com/don-tapscott/business-models-for-five-_b_895240.html.

6 IFPI, *Global Music Report: Music Consumption Exploding Worldwide* (2016a), www.ifpi.org/downloads/ GMR2016.pdf.

7 RIAA, "Who Music Theft Hurts," 2015, http://riaa.com/physicalpiracy. php?content_selector=piracy_details_ online.

8 W. Scholes, "Piracy's Ripple Effect on the Global Economy," *The Diplomatic Courier*, January 14, 2014, www.diplomaticourier.com/news/

sponsored/2011-piracy-s-ripple-effect-on-the-global-economy.

9 IFPI, *Record Industry in Numbers* (International Federation of Phonographic Industries, 2000); IFPI, "The Recording Industry's Ability to Develop the Digital Marketplace Is Undermined by Piracy," 2016, www.ifpi.org/music-piracy.php.

10 IFPI, Global Music Report.

11 K. Kelly, "Towards a Post-Napster Music Industry," *The New York Times* Magazine, March 17, 2002, 19–21.

12 Ibid.

13 N. Negroponte, *Being Digital* (Vintage, 1996), 58.

14 N. Negroponte, "Being Digital: A Book (P)review," *Wired* 3.02 (February 1995), www.wired.com/wired/archive/3.02/negroponte.html?pg=2&topic=.

15 Ibid.

16 K. Kelly, *New Rules for the New Economy: 10 Ways the Network Is Changing Everything* (Fourth Estate, 1999).

17 K. Negus, *Producing Pop: Culture and Conflict in the Music Industry* (Arnold, 1992).

18 P. Théberge, "Plugged In: Technology and Popular Music," in *The Cambridge Companion to Rock and Pop*, ed. S. Frith, W. Straw and J. Street (Cambridge University Press, 2001), 3–25; P. Bakker, "File-sharing: Fight, Ignore or Compete. Paid Download Services vrs. P2P Networks," *Telematics and Infomatics* 22, nos. 1–2 (February–May 2005): 41–55.

19 R. Burnett, *The Global Jukebox: The International Music Industry* (Routledge, 1996), 148.

20 M. McLuhan, *The Gutenberg Galaxy: The Making of Typographic Man* (Mentor, 1962); M. McLuhan, *Understanding Media: The Extensions of Man* (Routledge, 1964); A. Toffler, *Future Shock* (Pan, 1970); A. Toffler, *The Third Wave* (Bantam Books, 1980).

21 M. Lister, J. Dovey, S. Giddings, I, Grant and S. Kelly, *New Media: A Critical Introduction*, 2nd ed. (Routledge, 2008).

22 R. Williams, *Television: Technology and Cultural Form*, ed. Ederyn Williams (1974; Routledge, 2003).

23 B. Winston, *Hardware Software: A Background Guide to the Study of the Mass Media* (Davis-Poynter, 1974); B. Winston, "How Are Media Born and Developed," in *Questioning the Media*, 2nd ed., ed. J. Downing, A. Mohammadi and A. Sreberny-Mohammadi (Sage, 1995), 54–72; B. Winston, *Media, Technology and Society: A History from the Telegraph to the Internet* (Routledge, 1998).

24 Winston, *Media, Technology and Society*.

25 Ibid., 11.

26 P. Preston, *Reshaping Communications* (Sage, 2001); R. Burnett and P.D. Marshall, *Web Theory: An Introduction* (Routledge, 2003).

27 Théberge, "Plugged In," 21.

28 T. Gillespie, *Wired Shut: Copyright and the Shape of Digital Culture* (MIT Press, 2007), 11.

29 T. McCourt and P. Burkart, "When Creators, Corporations and Consumers Collide: Napster and the Development of On-line Music Distribution," *Media, Culture and Society* 25 (2003): 340.

30 P. Resnikoff, "The RIAA: Just How Many Lawsuits and Letters," *Digital Music News*, June 28, 2009, www.digitalmusic news.com/stories/062809riaa.

31 D. Sterk, "P2P File-sharing and the Making Available War," *Northwestern Journal of Technology and Intellectual Property* 9, no. 7 (Spring 2011): 495–512.

32 L. Lessig, *The Future of Ideas* (Vintage, 2001).

33 A. Gowers, *Gowers Review of Intellectual Property* (Her Majesty's Stationery Office, 2006).

34 For example, A. Kassabian, *Hearing Film: Tracking Identification in Contemporary Hollywood Film Music* (Routledge, 2001); A. Kassabian, "Ubiquitous Listening," in *Popular Music Studies*, ed. D. Hesmondhalgh and K. Negus (Oxford University Press, 2002), 131–142; A. Kassabian, "Would You Like World Music with Your Latte?: Starbucks, Putumayo and Distributed Tourism," *Twentieth Century Music* 1, no.2 (2004): 209–223.

35 IFPI, Global Music Report.

36 See Rogers, *The Death and Life of the Music Industry in the Digital Age*, 106–111 for a list of examples.

37 CISAC, *Global Collections Report 2015* (2015), file:///C:/Users/rogersj/Downloads/CISAC_Collections+Report_2015-ENG.pdf.

38 PRS for Music, *Economic Insight* 15, July 20, 2009.

39 D. Harker, *It's a Jungle Sometimes: The Music Industry, the Crisis and the State* (1998), http://www2.hu-berlin.de/fpm/textpool/texte/harker_the-music-industry-the-crisis-and-the-state.htm.

40 J. Alderman, *Sonic Boom: Napster, P2P and the Future of Music* (Fourth Estate, 2002), xiii.

41 Ibid.

42 See, for example, J. Rogers, "De-constructing the Music Industry Ecosystem," in *Media Convergence and De-convergence*, ed. S. Sparviero, G. Balbi and C. Peil (Palgrave Macmillan, 2017).

43 Media Research cited in P. Resnikoff, "The Music Industry Has Only Declined 3 per cent since 2000 Research Shows," *Digital Music News*, June 5, 2014, www.digitalmusicnews.com/2014/06/05/music-industry-declined-3-since-2000-research-shows/.

44 D.R. Winseck, "Political Economies of the Media and the Transformation of the Global Media Industries: An Introductory Essay," in *The Political Economies of Media: The Transformation of the Global Media Industries*, ed. D.R. Winseck and Dal Yong Jin (Bloomsbury, 2011), 3–48.

45 Vivendi, "Vivendi Earnings" press release, February 29, 2008, www.vivendi.com/wp-content/uploads/2012/03/PR290208_Results2007.pdf; Vivendi, "Vivendi 2008 Results and 2009 Outlook" press release, March 2, 2009, www.vivendi.com/wp-content/uploads/2012/03/EN-_090227_FY-08-final_ul-March-2-2009.pdf; Vivendi, "2009 Vivendi Earnings" press release, March 1, 2010, www.vivendi.com/wp-content/uploads/2012/03/PR100301_Results.pdf; Vivendi, "2010 Vivendi Earnings" press release, March 1, 2011, www.vivendi.com/wp-content/uploads/2012/03/PR110301_resultats_annuels_2010.pdf; Vivendi, "2012 Vivendi Earnings" press release, February 26, 2013, www.vivendi.com/wp-content/uploads/2013/02/20130226_VIV_PR_R%C3%A9sultats-2012.pdf; Vivendi, "Investor Presentation March 2014," 2014, www.vivendi.com/wp-content/uploads/2014/04/20140305_VIV_Investor-Presentation_March-2014.pdf; Vivendi, "2014 Vivendi Earnings" press release, February 27, 2015, www.vivendi.com/wp-content/uploads/2015/02/20150227_VIV_CP_Annual_Results.pdf; Business Wire, "Vivendi Universal Reports Full Year 2005 Revenues Up 9% and 7% on a Comparable Basis," *Business Wire*, January 30, 2006, www.businesswire.com/news/home/20060130005463/en/Vivendi-Universal-Reports-Full-Year-2005-Revenues#.Va5Rs_n4G5l.

46 Warner Music Group, "Investor Relations" press release, December 1, 2005, http://investors.wmg.com/phoenix.zhtml?c=182480&p=irol-newsArticle&ID=791605; Warner Music Group, "Investor Relations" press release, November 29, 2007, http://investors.wmg.com/

phoenix.zhtml?c=182480&p=irol-newsArticle&ID=1082464; Warner Music Group, "Investor Relations" press release, November 25, 2008, http://investors.wmg.com/phoenix.zhtml?c=182480&p=irol-newsArticle&ID=1229864; Warner Music Group, "Investor Relations" press release, November 24, 2009, http://investors.wmg.com/phoenix.zhtml?c=182480&p=irol-newsArticle&ID=1358713; Warner Music Group, "Investor Relations" press release, November 17, 2010, http://investors.wmg.com/phoenix.zhtml?c=182480&p=irol-newsArticle&ID=1497315; Warner Music Group, "Warner Music Group Corp. Reports Results for Fiscal Fourth Quarter and Full Year Ended September 30, 2014," 2014, www.wmg.com/news/warner-music-group-corp-reports-results-fiscal-fourth-quarter-and-full-year-ended-september-3-1.

47 Sony, *Annual Report 2011* (2011), www.sony.net/SonyInfo/IR/financial/ar/report2011/SonyAR11-E.pdf; T. Ingham, "Why Sony Music and Sony/ATV Are on Course for a Big Financial Year," *Music Business Worldwide*, March 22, 2015, www.musicbusinessworldwide.com/why-sony-music-and-sonyatv-are-on-course-for-big-financial-years/.

48 M. Mulligan, "The Death of the Long Tail," *Music Industry Blog*, March 4, 2014, https://musicindustryblog.wordpress.com/2014/03/04/the-death-of-the-long-tail/.

49 See Rogers, "De-constructing the Music Industry Ecosystem" for an overview of recent ownership trends in various music industry sub-sectors.

9 | FREE SOFTWARE AND OPEN SOURCE MOVEMENTS FROM DIGITAL REBELLION TO AARON SWARTZ

Responses to government and corporate attempts at suppression and enclosure

Paul McKimmy (with a coda by Bob Jolliffe)

Introduction

The free software and open source software movements have proven prescient precursors to today's multi-faceted movements against the over-broad privatization of culture and restrictions on expression. Richard Stallman's pivotal decision to lead an organized opposition against the evolving culture and methods of proprietary software paved the way for those with even wider concerns about the stifling effects of copyright and other forms of intellectual property. Today's various movements – including free expression, free culture, free content, open access and free software – owe some of their momentum to the pioneering software hackers who fought to keep code "open" and defend the rights of users to study, change, modify and distribute modifications to the works of others.

As we consider the future of democracy in the United States, we need to consider these movements in the context of the loud and powerful lobbies of corporate interests. The current state of lopsided influence is clearly evidenced in existing laws that benefit corporate content providers at the expense of citizens, in the continuous expansion of copyright terms, and in proposed international agreements like the Trans-Pacific Partnership (TPP). Before considering current conflicts in these areas, it is instructive to understand the history of opposition movements, beginning with free software.

Software and shared code

The Free Software movement began in opposition to the loss of access to software source code, as enforced through copyright.

Source code is the human-readable form of the instructions that control computerized devices. "These machines run us. Code runs these machines," says Lawrence Lessig in his Introduction to Richard Stallman's *Free Software, Free Society*.[1] Stallman, credited as the father of the free software movement, describes the sharing of source code as common within the programming community prior to the 1980s. Colleagues could read, change, and re-use one another's work. Open sharing of code was "as old as computers, just as sharing of recipes is as old as cooking."[2] Stallman encountered what he termed the "proprietary-software social system" during the early 1980s. This system denied him the right to view or change the software that operated modern computers of the day, suppressing such use through the legal power of copyright. Proprietary software distribution provides just the executable form of the software, as derived from source code. Anyone can create the executable version from the source; but the reverse is not true. Stallman's response was to question directly the right of software publishers to restrict code, framing his challenge with the ethical obligation to help others through sharing.[3]

It is the ethical challenge to non-free or closed source code that differentiates the free software movement from its progeny, open source software. In practice, both encompass nearly the same code, as the definitions of free software and open source software embrace virtually the same software licenses. The latter, however, defines open source not with a moral lens, but as a practical approach to effective software development. "Open source" was coined by strategists to intentionally distinguish it from the "philosophically- and politically-focused label 'free software'."[4] Both movements have long wrestled with business models where freely sharing code enables profitable ventures. There are several strategies: provision of consulting services based on freely licensed software; support services for enterprise use of free software; and open core – where value-add extensions are sold, but not as part of the freely licensed core software.[5] Despite the commercial success of Redhat and other open source software businesses, proprietary software development still dominates the market.

The Free Software Foundation's (FSF) and Open Source Initiative's (OSI) definitions of their respective terms read very differently, yet the OSI states they are "two terms for the same thing: software released under licenses that guarantee a certain, specific set of freedoms."[6] Stallman asserts that they are "almost the same category," but with fundamentally different values (and exceptions considered open source, but not free). "Open source is a development methodology; free software is a social movement."[7]

Whether termed free or open source software, both exist in contrast to proprietary software models. Both are viewed skeptically by some; however, they succeed in providing an avenue for continued collaboration and innovation independent of organizational boundaries. Free and open source software alternatives for personal and enterprise software are widely available today. As examples, this chapter was written using a Linux-based operating system, on Libre-Office word processor, with Zotero for citation management – the source code for all of this software is freely available online.

Intellectual property and societal benefit

A key argument for the ethical imperative to share is to increase societal benefit. In Stallman's argument, societal benefit outweighs individual benefit; and we should therefore find ways and means to develop and distribute software that benefits everyone. Essentially, software should become a public good – a good that is valuable, but "cannot be owned, controlled or provided by a single person."[8] There are difficulties with this perspective, however, especially relating to the cost of and motivation for development efforts.

In his book *Intellectual Property and Open Source*, Van Lindberg states that information is a public good that is susceptible to problems with development costs and the value of secrets. An inherent dilemma exists in the opposing costs of knowledge creation and consumption; the former is expensive, the latter is cheap.[9] New knowledge, information, and creative works are costly to create. Research, analysis, time, artistic expression and other work are involved in the generative and creative effort. The costs of consuming them are low – once knowledge, information and creative works exist in some fixed form, today's replication and distribution technologies make consumption very inexpensive. The creator bears the development cost, but the consumer gets a free ride. The second dilemma with information as a public good is that knowledge is more valuable to the individual when held secretly, whereas shared knowledge is more valuable to society. By releasing secret knowledge, the individual loses value even though society gains. The natural motivation, barring other factors, is therefore to hold knowledge secretly.

The function of intellectual property (IP) law is to allow us to share our secrets while controlling how they are used. Authors and inventors receive exclusive control over their knowledge for a limited period, allowing them to reap benefits. In exchange, they share their works publicly – that is the bargain. "After the limited times decreed by the Constitution and by Congress, the knowledge reverts to its natural state as a public good; the freed knowledge is said to be in the 'public domain'."[10]

The power to restrict software use is primarily embodied in copyright law, though patent and trademark law also factor. Collectively, copyright, patent, trademark and trade secret laws are commonly referred to as intellectual property. Maximalist perspectives treat IP as foundational to our economy, and to our rights and identities as creators. Minimalists may view IP as a self-contradiction, holding that knowledge cannot be owned, or that IP unduly restricts creative expression.[11] Opinions on the validity, utility and desirability of IP, especially copyrights and patents, vary to extremes. The term "intellectual property" itself is charged. As an umbrella term, IP encompasses separate and distinct concepts (copyright, patents, trademarks and trade secrets) that have distinct legal treatments and histories. The FSF notes "intellectual property" under "Words to Avoid Because They Are Loaded or Confusing."[12]

Copyright is a monopoly on the right to copy, distribute and adapt a work within a legal jurisdiction, assigned to the creator of an original work. In the United States, the Constitution itself grants congress the power "to promote the Progress of Science and useful Arts, by securing for limited Times to Authors and Inventors the exclusive Right to their respective Writings and Discoveries."[13] Copyright is a federal law, embodied in Title 17 of the US Code, interpreted by the Federal courts. The term of US copyright protections has been expanded several times through congressional acts – a pattern of concern for public domain advocates and IP minimalists. Computer code, as a form of personal expression, is subject to copyright law and its monopoly terms.[14]

Copyright is built upon the notion that securing a monopoly for authors will promote the progress of science and useful arts. But what happens when copyright interferes with such progress? If learning from and building upon others' code is essential, or simply more valuable to progress than are monopoly rights as incentive for creating code, then copyright restrictions are something to overcome rather than embrace. From the FSF's perspective, it's also an ethical imperative.

Digital rebellion with software licenses

The GNU Project was Stallman's seminal act of digital rebellion. The effort was to build a free software replacement for the non-free Unix operating system, and in 1985 he invited the world to participate by issuing the GNU Manifesto.[15] Stallman asserts that "software should not have owners," yet the system of copyright confers ownership, allowing programmers to withhold the software's benefit from the rest of the public.[16] He offers several arguments as to why copyright on software is inappropriate, centering on the fact that digital technology makes copying and sharing nearly cost-free and effortless. He argues that the law is not an unquestionable view of morality, that there are no natural rights to control what one creates and that abolishing software ownership would not stifle development of the software our society really needs.[17] GNU was to be such software – a computer operating system that could run Unix programs, but allow the programming community to make improvements, maintain "solidarity with other users" and to give GNU away.[18] The vision was to eliminate proprietary software.

Proprietary software's reliance on copyright inspired another digital rebellion that turns copyright on its head. Stallman's solution to overcoming copyright was "copyleft." Any free software license guarantees users the freedoms to use, study, copy and share, modify and distribute derivative works. Copyleft licenses additionally dictate that all modified and extended versions be free as well.[19] Stallman adopted the phrase "all rights reversed" to describe the concept.[20] His implementation is the GNU General Public License, or GPL.[21] The GPL was updated in 1991 and again in 2007 to combat new and emerging legal threats to copyleft (software patents and hardware restrictions on free software). Now in version 3, GPL accounts for 30 percent or more of all open source projects today.[22]

While software published under the GPL has proven popular and successful, copyleft has seen its share of criticism. At times pejoratively termed a "viral license," it has been criticized as posing a threat to the intellectual property of any organization making use of it.[23] Stallman's vision of a restrictions-free operating system was first realized when GNU software was combined with Linus Torvald's Linux kernel in 1991. Originally under a license that forbade commercial use, the Linux kernel vo.12 embraced copyleft[24] when Torvalds initiated a switch from his original license to the GNU GPL.[25] GNU, in combination with the Linux kernel, provided a complete free software operating system.[26]

Linux-based operating systems (Linux) have since become widespread; especially in server, supercomputer and mobile computing. Linux systems serve the majority of websites worldwide,[27] run nearly all existing supercomputers, and Android, a Linux-based system, is estimated at nearly two-thirds of the mobile computing market share today.[28] Former Microsoft CEO Steve Ballmer once remarked that "Linux is a cancer that attaches itself in an intellectual property sense to everything it touches. That's the way that the license works."[29] Stallman chose to describe the GPL as a spider plant which "goes to another place if you actively take a cutting."[30] Despite its relatively small use in desktop computing, the massive worldwide use of Linux makes it a runaway success story for copyleft.

Where copyright provides a monopoly on a creator's expression of an idea, patents provide a monopoly on the idea itself. They are time-limited monopolies on inventions or technological developments that must be "useful," "novel" and "non-obvious." Unlike copyright, patents must be approved through an application process that requires full disclosure of the idea and describes the best way to implement it.[31] A relatively recent phenomenon in the United States, software was considered un-patentable prior to a 1981 Supreme Court ruling, *Diamond vs. Dierh*. This ruling established that software innovations could be patented within "broader patenting of larger, more specific processes." A 1994 Federal Circuit decision, *In re Alappat* held that programming creates a "new machine" by changing a general purpose computer into a special purpose computer – further strengthening the status of software patents.[32] Throughout the 1990s, patent law continued to evolve in favor of software patents, increasingly becoming a threat to free and open source software.

There are many arguments against software patents. The End Software Patents campaign curates a list of reasons for abolishment. Open source advocates claim that the US Patent and Trademark

Office has allowed obvious, trivial patents, that patents hinder the standards setting process, and that patents hamper the innovation process in software development.[33] When small pieces of software that are adaptable to many applications are patented, it is increasingly likely that each program will infringe someone's patent.[34] How can any programmer hope to know whether code they write on any given day infringes one of the hundreds of thousands[35] of US software patents (let alone patent applications that may be approved and are yet unpublished)? "In software, it's easy to implement thousands of ideas together in one program: If 10 percent are patented, that means hundreds of patents threaten it."[36] And in what circumstances would a software developer intentionally search existing patents for a means to implement functionality in software (expecting, therefore, to seek license terms with the patent owner for the right to implement that functionality)? The threat of patent litigation, rather than encouraging innovation, frequently has the opposite effect in software development.

Stallman has been an outspoken opponent of software patents, stating "All software developers are threatened by software patents and even software users are threatened by software patents."[37] The third iteration of GPL was introduced, in part, to provide stronger protection against patent threats. When a programmer conveys software that they've written or modified under GPLv3, they must "provide every recipient with any patent licenses necessary to exercise the rights that the GPL gives them." "If any licensee tries to use a patent suit to stop another user from exercising those rights, their license will be terminated."[38]

Software patents present a complex, difficult problem to free and open source software developers – both legally and practically. The existence of thousands of software patents makes retroactive invalidation unlikely. One simple idea is to limit legislatively the effect of infringement by software rather than invalidating patentability. Stallman advocates that "We should legislate that developing, distributing, or running a program on generally used computing hardware does not constitute patent infringement."[39]

Cultural rebellion with content licenses

While software could be developed under free or open source licenses, other types of expression lacked structures to overcome the stifling effects of copyright. Culture is the accumulation of human intellectual achievement and expression, software included. Our culture "consists *entirely* of shared copyrightable expression."[40] If our expressions of art, discovery and ideation build upon others' expressions, how then do we generate new knowledge without continuously tripping over someone else's copyrights?

The public domain, or cultural commons, is that body of content in which copyright has expired or been deliberately relinquished by creators. The public domain is considered by many as a critical springboard from which to inspire and derive new works. "Our art, our culture, our science depend on this public domain," writes James Boyle, Duke Law professor.[41] The expiration, or deliberate revocation, of a copyright places the protected work into the public domain where it is available for others to use, modify and distribute without restrictions.

The framers of our constitution specified "securing for limited times" the rights of authors. At what point does the span of that limited time period become, for purposes of derivative works, counterproductive to societal benefit? A series of congressional acts has now extended the period of copyright protections to what many consider counterproductive terms. The first federal copyright act, the Copyright Act of 1790, granted protections for 14 years, with the right to renew for another 14 should the copyright holder still be alive. Under current law, works created on or after January 1, 1978 are protected for the life of the author plus 70 years; or where the work was made for hire (i.e. corporate ownership), copyright duration is the shorter of 95 years from publication or 120 years from creation.[42] Clearly, the term of copyright protection has dramatically shifted, consequently impacting the scope and content of the public domain.

A protest movement has formed, opposing the continuous expansion of copyright, the resulting reduction of the public domain and the consequential hindrance to free experimentation and expression based on others' ideas. "The notion that intellectual property rights should never expire, and works never enter the public domain – this is the truly fanatical and unconstitutional position," says Jonathan Zittrain, a co-founder of the Berkman Center for Internet and Society at Harvard Law School.[43] Termed the "free culture movement" by Lawrence Lessig, Stanford Law professor, the reformers of this movement have taken action to protect the erosion of the public domain. They fear the continuous expansion of copyright and concomitant erosions of our rights to access and use cultural works.

An initial rebellion in free culture occurred at the same time the Open Source Initiative was formed. The Open Content Project, started by David Wiley in 1998, advocated an Open Content License (OPL) for other forms of content beyond software.[44] The project specifically cited Stallman's GNU Manifesto as inspiration. The OPL was "created to provide instructional designers and content specialists the same benefits, protections and assurances programmers gain from Free Software licenses."[45] The project cited "learning objects" such as graphics, images, sound, video, models, lecture notes, tutorials and anything else "referenced during technology supported learning" as example material for OPL coverage. The term "open content" has evolved since the original OPL and now includes many content types with varying degrees of "openness." The OpenContent website now offers a 5 Rs framework to assess the extent to which content is open. The five "R"s refer to the right to retain, reuse, revise, remix and redistribute content created by others.[46]

Established in 2001, Creative Commons succeeded the Open Content Project. It released its first set of copyright licenses in 2002 – inspired in part by the FSF's GPL. Creative Commons licenses help creators license works freely for certain uses, on certain conditions, or dedicate works to the public domain. There are over a billion "CC-licensed" works today, hosted on content platforms that include flickr, Wikipedia, vimeo, and YouTube.[47] The organization now hosts projects in open access (scholarly works), open educational resources (teaching, learning and research materials) and open science (data) among others.

Additionally, a Free Cultural Works project was started in 2006 by Erik Möller and Benjamin Mako Hill. This project defined the term "free content" or "free cultural work" similar to the terms used in the Free Software Definition. Free cultural works use an approved Free Culture license, or are in the public domain.[48] Notably, they must allow for commercial use. Creative Commons Attribution, Attribution-ShareAlike, and CC0 Public Domain Dedication licenses qualify as Free Culture licenses, and are promoted by Creative Commons with a Free Cultural Works logo. All three allow for commercial uses of the licensed work.

The open access movement

While content licenses provide one approach to broadening the available commons for creative inspiration, remix and derivative works, the traditional process of publishing scholarly works (primarily books and journals) left most research-based and peer-reviewed material subject to publisher-imposed fees and access restrictions. Internet technologies, however, had changed the scope and capabilities of the publishing process and opened the way to new distribution methods. The open access (OA) movement began to take off around 2000, as scholars began exploring alternative means of making scholarship available. The movement is concerned with making peer-reviewed research literature freely available online to all those able to access the internet. While some regard it as a movement, it also represents alternate economic, distribution, marketing and promotion models.[49]

The Budapest Open Access Initiative, an early advocate, authored the most influential definition of open access as literature characterized by:

> free availability on the public internet, permitting any users to read, download, copy, distribute, print, search, or link to the full texts of these articles, crawl them for indexing, pass them as data to software, or use them for any other lawful purpose, without financial, legal, or technical barriers other than those inseparable from gaining access to the internet itself.[50]

A subsequent definition, the Bethesda Statement on Open Access Publishing, further requires copyright owners to grant "free, irrevocable, worldwide, perpetual" rights, which include making derivative works.[51] Creative Commons Attribution and a variety of other licenses may be used to satisfy this definition.[52] Peter Suber, Director of Harvard Open Access Project, defines open-access literature simply as "digital, online, free of charge, and free of most copyright and licensing restrictions."[53]

The case for open access to literature can be made on economic, cooperative, political or moral grounds. Open access benefits teachers, researchers, students and the public who have interests in the content. It also increases the presence and impact of published works while adding little to the publishing costs.[54] Advocacy for OA has stemmed from many sources, including the international Right to Research Coalition, comprised of diverse student organizations. Recent research suggests that OA has entered the mainstream of scholarly communication, and in fact may represent the majority of papers published in many fields (general science and technology, biomedical, biology, mathematics and statistics). However, it is at times greeted with skepticism by researchers who are used to the traditional methods of journal publication, especially where quality control, particularly rigorous peer review, might be questioned.[55]

A primary argument for OA is that research generated using public funds ought to be made publicly available, without fees or financial hurdles for access. Over the past several years, an increasing number of policy mandates have been introduced, especially in universities and research institutions, which have made significant contribution to the uptake of OA. The Registry of Open Access Repository Mandates and Policies (ROARMAP) is an international registry that charts the growth of policies requiring (or requesting) researchers to provide open access to their peer-reviewed articles. Nearly 800 such policies are registered at this time, showing significant growth since tracking began in 2005 when 132 policies were recorded.[56]

Freedom of information and freedom of expression

While open access literature focuses on the unrestricted distribution of scholarly works, the related Freedom of Information movement centers on the public's right to access information of all types – especially focusing on governmental transparency and the avoidance of censorship and surveillance. The term "freedom of information" once was specific to government policies regulating access to state-held data, but is gaining a "radical" new definition in online spaces. It is now also used to describe the protection of freedom of speech as applied to both content and means of expression.[57] It thereby encompasses a movement for freedom of expression, which resists attempts to control communications. Freedom of expression is a right recognized under the Universal Declaration of Human Rights, adopted by the United Nations in 1948. Article 19 states that "Everyone has the right to freedom of opinion and expression; this right includes freedom to hold opinions without interference and to seek, receive and impart information and ideas through any media and regardless of frontiers."[58] Both freedom of expression and freedom of information are commonly cited democratic ideals, upholding the values of open debate and discussion. The right to communications privacy, protection from surveillance, opposition to censorship and opposition to expansion of intellectual property protections are hallmarks of these movements. Amnesty International, for example, asserts that governmental surveillance activities are targeted based on peoples beliefs, especially toward activists and protesters, the results of which may be violations of privacy and free expression rights.[59] In online communities, the idea of freedom of information is founded on the argument that communication in any form should not be restricted.[60]

Communications privacy through the internet relies upon anonymity, which typically requires the use of encryption. Encryption software is instrumental to our ability to communicate without surveillance and avoiding censorship in various forms. Hence, encryption, and the right to use it, are key elements for the Freedom of Information movement. Formerly regulated on the US munitions list,[61] cryptographic technologies are used in secure communications (such as PGP), secure connections between computer networks (such as SSL), anonymous internet use (such as the Tor network) and many forms of securing data against unauthorized access (such as True-Crypt and VeraCrypt, its successor project).

Advocates for both intellectual property reform and Freedom of Information share concern over the control of communications media. Both legislation and access control technologies are used to control data access and transmission. The Digital Millennium Copyright Act of 1998 (DMCA), for example, criminalizes the act of circumventing access controls on copyrighted works – regardless of any actual infringement of copyright. These controls – known as digital rights management or digital restrictions management, depending on your perspective[62] – are commonly known as DRM. Opponents of DRM, including the FSF,[63] cite a litany of harms occurring from such restriction, including interference with users' legal rights such as making backups, converting formats, uses protected by fair use doctrine and DRM's innate ability to cede device control to an external party. The criminalization of technology, devices or services intended to circumvent DRM seems a clear case of legislative overreach benefiting only those companies that license and distribute copyrighted content. This occurs at the expense of users.

Criminalizing specific technology, in the name of IP protection, is conflated with defining and enforcing legal use of content.

The Electronic Frontiers Foundation (EFF), founded in 1990, is a non-profit organization, opposing governmental and business threats to "our right to communicate."[64] It opposes DRM. The EFF has been instrumental in establishing that governmental seizure of electronic communications requires a warrant. It obtained a ruling that software code is speech protected by the First Amendment, which resulted in the right to publish encryption software without governmental permission. In addition to supporting our rights to communicate privately, the EFF clearly expresses that intellectual property ownership is at odds with "the right to think and speak freely."[65]

The Pirate Parties are another advocate for user control over communications; a rebellion against the status quo using existing political processes. Founded to advocate for the revision of current intellectual property regimes,[66] Pirate Parties International (PPI) is a non-profit, non-governmental organization formed in 2010 serving to organize worldwide Pirate Parties, which are political incarnations achieving their goals through established political systems as opposed to activism. It currently represents 43 countries including the United States Pirate Party. PPI advocates for "protection of human rights and fundamental freedoms in the digital age, consumer and authors rights-oriented reform of copyright and related rights, support for information privacy, transparency and free access to information."[67]

The US Pirate Party's platform includes the reduction of copyrights to 14 years and the expiration of patents that don't result in significant progress within four years.[68] The party's "Frequently Asked Questions" page states that "We affirm that current copyright law is not good for the public *or* for creative professionals, and only actually benefits a small minority of corporate executives. We support reforms to copyright law which legalize the freedom to share, while more effectively helping creative professionals make a living."[69] Governmental transparency, protection of privacy and civil liberties are also priorities.[70] The Pirate Parties are political incarnations of the freedom of expression movement, using established political systems, as opposed to activism, to achieve their goals.

The Aaron Swartz case

Aaron Swartz (1986–2013) was an American programmer, activist and political organizer. He committed suicide at age 26 while under federal indictment for alleged computer crimes.[71] Swartz was regarded as a gifted coder, involved in the interpretation and development of both legal and programming code. As legal code alternatively protects, restricts and incubates computing code, his tragedy represents the loss of one who could authoritatively influence the development of both. Aaron's case illustrates the confluence of various IP backlash movements and serves as a cautionary tale against a future with unconstrained manipulation of the legal system by entrenched interests.

A computing expert from an early age, Swartz was involved in programming several notable open source software projects – several of which are aligned with the interests of the Freedom of Information movement. He was a major contributor to the Markdown markup language (for generating HTML code).[72] He co-wrote DeadDrop, an open source software platform for secure, anonymous communications between journalists and whistleblowers (now called Securedrop).[73] Swartz also co-designed Tor2web, which provides access to the Tor network from a basic web browser.[74]

In 2010, Swartz co-founded Demand Progress, an advocacy group now boasting more than two million members. Demand Progress focuses on free expression and privacy, open government, and money-in-politics reform. It helped defeat the Stop Online Piracy Act (SOPA), an internet censorship bill. It also lead efforts to block the Cyber Intelligence Sharing and Protection Act (CISPA), an online surveillance bill.[75]

A fierce advocate for open access and freedom of information, Swartz developed software to address conditions he viewed as unfair. In 2008, he worked with Carl Malamud of Public.Resource.Org to download and publish federal court documents (motions, legal briefs, scheduling orders, etc.) that were otherwise accessible only through the Administrative Office of the US Courts' PACER (Public Access to Court Electronic Records) paywall. PACER requires payment for access to public records of the court system, which Swartz and others considered an injustice. Federal court documents are not subject to copyright.[76] After publishing 2.7 million documents, the library access system leveraged by Swartz was shut down and he was investigated by the FBI. In this case, no charges were filed.

Swartz was also angered by the idea that, in accepted publication practices, publishing firms charged fees to access the academic papers produced by taxpayer-funded scientific research. In 2008, he co-wrote the Guerilla Open Access Manifesto, which calls for activists to "liberate" information locked up by publishers by sharing it. His manifesto states that those with access to knowledge resources have a moral obligation to share those resources to the rest of the world. It labels restricted access to information as "private theft of public culture," and calls out corporate greed and politicians who are "bought off" to pass laws granting exclusive copyrights. Moreover, it encourages civil disobedience, including publishing "secret data-bases" and scientific journals online. Such content, of course, is protected by copyright.[77]

In 2011, Swartz was arrested on breaking-and-entering charges after connecting a computer to the MIT network in an unmarked closet and downloading academic journals systematically from JSTOR using a guest account issued to him by MIT. Federal prosecutors then charged him with wire fraud and violations of the 1986 Computer Fraud and Abuse Act (CFAA), carrying cumulative maximum penalties of 35 years in prison and $1 million in fines. Swartz declined a plea bargain that called for six months in federal prison, and the prosecution rejected his counter offer.[78] He hanged himself while under federal indictment.

After his suicide, a bill dubbed "Aaron's Law Act of 2013" was introduced to reform the CFAA, but it was not enacted. The CFAA has been criticized as outdated and prone to overzealous prosecution for non-malicious computing offenses. The Electronic Frontiers Foundation cites continued misuses of the CFAA across the country.[79] Senator Ron Wyden, sponsor of a 2015 re-introduction of Aaron's Law, stated "The CFAA is so inconsistently and capriciously applied it results in misguided, heavy-handed prosecution. Aaron's Law would curb this abuse while still preserving the tools needed to prosecute malicious attacks."[80]

Today: corporate influences challenge our freedoms

Undaunted by public outcry or grassroots opposition, corporate pressure to expand and enforce IP restrictions continues. Driven by the influence of political donations and by armies of lobbyists, corporate agendas frequently stand at odds with public interests. These agendas include harmful efforts such as continuous expansion of copyright duration, criminalization of DRM circumvention, and legal obstacles to policies that require source code disclosure. When public interests are muted by the influence of corporate political contributions and lobbying, democracy fails us.

The Center for Responsive Politics produces and disseminates data on money in politics to "champion transparency, and expose disproportionate or undue influence on public policy."[81] The Center tracks data on lobbying, lobbyists, political donations and the political action committees (PACs) that control "the most corporate of money."[82] The official figures based on data from the Senate Office of Public Records show that 11,143 registered lobbyists spent $3.12 billion in 2016.[83] However, the research of James Thurber of American University suggests that the true number of working lobbyists is closer to 100,000.[84] Legal loopholes, poor enforcement, faux-grassroots campaigns and an Obama administration executive order disincentivizing registration have combined to produce "near-total collapse" of the system designed to monitor federal lobbying. In short, federal lobbying has gone underground and continued to grow.[85] The interests of the public must certainly suffer under the influence of such well-funded and omnipresent lobbying efforts by special interest groups.

The 2010 Supreme Court case, *Citizens United vs. Federal Election Commission* (*Citizens United*), opened a floodgate of corporate influence by removing campaign contribution limits for non-profits, corporations and other associations.[86] *Citizens United* struck down earlier prohibitions against using corporate funds for advocacy and electioneering communications.[87] "Thanks to *Citizens United*, supporters can make the maximum $5,200 donation directly to a candidate, then make unlimited contributions to single-candidate super PACs."[88] Corporations, are permitted to sponsor political action committees, directly influencing federal elections.[89] With such unrestricted political influence, *Citizens United* creates near certainty that corporate interests will be heard over those of public citizens.

Several trade agreements considered by the US government have exemplified US corporate perspectives, and attempted to spread them to the international sphere. The Trans-Pacific Partnership[90] was a controversial pact between 12 countries: the United States, Japan, Malaysia, Vietnam, Singapore, Brunei, Australia, New Zealand, Canada, Mexico, Chile and Peru. The signatories intended to eliminate or reduce tariffs and restrictive policies on goods, while cooperating on issues such as employment practices, competition policies and treatment of IP.[91] Negotiated as one of President Obama's initiatives, the United States withdrew from the negotiating process as President Trump's first executive order.[92]

While its goals may have seemed supportable on the surface, core aspects of the TPP represented the antithesis of ideals held by the free software, free culture and freedom of expression movements. Of significant concern is the secrecy in which the TPP was negotiated. Negotiations took place behind closed doors from 2010 until the release of the TPP text in 2015. However, corporate lobbyists had ready access to the draft text and dedicated massive lobbying resources to influence the TPP's copyright rules.[93] The public was kept in the dark. Even members of Congress were only allowed to view select portions, under supervision.[94] WikiLeaks released a leaked draft of the IP chapter in 2013, stating that the United States was attempting to enforce its highly restrictive vision of IP on the world. Ironically, the TPP's stated purposes include enhancing innovation and promoting transparency and good governance.[95]

The TPP would have created digital policies that benefit corporations at the expense of the public. Chapter 18 of the TPP requires signatories to impose penalties for copyright infringement, including imprisonment and fines sufficient to deter future acts of infringement. It stipulates that the length of copyright protections will be 70 years after the death of the creator[96] – pushing extended copyright terms to countries beyond the United States. TPP also makes circumvention of DRM punishable by civil and/or criminal penalties (Articles 18.68 and 18.74),[97] compelling DMCA-like restrictions in partner countries and treating circumvention as an separate offense from infringement.

The Recording Industry Association of America (RIAA) reported $4,392,911 on 2016 lobbying expenditures, and made $168,454 in political contributions.[98] The Motion Picture Association of America (MPAA) reported $2,580,000 in lobbying and $239,573 in political contributions.[99] Both organizations are representative of powerful industry lobbies, and both were vocally supportive of the copyright and DRM terms represented by the TPP.

These extensions of US-like copyright and DRM policies met with condemnation from EFF,[100] FSF[101] and other activists. Evan Greer, of Fight for the Future (FFF) said "While claiming to champion an open Internet, the Obama administration is quietly pushing for extreme, SOPA-like copyright policies that benefit Hollywood and giant pharmaceutical companies at the expense of our most basic rights to freedom of expression online."[102] Julian Assange, founder and editor-in-chief of WikiLeaks, stated

the TPP's intellectual property regime would trample over individual rights and free expression, as well as ride roughshod over the intellectual and creative commons. If you read, write, publish, think, listen, dance, sing or invent; if you farm or consume food; if you're ill now or might one day be ill, the TPP has you in its crosshairs.[103]

TPP also represented a lost opportunity for debate and progressive reform in IP treatment. It did nothing to address patenting in software – a failure to address one of the great threats to free software development and technological innovation. TPP would have outlawed a country from adopting rules for software sales that include mandatory code review or release of source code – prohibiting open source mandates[104] that might leverage governmental spending to create greater value for citizens.

The Transatlantic Trade and Investment Partnership (TTIP), a separate international treaty, is also being negotiated in secret. TTIP is a multi-trillion dollar treaty between the United States and the European Union that remains closely guarded by the negotiators, though big corporations are given special access to its terms. It also contains terms that provide for policing the internet on behalf of the content industry.[105]

The closed-door negotiations, direct influence by lobbyists and lack of scrutiny by legitimate dissenting interests make TPP and TTIP's demonstrative cases of political corruption. The process and content of the TPP fly in the face of democratic values such as open debate, transparency and elected representation. The TPP effectively entrenched the interests of Hollywood and big media, extending the United States' controversial copyright and anti-circumvention treatments to 11 other nations. When lobbyists gain such direct access and influence over international agreements outside the public view, it is an indictment of a political system that has lost its way, prioritizing economic benefits of the powerful over the best interests of the people.

Summation and moving forward

The impacts of over-broad IP restrictions on individual's computing, communications and information-sharing activities are being felt everywhere. The ideals of unrestricted collaboration and free expression originating in the free software movement are articulated and sought by activists in academia, research, creative enterprise and a variety of free speech advocates. Standing in opposition, are business and governmental interests seeking not just to control information ownership, but the means to restrict access through measures such as closed source code, IP monopoly, encryption and digital rights management.

While "radical" idealists may be criticized for opposing intellectual property in both concept and statute, many activist responses actually rely on it. Creative Commons and open source software licenses rely on copyright to achieve their ends; they do not seek to abolish copyright (or patents for that matter), but to balance private interests with public good. Both activists and IP stalwarts claim to desire incentives for innovation and creative effort, protecting creators while benefiting society. A core issue is balancing public good against private interest in establishing reasonable standards and periods of protection.

There are issues and actions that must to be debated – not by lobbyists and lawmakers behind closed doors, but by all of us who care deeply about preserving a free and democratic society in the digital age. And legislative actions must follow. A prescription for action might include:

First, revise the Computer Fraud and Abuse Act. With its disproportionate penalties, ambiguous terminology and prosecutorial overreach, it requires revisions to focus on malicious activity and prevent abuse. Aaron's Law needs to be enacted.

Second, our money-in-politics problem requires decisive action. In deciding *Citizens United*, the Court relied on a theory of corporate personhood which sees the existence of human beings and corporations as legally and factually indistinguishable. This stance is flawed for several reasons, not the least of which is its inconsistency with the meaning and purpose of the US Constitution.[106] A constitutional amendment repudiating corporate personhood should be broadly discussed and implementation considered. Thoughtful and unconventional solutions to campaign finance reform (such as universally anonymous donations) need to be considered. Without addressing this issue, the wealth and power of corporations will continue to drown out the voices of those opposing their special interests.

Third, negotiate a return to sensible copyright terms. Protect the public domain and protect our right to ideate and create freely by reducing the monocracy of copyright to terms that enable creators to monetize their work without locking it away for generations. A publicly palatable solution exists between the Pirate Party's 14-year ideal and the 120-year maximum under current law.

Fourth, eliminate the deleterious effects of patents on software development by legislating that developing, distributing or running a program on generally used computing hardware does not constitute patent infringement. As Stallman points out, there may be precedent for this approach in the legal protections afforded surgeons from patented surgical procedures; and it fixes the effect on software innovation without tinkering with the patent system itself.[107]

Fifth, revoke the Digital Millennium Copyright Act. Decriminalize DRM circumvention, protecting our right to control the devices we own.

Sixth, support the FSF, EFF, FFF and other organizations that seek to make the voices and interests of citizens heard over the din of corporate money.

Finally, consider open source software mandates for publicly funded institutions. Where effective solutions exist or where such solutions can be developed through minimal effort, the cost savings and societal benefits to bolstering open source use is in the public interest. Such efforts exist, but require both public support and defense against the powerful voice of corporations that stand in their way.

Clearly, controversy surrounds the appropriate scope, strength and benefit of copyright and other intellectual property law. The agendas of politically powerful corporate interests, however, can be countered by grassroots online activism. Protests, whether through social movements (free software, free culture), alternative processes (open source, open access), civil disobedience or use of established political processes (Pirate Parties), can shape the discussion into a more balanced dialogue.

CODA: WHAT'S RADICAL ABOUT FREE/OPEN SOURCE SOFTWARE?

Bob Joliffe

Editor's note: Having considered such an important national case study as advanced in the preceding pages by Paul McKimmy, here we offer a brief international perspective and some reflections on the radical potentials of FOSS, courtesy of Bob Jolliffe (University of Oslo, and formerly University of South Africa).

This is a welcome opportunity and challenge to reflect briefly on more than 25 years of engagement with Free and Open Source Software (FOSS) – at various times as a practitioner, teacher, advocate and activist. Much of the FOSS story which unfolded over this period has already been narrated in the excellent chapter above by Paul McKimmy. That chapter is a thorough and thoughtful account which I will try to extend in two ways. I want to try to delve just a little beneath the surface appearance of what we understand as FOSS in order to grasp what it is that might be *radical*; and to do that from my quite different geo-political perspective (most of my FOSS work has been in Africa).

What is a radical perspective? For Marx, a truly radical idea was one which is potentially transformational in a practical and material sense and which has the real, existing human condition as its central object and subject. This is what Gramsci in his *Prison Diaries* was later to refer to as a *theory of praxis.*

It is a useful perspective to keep in mind as we examine radical claims around FOSS and IP more generally. I have found that for many IP activists, intellectual property itself is often seen as a (*the?*) central social pathology, in need of radical alternatives. The FOSS story is then projected as a real historic model of what such radical alternatives might look like. The danger here is twofold: (i) IP is not the *root of the matter,* though it is symptomatic of (and instrumental in) broader contradictions of use and exchange value and human alienation in capitalist society; and (ii) some of the more radical claims of FOSS have indeed been suggestive of broader societal transformation at the level of the individual, the class structure of production and the relations between nations in narratives of development. To view it simply as an interesting and creative example of circumventing IP norms misses an important and radical opportunity.

Here, I outline three *radical* claims related to FOSS.

The free, creative, laboring human being Making software is a creative human activity. Yet, at the time that FOSS was beginning to emerge in the 1980s and 1990s, dominant software engineering methods were using Taylorist ideas to reduce the scope of creativity and by so doing attempt to increase the reliability and correctness of software production – separating designers from coders and valorizing the former against the latter. With the industrialization of software production, coders were systematically alienated from the product of their own labor, and hence from one another and the world around them. It was capital's first instinct to organize software production in a similar way to the division of labor in material industry.

The early FOSS movement presented a radical, non-alienating alternative. It was in this sense a child of the internet (though in a dialectic twist, also its creator). It was perhaps the first example of the creative potential of this new network. Outside the confines of "the factory," software creators found one another, developed tools collaboratively in order to collaborate, using the primitive tools of the early internet to build and refine the internet. Eben Moglen described the creative power that was being unleashed in his famous corollary to Faraday's law: if you wrap the internet around the planet, then spin the planet, creativity will flow.

In this narrative, the human creator is cast as the central subject-object, and through his (and it is usually his, rather than her) creative activity he becomes more free whilst also creating conditions which allow others to do the same.

What is this new free man like? There is no more eloquent account of the liberating effect of free, *technical* labor than Primo Levi's ode to technical work – the collection of short stories *The Wrench*. Levi, as an Auschwitz survivor, was keenly aware of, and probably haunted by throughout his life, the inhuman brutality of labor in the death camps that consumed the life force of inmates under the slogan of "Arbeit macht frei." Yet in *The Wrench*, Levi presents a touching, beautiful account of liberating technical labor. One pivotal passage relates to how the "hero," Falzone, learns to weld at the new Fiat factory near his home. He describes the sense of joy at this accomplishment in a *physical* way – people who could weld walked differently. There was a swagger! It is a wonderful account of Homo Faber or man as a tool making animal, man as maker, reaching fulfillment through labor. It is his response to the deathly labor of Auschwitz.

Many FOSS programmers have shared this joy of accomplishment, and the fact of open source code makes their contributions visible, at least to their peers. Like the welders from Fiat, they effect a swagger, even if it is only one their peers might recognize.

The *maker* movement is an interesting new cultural phenomenon bringing Western human beings (largely men) back in touch with tactile creativity – it is closely linked with technology and there are interesting parallels with the FOSS hacker culture. Across political perspectives, FOSS provided individual makers with the tools and inspiration to create, and bound them into a community of fellow creators. In this narrative, software production approaches art. Beautiful code!

The notion of FOSS as nurturing a free, laboring, creative individual is a romantic, humanist one which is perhaps all the more radical because of it. But there are of course problems with the account. At a fundamental level, I am not sure that the free, laboring, FOSS programmer ever really exists, other than as a creature of hopeful and fleeting imagination. Again, as Marx reminds us, it is not the study of Robinson Crusoe's solitary producers which leads us beyond appearances to the essence of political economy. For that we need to understand social production happening within actual society. And that society is characterized and deeply penetrated by a capitalist mode of production. Whereas that does not preclude the contingency of human agency in battle against structure, it does need to be taken into account.

A post-capitalist mode of production? Another radical claim seen in the works of Christian Fuchs, Paul Mason (and others) is that open source, free software and other forms of peer production offer a glimpse of a new post-capitalist mode of production. For those of us who still believe that capitalism represents the biggest threat to humanity in every sense, this is an enticing claim.

They draw some inspiration for this from Marx's *Grundrisse* and in particular the Fragment on Machines. The *Grundrisse* is also a source of theoretical inspiration of Antonio Negri of the Italian autonomistas and more recently the Occupy movement and the *Empire* series with Michael Hardt. It is a serious and interesting contemporary claim that needs more exploration than I have space for here. But in short, I think it is largely unfounded.

If anything, capitalism has shown itself predictably agile at adapting to the disruptive challenges posed by the free, creative, laboring individual of the previous section. Far from being a counterpoint to corporate interests, today there are no serious technology companies which are not deeply invested in FOSS. In other words there is considerable overlap between corporate interests and FOSS community interests. For the Irish academic, Brian Fitzgerald, Free Software and its early ideological tussles with OSS 1.0, were simply the immature stirrings of a movement which, once it demonstrated market potential, needed to be tamed and made "*commercially viable.*" Fitzgerald agrees with Christopher May who, writing about the potential of FOSS in Africa,[108] claims that FOSS is not anti-capitalist so much as *differently* capitalist. He makes an analogy with the time proven business strategy of "giving away the razor to sell the blades."

The trend is increasingly clear to see. For example, despite quite notable exceptions, it becomes harder to find fully functional FOSS software outside the realm of developer tools and libraries. The popular nginx web server, the mysql database, new analytics and visualization frameworks like splunk are all available for download in their FOSS versions. But for key additional functionalities required for production-level use, the user is invited to pay a license or subscription fee for proprietary extensions.

And so FOSS (or preferably now, just OSS), becomes simply a new and better way of doing business. There are winners and losers, but certainly capitalism as a mode of production is not shaken.

FOSS and post-colonial empowerment of the periphery Many so-called developing countries on capitalism's global periphery saw in FOSS an opportunity to challenge critical dependency in information technology, particularly a crippling dependency on Microsoft desktop licenses. An analysis of this perspective requires stepping back/up/away from the individual and class and picturing the world in terms of a community of nations which exist in terms of particular power relations to one another. The nation state becomes the unit of analysis – like the recent (reinvigorated) America First movement.

South Africa, for example, found itself in 2003 (i) increasingly reliant on computer software, (ii) caught in a deadly embrace with Microsoft at a time when the Rand was hit by global currency speculation and collapse and (iii) developing an innovation policy around the notion of developmental state. FOSS provided some potential of a way forward. The South African cabinet adopted a policy which favored FOSS in all new procurement. The rationale was mixed, but primary concerns were economic efficiencies, national security and promoting local innovation. Similar sentiments were held in Peru, Brazil and elsewhere. FOSS was not exclusively about the freedom of the individual but also about the sovereignty of states and their capacity to deliver on emancipatory and transformational social goals using the new ICTs without becoming ever more entrapped in dependent relations.

An interesting difference in the way FOSS was perceived related to the question of cost (and total cost of ownership, or TCO, in particular). Incumbent proprietary vendors were winning lobby-ist battles amongst governments in Europe and North America, claiming that in the grander scheme of enterprise software deploy-ments, the costs of license fees were insignificant compared to maintenance, training, support, customization, etc. Rishab Ghosh, an Indian researcher based in Maastricht, conducted a number of global studies and published results showing the same parameters do not hold true in many poorer countries in the South. Using GDP as a normalizer he showed that a desktop software license in the United States cost the equivalent of 0.19 months of work. The same software in Burundi would cost the equivalent of 67 months.[109]

Activists within governments and civil society on the periphery collaborated to realize the ambition of FOSS on the desktop with limited success. The onslaught from corporate lobbyists (both foreign and local comprador) was swift and relentless.

Despite failings, the advancing of a state-supported FOSS agenda in South Africa and elsewhere has not been without successes. FOSS-centered innovation and development are now slowly becoming more commonplace around Africa, in the university sector, civil society and the private sector. FOSSFA (the Free and Open Source

Foundation for Africa) has been actively organizing a continent-wide community for over a decade.

FOSS solutions have been particularly prominent in areas like health information systems, where projects such as the District Health Information System[110] have been strengthening health systems in countries across the world.

Notes

1 R.M. Stallman, J. Gay and L. Lessig, *Free Software, Free Society: Selected Essays of Richard M. Stallman* (CreateSpace Independent Publishing Platform, 2009), 11.

2 Ibid., 17.

3 Ibid.

4 Open Source Initiative, "History of the OSI," (n.d.). Retrieved August 30, 2016, from https://opensource. org/history.

5 G. Ingersoll, "Refactoring Open Source Business Models," *Opensource. Com*, April 20, 2016, https://opensource. com/business/16/4/refactoring-open-source-business-models.

6 Open Source Initiative, "Frequently Answered Questions," (n.d.). Retrieved August 30, 2016, from https:// opensource.org/faq#free-software; Open Source Initiative, "The Open Source Definition," (n.d.). Retrieved September 23, 2016, from https:// opensource.org/osd; Free Software Foundation, "What Is Free Software?" (n.d.). Retrieved August 30, 2016, from www.gnu.org/philosophy/free-sw.en. html.

7 R. Stallman, "Why Open Source Misses the Point of Free Software," (n.d.). Retrieved August 30, 2016, from www.gnu.org/philosophy/open-source-misses-the-point.html.

8 V. Lindberg, *Intellectual Property and Open Source: A Practical Guide to Protecting Code* (O'Reilly Media, 2008), 11.

9 Ibid., 12.

10 Ibid., 13–14.

11 Ibid., 2.

12 GNU Project, "Words to Avoid (or Use with Care) Because They Are Loaded or Confusing," (n.d.). Retrieved August 23, 2016, from www. gnu.org/philosophy/words-to-avoid. html#IntellectualProperty.

13 US Constitution, Article 1, Section 8.

14 Lindberg, *Intellectual Property and Open Source*, 71.

15 R. Stallman, "The GNU Manifesto," (n.d.). Retrieved August 30, 2016, from www.gnu.org/gnu/manifesto. en.html.

16 Stallman et al., *Free Software, Free Society*, 47.

17 Ibid., 48–51.

18 Stallman, "The GNU Manifesto."

19 GNU Project, "What Is Copyleft?" (n.d.). Retrieved August 31, 2016, from www.gnu.org/copyleft/.

20 C. DiBona and S. Ockman, *Open Sources: Voices from the Open Source Revolution* (O'Reilly Media, 1999), 59.

21 GNU Project, "GNU General Public License," (n.d.). Retrieved August 31, 2016, from www.gnu.org/copyleft/ gpl.html.

22 S. Wilson, "Open Source Software Licensing Trends," OSS Watch Team Blog, (n.d.). Retrieved August 31, 2016, from https://osswatch.jiscinvolve.org/ wp/2015/02/05/open-source-software-licensing-trends/.

23 "Speech Transcript – Craig Mundie, The New York University Stern School of Business | News

Center," May 3, 2001. Retrieved September 1, 2016, from http://news. microsoft.com/speeches/speech-transcript-craig-mundie-the-new-york-university-stern-school-of-business/ #sm.00011cfrz2p3lepmtol2ie2a0taze.

24 Linus Torvalds Interview, February 10, 2007. Retrieved from https://web.archive.org/web/20070210224351/http://hotwired.goo.ne.jp/matrix/9709/5_linus.html; L. Torvalds, "Release Notes for Linux v0.12." [Linux Kernel Archives]. Retrieved August 30, 2016, from www.kernel.org/pub/linux/kernel/Historic/old-versions/RELNOTES-0.12.

25 Torvalds, "Release Notes for Linux v0.12."

26 GNU Project, "Overview of the GNU System," (n.d.). Retrieved August 23, 2016, from www.gnu.org/gnu/gnu-history.html.

27 W3Techs, "Usage Statistics and Market Share of Unix for Websites, September 2016," September 1, 2016. Retrieved September 1, 2016, from https://w3techs.com/technologies/details/os-unix/all/all.

28 "Operating System Market Share," (n.d.). Retrieved September 1, 2016, from www.netmarketshare.com/operating-system-market-share.aspx?qprid=8&qpcustomd=1.

29 "Microsoft CEO Takes Launch Break with the Sun-Times," June 1, 2001. Retrieved September 1, 2016, from https://web.archive.org/web/20010615205548/http://suntimes.com/output/tech/cst-fin-micro01.html.

30 S. Williams, *Free as in Freedom* (2002). Retrieved from www.oreilly.com/openbook/freedom/ch02.html.

31 Lindberg, *Intellectual Property and Open Source.*

32 A. Layne-Farrar and D.S. Evans, "Software Patents and Open Source: The Battle Over Intellectual Property Rights,"

2004. Retrieved from http://papers.ssrn.com/abstract=533442.

33 Ibid.

34 J.E. Bessen and R.M. Hunt, "An Empirical Look at Software Patents," *SSRN Electronic Journal*. https://doi.org/10.2139/ssrn.461701.

35 R. Stallman, "Software Patents: Obstacles to Software Development," March 25, 2002. Retrieved September 1, 2016, from www.gnu.org/philosophy/software-patents.en.html.

36 R. Stallman, "Let's Limit the Effect of Software Patents, Since We Can't Eliminate Them," (n.d.). Retrieved September 2, 2016, from www.wired.com/2012/11/richard-stallman-software-patents/.

37 Stallman, "Software Patents: Obstacles to Software Development."

38 Smith, "A Quick Guide to GPLv3," (n.d.). Retrieved September 2, 2016, from www.gnu.org/licenses/quick-guide-gplv3.html.

39 Stallman, "Let's Limit the Effect of Software Patents, Since We Can't Eliminate Them."

40 Lindberg, *Intellectual Property and Open Source*, 73.

41 R.S. Boynton, "The Tyranny of Copyright?" *The New York Times*, January 25, 2004.

42 U.S. Copyright Office, "Copyright Basics," (n.d.), 5.

43 Boynton, "The Tyranny of Copyright?"

44 "OpenContent License," July 14, 1998. Retrieved September 7, 2016, from https://web.archive.org/web/19990129013417/www.opencontent.org/opl.shtml.

45 "OpenContent - Frequently Asked Questions," January 28, 1999. Retrieved September 7, 2016, from https://web.archive.org/web/19990128185303/www.opencontent.org/faq.shtml.

46 D. Wiley, "Defining the 'Open' in Open Content and Open Educational Resources," (n.d.). Retrieved September 7, 2016, from http://opencontent. org/definition/.

47 "Creative Commons Platforms," (n.d.). Retrieved September 7, 2016, from https://creativecommons. org/about/platform/.

48 "Definition of Free Cultural Works," (n.d.). Retrieved September 7, 2016, from http://freedomdefined. org/Definition.

49 G. Hall, "Pirate Radical Philosophy," *Radical Philosophy*, (n.d.), 36. Retrieved from www. radicalphilosophy.com/commentary/ pirate-radical-philosophy-2.

50 "Budapest Open Access Initiative | Read the Budapest Open Access Initiative," (n.d.). Retrieved August 30, 2016, from www. budapestopenaccessinitiative.org/read.

51 "Bethesda Statement on Open Access Publishing," June 20, 2003. Retrieved September 13, 2016, from http://legacy.earlham.edu/~peters/fos/ bethesda.htm.

52 Charles W. Bailey, "What Is Open Access?" February 7, 2007. Retrieved August 25, 2016, from http://digital-scholarship.org/cwb/WhatIsOA.htm; L. Liang, "Guide to Open Content Licenses," (n.d.). Retrieved September 13, 2016, from https://archive.org/stream/ media_Guide_to_Open_Content_ Licenses/Guide_to_Open_Content_ Licenses_djvu.txt.

53 Peter Suber, "Open Access Overview (Definition, Introduction)," June 19, 2007. Retrieved July 22, 2010, from www.earlham.edu/~peters/fos/ overview.htm.

54 J. Willinsky, *The Access Principle: The Case for Open Access to Research and Scholarship* (MIT Press, 2006).

55 S. Pinfield, "Making Open Access Work: The 'State-of-the-Art' in Providing Open Access to Scholarly Literature," *Online Information Review* 39, no. 5 (2015): 604–636. https://doi. org/10.1108/OIR-05-2015-0167.

56 ROARMAP, "Welcome to ROARMAP," (n.d.). Retrieved September 13, 2016, from http://roarmap.eprints. org/.

57 J.L. Beyer, "The Emergence of a Freedom of Information Movement: Anonymous, WikiLeaks, the Pirate Party, and Iceland," *Journal of Computer-Mediated Communication* 19, no. 2 (2014): 141.

58 United Nations, "The Universal Declaration of Human Rights," (n.d.). Retrieved September 22, 2016, from www.un.org/en/universal-declaration-human-rights/index.html.

59 "Freedom of Expression," (n.d.). Retrieved September 15, 2016, from www.amnestyusa.org/our-work/issues/ security-and-human-rights/freedom-of-expression.

60 Beyer, "The Emergence of a Freedom of Information Movement," 141.

61 Electronic Privacy Information Center, "International Traffic in Arms Regulations," (n.d.). International Traffic in Arms Regulations. Retrieved September 22, 2016, from https://epic. org/crypto/export_controls/itar.html.

62 Digital Restrictions Management, "What Is DRM?," (n.d.). Retrieved September 21, 2016, from http://drm. info/what-is-drm.en.html.

63 Defective by Design, "DRM Frequently Asked Questions," (n.d.). Retrieved September 21, 2016, from www.defectivebydesign. org/faq#free%20software.

64 "A History of Protecting Freedom Where Law and Technology Collide," October 7, 2011. Retrieved September 12, 2016, from www.eff.org/about/history.

65 Ibid.

66 Beyer, "The Emergence of a Freedom of Information Movement," 144.

67 Pirate Parties International, "ABOUT PPI," (n.d.). Retrieved August 27, 2016, from https://pp-international. net/about-ppi/.

68 J. Downie, "Avast Network," January 23, 2011. Retrieved September 13, 2016, from https://newrepublic. com/article/81963/pirate-party-wikileaks.

69 United States Pirate Party, "FAQ," (n.d.). Retrieved August 27, 2016, from https://uspirates.org/faq/.

70 United States Pirate Party, "About," (n.d.). Retrieved August 27, 2016, from https://uspirates.org/about/.

71 S. Gustin, "Aaron Swartz, Tech Prodigy and Internet Activist, Is Dead at 26," *Time*, January 13, 2013. Retrieved from http://business.time. com/2013/01/13/tech-prodigy-and-internet-activist-aaron-swartz-commits-suicide/.

72 "Markdown (Aaron Swartz: The Weblog)," (n.d.). Retrieved September 14, 2016, from www.aaronsw. com/weblog/001189.

73 M. Kassner, "Aaron Swartz Legacy Lives on with New Yorker's Strongbox: How it works," *TechRepublic*, May 20, 2013. Retrieved from www.techrepublic. com/blog/it-security/aaron-swartz-legacy-lives-on-with-new-yorkers-strongbox-how-it-works/.

74 Katie Dean Email, "Open Source Opens Education," *Wired Magazine*, March 13, 2000. Retrieved from www. wired.com/print/culture/lifestyle/news/2000/03/34807.

75 "About Demand Progress," (n.d.). Retrieved September 14, 2016, from https://demandprogress.org/about/.

76 T.B. Lee, "The Inside Story of Aaron Swartz's Campaign to Liberate Court Filings," February 8, 2013. Retrieved September 14, 2016, from http://arstechnica.com/tech-policy/2013/02/the-inside-story-of-aaron-swartzs-campaign-to-liberate-court-filings/.

77 A. Swartz, "Guerilla Open Access Manifesto," 2008. Retrieved August 25, 2016, from https://archive.org/stream/GuerillaOpenAccessManifesto/Goamjuly2008_djvu.txt.

78 J. Naughton, "Aaron Swartz Stood up for Freedom and Fairness – and Was Hounded to His Death," *The Guardian*, February 7, 2015. Retrieved from www. theguardian.com/commentisfree/2015/feb/07/aaron-swartz-suicide-internets-own-boy.

79 C. Cohn, "Aaron's Law Reintroduced: CFAA Didn't Fix Itself," April 29, 2015. Retrieved September 14, 2016, from www.eff. org/deeplinks/2015/04/aarons-law-reintroduced-cfaa-didnt-fix-itself.

80 "Wyden, Lofgren, Paul Introduce Bipartisan, Bicameral Aaron's Law to Reform Abused Computer Fraud and Abuse Act," Senator Ron Wyden, April 21, 2015. Retrieved September 14, 2016, from www.wyden.senate.gov/news/press-releases/wyden-lofgren-paul-introduce-bipartisan-bicameral-aarons-law-to-reform-abused-computer-fraud-and-abuse-act-.

81 OpenSecrets, "About OpenSecrets.org," (n.d.). Retrieved February 14, 2017, from www. opensecrets.org/about/.

82 OpenSecrets, "Influence & Lobbying," (n.d.). Retrieved February 14, 2017, from www.opensecrets. org/influence/.

83 OpenSecrets, "Lobbying," (n.d.). Retrieved February 14, 2017, from www. opensecrets.org/lobby/.

84 "Where Have All the Lobbyists Gone?" *The Nation*, (n.d.). Retrieved February 9, 2017, from www.thenation. com/article/shadow-lobbying-complex/.

85 Ibid.

86 "How Citizens United Has Changed Politics in 5 Years," (n.d.). Retrieved February 14, 2017, from www. usnews.com/news/articles/2015/01/21/5-

years-later-citizens-united-has-remade-us-politics.

87 M.J. Allman, "Swift Boat Captains of Industry for Truth: Citizens United and the Illogic of the Natural Person Theory of Corporate Personhood," *Florida State University Law Review* 38 (2010): 387.

88 Ibid.

89 R. Jacobs and J. Ryan, "Regulatory: 4 Ways Corporations Can Participate in Federal Elections," *Inside Counsel*, March 14, 2012. Retrieved February 14, 2017, from www.insidecounsel.com/2012/03/14/regulatory-4-ways-corporations-can-participate-in.

90 "Text of the Trans-Pacific Partnership," *New Zealand Foreign Affairs and Trade*, (n.d.). Retrieved September 22, 2016, from www.mfat.govt.nz/en/about-us/who-we-are/treaty-making-process/trans-pacific-partnership-tpp/text-of-the-trans-pacific-partnership/.

91 "TPP: What Is It and Why Does It Matter?" *BBC News*, July 27, 2016. Retrieved from www.bbc.com/news/business-32498715.

92 J. Diamond and D. Bash, "Trump Signs Order Withdrawing from TPP," *CNN*, January 24, 2017. Retrieved February 7, 2017, from www.cnn.com/2017/01/23/politics/trans-pacific-partnership-trade-deal-withdrawal-trumps-first-executive-action-monday-sources-say/index.html.

93 "A New Infographic on TPP and Your Digital Rights," February 19, 2016. Retrieved September 22, 2016, from www.eff.org/deeplinks/2016/02/new-infographic-tpp-and-your-digital-rights.

94 A. Hern and D. Rushe, "WikiLeaks Publishes Secret Draft Chapter of Trans-Pacific Partnership," *The Guardian*, November 13, 2013. Retrieved from www.theguardian.com/media/2013/nov/13/wikileaks-trans-pacific-partnership-chapter-secret.

95 "Summary of the Trans-Pacific Partnership Agreement," (n.d.). Retrieved September 22, 2016, from https://ustr.gov/about-us/policy-offices/press-office/press-releases/2015/october/summary-trans-pacific-partnership.

96 "Text of the Trans-Pacific Partnership," 18–34.

97 Ibid., 18–36.

98 OpenSecrets, "Lobbying."

99 Ibid.

100 Electronic Frontiers Foundation, "Trans-Pacific Partnership Agreement," (n.d.). Retrieved September 22, 2016, from www.eff.org/issues/tpp.

101 Donald Robertson, "The Sharks Move In; Lobbyists Pushing Forward on TPP Agreements," *Free Software Foundation*, November 24, 2014. Retrieved September 22, 2016, from www.fsf.org/blogs/licensing/the-sharks-move-in-lobbyists-pushing-forward-on-tpp-agreements.

102 Hern and Rushe, "WikiLeaks Publishes Secret Draft Chapter of Trans-Pacific Partnership."

103 Ibid.

104 Electronic Frontiers Foundation, "Trans-Pacific Partnership Agreement."

105 WikiLeaks, "Transatlantic Trade and Investment Partnership," May 9, 2016. Retrieved September 23, 2016, from https://wikileaks.org/ttip/.

106 Allman, "Swift Boat Captains of Industry for Truth."

107 Stallman, "Let's Limit the Effect of Software Patents, Since We Can't Eliminate Them."

108 C. May, "Escaping the TRIPs Trap: The Political Economy of Free and Open Source Software in Africa," *Political Studies* 54, no. 1 (2006): 123–146.

109 Rishab Aiyer Ghosh, "Licence Fees and GDP per Capita: The Case for Open Source in Developing Countries," *First Monday* 8, no. 12 (December 1, 2003). doi: http://dx.doi.org/10.5210/fm.v8i12.1103.

110 http://dhis2.org.

SECTION THREE

LAW, POLICY AND JURISDICTION

After all is said and done, it still remains to examine what intellectual property law actually is. Furthermore, we must consider what the distinctions and similarities are between national and international intellectual property regimes, including treaties and policies of various bodies and jurisdictions.

It is necessary to examine, even if only on an introductory level, the IP laws particular to certain countries, such as the United States, their international ramifications through organizations such as the World Intellectual Property Organization (WIPO) as well as the difficulties they encounter when confronted by "piracy." Not only can these laws, treaties and industrial practices be understood by the lay person – as long as they are properly explained, but the gaps and inconsistencies between them and public perception of them can also be explained.

Section 3 begins by advancing a call for the reconceptualization of WIPO, reconfiguring its nucleus as to fundamentally revise its purpose away from the protection of property rights, and more towards the aims and agendas of a range of other United Nations organizations that deal with health, sustainable industrial development, education, science, culture and more.

Beyond this, key claims that lie at the heart of intellectual property law are dismantled and scrutinized. The manipulation of the IPR domain by powerful interests is foregrounded against the stark lack of evidence that intellectual property law fulfills its promise to serve as the mechanism to motivate and encourage the generation of literary and scientific works, etc., and reform proposals are advanced for a fairer and more equitable approach to intellectual property rights.

Finally, the re-emergence and reconceptualization of the "pirate" in the contemporary environment is unpacked to clarify the concept and expose its misuse in bolstering the interests of the privileged.

10 | RETHINKING THE WORLD INTELLECTUAL PROPERTY ORGANIZATION[1]

Debora J. Halbert

Introduction

The World Intellectual Property Organization (WIPO) head-quarters, located in Geneva Switzerland, stands as testimony to the artistic world WIPO seeks to facilitate. As former Director General of WIPO, Arpad Bogsch notes in his commemorative book on WIPO's first 25 years:

> The blue glass façade of the tower-like main part are a landmark of Geneva. The marble floors and decoration of the lobby as well as the mosaic covering the inside of its cupola are masterpieces from two specialized old firms of Rome. The main conference room, with a view on oak trees, and its decoration, are the delight of most delegates. More than a hundred works of art (sculptures, paintings, textiles), many of them gifts from governments and organizations, embellish several parts of the interior.[2]

For Bogsch, the WIPO building and its art demonstrates why protecting intellectual property is essential – to protect those who create. However, the protection of creativity offered by WIPO tends to conflate the reasons for creation with the economic incentives attached to protecting commercial or industrial property from theft. The art described by Bogsch and a drug invented by employees of a pharmaceutical company are each protected by a type of intellectual property, yet the motivation for their creation and how they were inspired could not be more different. WIPO, however, tends to wrap all types of creative work under the rubric of the individual creation as described above, and embrace the associated assumption that without the protection of intellectual property, creators would have no incentive to create.[3]

It is WIPO's goal to ensure that intellectual property is protected in all member states and that all member states understand the importance of such protection. In achieving its goals, WIPO is responsible for the administration of the treaties under its jurisdiction and providing educational opportunities for those who seek to learn about the benefits of strong intellectual property protection, especially officials from the Global South.[4]

WIPO is an organization focused on the protection of intellectual property globally, but its own building and grounds problematize the value of IP as inspiring creativity. Two examples help make this point. First, upon entering WIPO's main entrance, one encounters the granite and marble foyer. One of the most prominent aspects of the foyer is the fountain that takes up an entire wall and is integrated into both the cupola and the granite floor. According to Pierre Braillard, the architect of WIPO's headquarters, the fountain:

> represents the emergence of the world from the mists, represented by white marble, beneath which water, the source of all life, appears as from a spring and trickles down the wall.
>
> Then comes the Earth itself represented by the grey rock. The water gives birth to plant life, which we see as marble that is first pale green and gradually darkens as that life becomes more dense.
>
> At the foot of the wall the water, representing human thought, collects in a marble basin from which five multi-colored ribbons spring forth, representing thought in the five continents. These ribbons, with their ever-changing colors, spread through the entire lobby. They wind in and out at the whim of mankind, broadening as they pass through centuries of enlightenment and narrowing during periods of intellectual austerity.
>
> This cycle, extending from the birth of the world to the present day, culminates in the apotheosis of a sunburst, representing the discovery of nuclear energy.[5]

Such a description locates human creativity and scientific ingenuity in the primordial and evolutionary structures of our humanity. It does not make an economic argument for the protection of intellectual property, but instead suggests that our essence as human beings is tied up with a creative process that is inseparable from a grand narrative of human history.

Second, one of the many fountains gracing the WIPO grounds highlights the complexity of creation and appropriation. This fountain circles the outside of the main conference room; it is 58 meters wide and 3.5 meters high. According to Braillard, the functional purpose of the fountain is to mitigate traffic noise. However, the water nymph sculptures in the fountain are castings of sculptures originally produced by Giambologna, a sixteenth-century Florentine sculptor and can be found in Neptune's fountain on the Piazza Signoria in Florence.

What can we learn from the sculptures in WIPO's fountain? Certainly, the motivations for creating the originals in sixteenth-century Florence had nothing to do with modern copyright. Additionally, they can be copied and brought to WIPO because intellectual property law does not stand in the way. The designers of WIPO's buildings and grounds utilize artistic work outside the realm of property rights while at the same time seeking to make such appropriations by others more difficult in the future. The water nymphs in the fountain may be a testimony to the creative genius of humanity, but they are not a testimony to the value of intellectual property rights.

WIPO's headquarters illustrates the disconnection that happens when one frames creative work primarily in economic terms as intellectual property instead of seeing it as associated with human ingenuity. A market-based system claims that the motivation for innovation is the possibility of economic rewards, but this rather superficial narrative does not fully account for the underlying impulse behind creation, nor does it provide the necessary conditions for future economic development and/or cultural creation. WIPO, however, is focused upon protecting a very narrow segment of human creativity – that done under the rubric of economic incentives.

This chapter seeks to look at WIPO's purpose and practices, along with its possible future. WIPO is an agency whose success relies upon adapting to the intellectual property landscape constructed by its member states. However not all 188 member states hold uniform views about the value or legitimacy of IP, nor is there consensus over the appropriate scope and depth of intellectual property protection. During the Cold War, WIPO dealt with differences surrounding IP as they played out between "communist" and "capitalist" countries. The politics of the Cold War have since been replaced with debates over the role of IP in a global free trade environment and the ongoing tensions between a globalized and developed world and the least developed nations of the Global South who have not benefited from globalization or neoliberal economic policies. The last three decades placed WIPO's efforts to educate people around the world about IP though their comic books, World IP day, summer institutes for legal scholars, reports and much more, within the paradigm of justifying constantly expanding IP protection.[6] Expansion is the result of efforts by the United States to forum shop for more comprehensive protection of what they see as an essential economic driver of the information age and the US economy. First, efforts to go beyond what WIPO could offer in terms of protection via the Berne and Paris Conventions were promulgated through the multilateral TRIPS agreement. When TRIPS proved too "flexible," the United States shifted to TRIPS plus bilateral agreements. The United States has entered into 41 bilateral treaties since signing TRIPS in order to ensure better IP protection abroad.[7]

Today we are faced with newly emerging efforts to develop more tailored "country club" agreements such as the Trans-Pacific Partnership (TPP) that bind trading partners to more comprehensive IP protection amongst more elaborate trade deals. Throughout the evolution of global IP, the role WIPO plays has remained consistent – as an advocate for IP protection because they claim it provides the underlying basis for economic development and creative innovation. WIPO remains committed to IP and its protection as the educational engine of IP boosterism upon which additional trade negotiations can be built.

Despite its pro-IP approach, as a specialized agency of the United Nations and thus responsible for the UN's efforts to encourage "development," WIPO could pursue a different approach to IP and development than the one it has taken so far. As its member countries shift their energies to other venues for defending their IP, something WIPO does not have the capacity to do anyway, this chapter argues that it is time for WIPO to reconsider its adherence to the strong IP approach. Instead WIPO should more critically evaluate the role IP plays in development and how it could support the efforts of the United Nations to foster the millennium goals in ways it currently does not. First, this chapter will briefly describe the history of WIPO, its current position and strategic directions. Then it will offer an alternative vision for what WIPO could be if it chose to balance protection of IP with other important development goals.

WIPO's history

The Bureaux Internationaux Réunis pour la Protection de la Propriété Intellectuelle (The United International Bureau for the Protection of Intellectual Property) began life protecting what was then called industrial property. The "PI" in BIRPI initially stood for *propriété industrielle* (industrial property) until the name was changed to intellectual property in the mid-1950s as the concept of intellectual property was popularized. During the 1950s, international agencies jostled to oversee intellectual property as part of their missions. The ultimate placement of IP protection with what became WIPO was not a foregone conclusion, but the result of adept political maneuvering. Jacques Secrétan, the director of BIRPI between 1953 and 1957[8] argued that while the International Bureau would forge working relationships with other organizations, they should ultimately be in charge of protecting and managing intellectual property internationally.[9] According to Secrétan, if different international organizations were given control over intellectual property issues, we would "end up with several contradictory conventions voted for by the same States."[10] UNESCO, the United Nations agency that hosted the University Copyright Convention and thus also had a claim to IP protection, also recognized the possible problem of multiple venues.[11] In fact, the existence of two different copyright treaties was a result of tension between the assorted views held about copyright protection. Specifically, the United States was not a member of the Berne Convention (and did not join it until 1989) because the Berne Convention protected moral rights, provisions favored by European countries but not included in US copyright law. Thus, the United States had created a separate intellectual property treaty through UNESCO called the Universal Copyright Convention.

The United Nations Conference on Trade and Development (UNCTAD) also had an interest in the protection of intellectual property as it related to technology transfer and development. During the meetings to create WIPO they put the issue of technology transfer on the table and WIPO agreed to help those in the least developed countries by providing the ability for them to attend meetings and work on plans for technology transfer.[12] It should be noted that UNCTAD sought to balance the enforcement of IP with other considerations related to development. Other agencies also had a stake, including the World Health Organization with whom Secrétan had signed a working agreement in the 1950s.[13]

The BIRPI leadership believed that having multiple centers for institutional authority would create contradictions that could not be tolerated because the clash would lead to different intellectual property-related outcomes depending upon the agency involved. Implicit in this argument was the assumption that only WIPO could focus on the protection of intellectual property whereas WHO, UNESCO or UNCTAD would balance intellectual property rights with their central missions of providing health care, cultural support or development. As I've argued elsewhere, reading the minutes of these early meetings, where those involved argued to elevate copyright and patent protection to a new privileged place, where it would be shielded from a requirement to consider balancing intellectual property rights with other interests, demonstrates that the protection of IP above all other possible rights was always contested and that this struggle, which remains ongoing today, is inherent in the tension upon which the agency made its initial claims for legitimacy.

While BIRPI and then WIPO publicly proclaimed a concern about discrepancies between agencies as a possible problem, this seems to be only one aspect of the ultimate agenda. After all, the existence of the UCC and the Berne Convention already created disparity of treatment between the different international conventions, given that the United States created the UCC because it would not agree to all the provisions in the Berne Convention. What becomes clear is that those advocating for WIPO understood their role as to produce the hegemonic discourse on intellectual property and consolidate control over this issue under the WIPO banner.[14] In order to do this, first BIRPI underwent the transformation to WIPO in 1970 and was then formally admitted as a special agency of the United Nations.

In its first report as a UN specialized agency, WIPO stated:

As in the case of all organizations of the United Nations system, one of the main objectives of WIPO is to assist developing countries in their development. WIPO assists developing countries in promoting their industrialization, their commerce and their cultural, scientific and technological development through the modernization of their industrial property and copyright systems and in meeting some of their needs in scientific documentation and the transfer of technology and technical know-how.[15]

As this quote suggests, WIPO couched its existence in terms of development, but its developmental strategy was to create intellectual property structures that met generic international "best practices" instead of facilitating the growth of intellectual property laws through the development of local initiatives on culture, health care and technology transfer. Thus, WIPO remained remote from the cultural lives of those they sought to help, favoring training IP practitioners and lawyers over other methods to spark development.

From the 1970s onwards, WIPO became the preeminent UN agency addressing issues related to intellectual property. While UNESCO continued to host the UCC, when the United States finally did join the Berne Convention in 1989 and the Soviet Union collapsed, the UCC became essentially irrelevant. That being said, WIPO's existence could have evolved quite differently if other United Nations agencies had been successful in integrating the issue of intellectual property into their missions instead of outsourcing it to a new agency. In other words, a very different history of international intellectual property could have been written if intellectual property had been diffused amongst other United Nations agencies who may have sought to balance its protection more intentionally with their other important goals – protection of health, education, culture and development. In the next section I will fast forward to what WIPO is doing today and how its goals have (or have not) shifted since its inception as a United Nations special agency.

WIPO today

Over the decades WIPO has sided with the maximalist approach to IP protection, perhaps to stay relevant to the changing geopolitics of IP, but also because of the way WIPO frames its mission and goals as an organization. Certainly, there are important critiques of treaties WIPO administers to consider.[16] Despite these critiques, WIPO has continued to build its programming upon the claim that strong IP protection will enhance economic development and that IP provides the necessary incentive to create. While economic development has always been part of WIPO's mission, developing nations and civil society groups have now challenged WIPO to demonstrate that their work can (and does) enhance economic development. In 2008/2009, WIPO reframed their strategic goals in the context of a strategic realignment program. In this section I'll briefly describe WIPO and its current trajectory.

WIPO's mission is "to lead the development of a balanced and effective international intellectual property (IP) system that enables innovation and creativity for the benefit of all."[17] As discussed in the last section, the possibility of development sparked by the protection of intellectual property is the justification for why WIPO achieved special organization status within the United Nations. However, "development" for WIPO has primarily taken the form of institution building to protect intellectual property. Even today, WIPO continues to assess itself based upon how often it communicates its message of strong intellectual property rights, not on if the institutions and legal framework it introduces around the world actually facilitate development.

However, with the introduction of the WTO and the TRIPS agreement in the mid-1990s, WIPO's position as the preeminent agency focused on intellectual property began to erode. In the context of a need to further expand and protect intellectual property globally, countries like the United States and its allies saw WIPO as mired in the concerns of the Global South and sought to stake out new negotiating territory where protection of IP could be made more absolute. While the evolution of the TRIPS agreement was not without significant controversy (global implementation of TRIPS was delayed by issues of development, with the least developed countries only meeting the TRIPS-related goals in 2006, ten years after TRIPS was signed) its adoption left WIPO seeking to clarify its role in the new multilateral world of IP as a trade issue.

TRIPS also raised considerable resistance to the idea that global harmonization of strong IP rights would ultimately be beneficial to the Global South. As a result, both the WTO and WIPO found themselves mired in the debates of their member states over the acceptable scope and depth of IP coverage while global civil society groups clearly favored a weakened IP regime. Within this larger political fight, the moment could have been ripe to change WIPO's positioning on matters of IP. For example, not only did WIPO introduce and take up issues of traditional knowledge during the 2000s, but in 2008 they also initiated a broader conversation about development and implemented their development agenda, at the behest of member states and civil society groups who sought to use WIPO to highlight the concerns of the Global South.

Despite these efforts, the underlying pro-IP approach taken by WIPO remains relatively untouched. In WIPO's 2006–2007 program and budget, five strategic goals are listed:

- to promote an IP culture;
- to integrate IP into national development policies and programs;
- to develop international IP laws and standards;
- to deliver quality services in global IP protection systems; and
- to increase the efficiency of WIPO's management and support processes.[18]

Each of these goals is accompanied by a description of programs deemed integral to accomplishing the goals, adding up to 31 independent programs proposed for the 2006/07 year.[19] The 2007 goal, to promote an IP culture, relies heavily upon developing an educational agenda. WIPO understood that policing the world was not sufficient – one must win the hearts and minds of the people through education. Thus, WIPO seeks to educate the world about the benefits of intellectual property because once people believe in the idea of intellectual property they will help make the world safe for it. To achieve this goal, WIPO hosts workshops, forums, training classes and even its own summer university program to communicate the value of intellectual property protection to the world at large.

Education is also central because WIPO does not claim, nor does it want to be the world police for IPRs. There is the understanding that WIPO will make the world safer for creative work by building the infrastructure necessary to protect intellectual property and developing rules and regulations for ensuring that "piracy" does not occur. Furthermore, there is the explicit argument made by WIPO that protecting IPRs is essential for future economic development. This line of reasoning is described in their pamphlet, *What Is Intellectual Property?* In this short pamphlet, WIPO first describes what intellectual property is and then argues that it should be promoted and protected because "the promotion and protection of intellectual property spurs economic growth, creates new jobs and industries, and enhances the quality and enjoyment of life."[20] One might note the irony in having to educate people about the centrality of a concept that is so crucial to economic development.

In December 2008 WIPO introduced nine strategic goals as part of the "first phase of a comprehensive strategic realignment process within the organization."[21] These goals include:

- Balanced Evolution of the International Normative Framework for IP
- Provision of Premier Global IP Services
- Facilitating the Use of IP for Development
- Coordination and Development of Global IP Infrastructure
- World Reference Source for IP Information and Analysis
- International Cooperation on Building Respect for IP
- Addressing IP in Relation to Global Policy Issues
- A Responsive Communications Interface between WIPO, its Member States and All Stakeholders.

While the language is different in the 2006 goals versus 2008, the concerted effort on the part of civil society groups and countries from the Global South to push WIPO to consider development in its assessment of itself has not resulted in a substantial difference between the earlier stated strategic goals and the ones issued in 2008. Rather, the central and underlying mission of the organization remains the same – to advocate for an international system of IP protection and continue to work on creating what they now call a "global IP infrastructure."

WIPO's foray into traditional knowledge has also met with limited success. As the issue of traditional knowledge rose in international importance and it became clear that many indigenous peoples felt their knowledge was appropriated, often through the very IP systems embraced by WIPO, an effort to develop a way of discussing traditional knowledge within the framework supported by WIPO commenced. The Intergovernmental Committee on Intellectual Property and Genetic Resources, Traditional Knowledge and Folklore was tasked with establishing some operational norms for protecting such knowledge.

Their efforts were, of course, framed by the prevailing language of IP and did not easily fit with systems of traditional knowledge. The challenge of translating traditional knowledge systems into one that only values creativity and knowledge that is commercialized proved difficult. In 2012, at least some indigenous peoples opted out of the process and stepped away from WIPO's efforts.[22] The work of the committee continues but remains controversial.[23]

In addition to its internal debates about development and traditional knowledge, WIPO today must also be considered in the context of the TRIPs agreement, but also in the context of the emergence of new plurilateral trade agreements that include even more restrictive IP provisions. These "country club" agreements include more select trading partners than do the broad multilateral efforts of the WTO and WIPO.[24] The exclusionary nature of these agreements is significant. The Trans-Pacific Partnership (TPP) for example, has excluded China while still capturing a significant portion of trans-Pacific trade.[25]

The Anti-Counterfeiting Trade Agreement (ACTA), the Trans-Pacific Partnership (TPP) and the Transatlantic Trade and Investment Partnership (TTIP) all involve closed-door negotiations and each agreement pushes the signatory governments to move beyond the flexibilities built into TRIPs to further expand IP protection.[26] Despite its many failures, as a multilateral effort, TRIPs did include a variety of flexibilities that the Global South was able to utilize. These new agreements are more restrictive, especially when it comes to issues such as public health and access to medicine. For example, the TPP does not include language ensuring generic medicine could make it to market as soon as the patent expired.[27] As Patel argues, the TPP puts IP rights well above human rights.[28] While ACTA was ultimately halted by massive global protests,[29] the TTP and the TTIP remain alive despite criticism of their IP provisions. The secrecy of the TPP (and the other agreements) has led to higher IP protection and enforcement standards than would have been generated if the "more transparent and multilateral World Intellectual Property Organization (WIPO)" had been used for negotiation.[30] All things considered, despite WIPO's commitment to what could be considered to be an IP maximalist approach, their multilateral membership means that such debates must happen more visibly than what is now the norm in trade negotiations. As a result, while WIPO is not without its problems, in the contemporary context it seems like a far better organization to balance competing IP interests than any of the newer international regimes favored by the United States and some of its trading partners.

I have elsewhere argued that one could test the viability of implementing intellectual property as a model of development by introducing the counterfactual – what would the world look like if WIPO didn't exist – and concluded that for the Global South there would be absolutely no difference.[31] In the post-development agenda era, WIPO has implemented a comprehensive assessment strategy that is intended to help demonstrate the value WIPO brings to the world via its approach to IP protection. This process is relatively convoluted and bureaucratized. Success is still measured in terms of reports written, new educational courses held, and organizational structures. Given that even with a push to consider development, it may be that WIPO cannot alter its path substantively. That being said, in the final section of this chapter I would like to sketch an alternative future of WIPO and how it might consider adapting to the needs of the Global South while working in conjunction with other UN agencies.

A different WIPO story

What if WIPO did not become a vertical silo of intellectual property protection, but instead worked with other UN agencies such as UNESCO, WHO and UNCTAD to integrate issues of copyright and patent protection into their everyday operation. In essence, what if we fragmented IP protection and allowed it to move forward only when paired with the goals of development and technology transfer? While the reasons developing countries joined WIPO remain unclear – though it is likely many joined either prior to full decolonization or in an effort to attain a level of international legitimacy – it is likely that an intended goal was to improve development in their home countries. It is also important to remember that WIPO's mission should be informed by the needs of all its member countries, not simply those with powerful industrial centers. To that end, and consistent with its mission under the UN, WIPO could begin with education, but not simply education in terms of intellectual property rights protection.

Instead, what if WIPO worked with the United Nations Education, Scientific and Cultural Organization (UNESCO) to build a clearinghouse for textbooks and scientific discoveries that could help develop the educational background for future innovation by providing the necessary materials for development? One of the key concerns raised by those seeking better access to knowledge (A2K) is that textbooks can be prohibitively expensive and that cracking down on photocopies in developing nations harms access to knowledge.

What if partnerships were made with existing educational institutions and with organizations working on providing education to ensure that illiteracy was reduced and education throughout the Global South was prioritized over efforts to halt access to the vital materials necessary to learn? What if, instead of fighting photocopy shops and actively supporting the copyright claims of the large multinational corporate owners of most textbooks, WIPO and UNESCO embarked upon an open access textbook program that would make foundational knowledge easy to access and available for free? Imagine a world where open access textbooks on medicine, engineering, social science, law, chemistry and much more were developed and distributed globally. Instead of working to protect the profits of publishing companies, what if knowledge were intentionally shared to improve development.

Associated with access to knowledge is the issue of domestic education in health, engineering and agriculture, all much needed areas within the developing world. UNESCO could take the lead on this project and WIPO would be vital in supporting UNESCO with the necessary technical information regarding how to structure an open access program and share knowledge. What if globally we were to recognize that the goals of education should take priority over the protection of intellectual property?

Complimenting the textbook strategy to facilitate development, WIPO could work with the United Nations Conference on Trade and Development (UNCTAD) to create an agricultural clearinghouse where appropriate agricultural technologies were licensed and shared with the developing world. Given the growing importance of food sovereignty and the concerns raised by ownership of seeds, such a project would stand in stark contrast to the corporatization of seeds and their control via restrictive licensing agreements. Instead of prioritizing seed monopolization, WIPO could side with farmer's rights and the Global South in its efforts to attain food security.[32] Furthermore, with a goal of providing appropriate technology, WIPO in association with UNCTAD could become an engine for appropriate and sustainable development instead of a vehicle for making profits for multinational corporations.

WIPO could also develop a technology transfer process associated with the new Patent Cooperation Treaty. The tech transfer process could provide developing countries with legal support in negotiating licensing agreements with companies in the industrialized North. Entire patent portfolios could be licensed when the resulting technology could improve development potential within the Global South. Instead of focusing on its Patents for Humanity project, which is a form of greenwashing for global multinationals, WIPO could work on extending technical knowledge as cheaply as possible to the Global South. Imagine a world where the Global South could leapfrog the environmentally destructive technologies of the industrial world and instead embrace new forms of energy generation, water purification, food production and more that would substantially improve the lives of those living in poverty today. WIPO, in association with the United Nations Industrial Development Organization (UNIDO), could provide expert assistance on the ground to build facilities and encourage innovation. Technologies could be licensed at affordable prices and with the intent of creating the necessary infrastructure for health care, transportation and industrial development. If WIPO used its role as a clearinghouse for patents to identify the types of technologies most suitable for a developing economy and work to provide these technologies to the Global South then more substantive development might be possible.

Finally, recognizing the importance of public health for a viable economy means that WIPO could work with WHO to ensure that access existed to essential medicines. WIPO could use their patent clearinghouse to identify the key medicines that could be licensed affordably and then work with other UN agencies to establish the necessary infrastructure throughout the Global South to produce these medicines locally and help facilitate a distribution network by supporting public health clinics, staffed by those who receive an education because it is now possible to afford the textbooks to study. Such access would not be determined by who could afford to pay for medicine, nor would basic health care as a human right take back seat to protection of pharmaceutical patents. Generics would be widely available and WHO could coordinate the distribution of these essential medicines to those in need.

In all cases, WIPO could understand its mission as supporting other UN agencies in their efforts to improve development. Instead of working to develop offices and model laws in developing countries to frame IP in terms beneficial to the United States and its most wealthy trading partners, WIPO could first work to create the conditions for development and then allow the laws that will govern IP to emerge out of the process itself. The economic literature demonstrated decades ago that only after sufficient economic development has been achieved will countries turn towards stronger IP protection.

When all is said and done, it isn't clear this rather idealistic scenario would facilitate development better than the reality. After all, UN agencies have been working on achieving their development goals for decades and have categorically failed if measured by economic conditions in the least developed countries. If anything, the failure to achieve economic development like that found in the developed world suggests that more is at work here than creating the conditions of protecting knowledge and innovation. Perhaps there is something inherently wrong with approaching development through the neoliberal model of free trade and structural adjustment. However, such a scenario goes well beyond the scope of intellectual property protection and needs to be saved for another day.

I want to conclude this chapter by bringing us full circle to Geneva. This chapter sought to examine the impact of WIPO on LDC countries. However, one must question the ability of an organization to encourage the spread of a message about the value of intellectual property internationally when violations of copyright law exist just down the street from their own headquarters. If one were to head through Geneva towards the city of Carouge, one would pass a bar called "Central Perk," where the sign reads, "we're your F.R.I.E.N.D.S." Despite the fact this Central Perk is a bar, not a coffee shop, and no one was especially friendly, it is clear that the name and likeness is appropriated from the popular hit television show *Friends*.

The presence of Central Perk is another irony of WIPO's existence. If Geneva is the headquarters of WIPO (and the WTO) and yet this bar can exist within a few miles from both headquarters, what really are these organizations doing? Of course, it is possible this local bar has permission from the television show to utilize their name and likeness, but I doubt it. Instead, it makes one wonder exactly how the world would be different if WIPO didn't exist, given that its presence has not even made an impact a few miles down the road.

Notes

1 Portions of this chapter appeared first in a paper presented at the CopySouth Working Group's meeting in 2012.

2 Arpad Bogsch, *The First Twenty-Five Years of the World Intellectual Property Organization from 1967 to 1992*, WIPO Publication No. 881 (E) (International Bureau of Intellectual Property, 1992), 71–72.

3 WIPO, *What Is Intellectual Property?* WIPO Publication No. 450 (E), http://www.wipo.int/edocs/pubdocs/en/intproperty/450/wipo_pub_450.pdf. Regarding Patents, WIPO states: "Without the rewards provided by the patent system, researchers and inventors would have little incentive to continue producing better and more efficient products for consumers" (p. 5). Regarding copyrights it states, "Giving authors, artists and creators incentives in the form of recognition and fair economic reward increases their activity and output and can also enhance the results" (p. 21).

4 For an important new work on WIPO see: Christopher May, *The World Intellectual Property Organization: Resurgence and the Development Agenda* (Routledge, 2007).

5 Pierre Braillard, "The Blue Tower of WIPO on the Place des Nations in Geneva," in *The First Twenty-Five Years of the World Intellectual Property Organization from 1967 to 1992*, ed. Arpad Bogsch, WIPO Publication no. 881 (E) (International Bureau of Intellectual Property, 1992), 96–97.

6 Matthew David and Debora Halbert, *Owning the World of Ideas: Intellectual Property and Global Network Capitalism* (Sage, 2015).

7 Katrina Moberg, "Private Industry's Impact on U.S. Trade Law and International Intellectual Property Law: A Study of Post-TRIPS U.S. Bilateral Agreements and the Capture of the USTR," *Journal of the Patent and Trademark Office Society* 96 (2014): 228–256.

8 The World Statesman, "International Organizations," World Intellectual Property Organization, http://www.worldstatesmen.org/International_Organizations2.html#WIPO.

9 Jacques Secrétan, Fourth William Henry Ballantyne Lecture, "The Work of the Berne Bureaux in the International Field at the Present Time," Lecture delivered to the British Group of the Association at the Old Hall, March 12, 1957. WIPO Library, 10.

10 Ibid., 18.

11 WIPO, "Records of the Intellectual Property Conference of Stockholm, June 11 to July 14, 1967," Geneva, 1971 (minutes for the meeting to create WIPO), 1088.

12 Ibid., 12–13.

13 Jacques Secrétan, "The Work of the Berne Bureaux," 10.

14 UNESCO clearly stated that they would not withdraw their own right to define copyright issues given that the mission of their organization was wrapped up with the protection of copyright. WIPO, "Records of the

Intellectual Property Conference of Stockholm, June 11 to July 14, 1967," Geneva, 1971 (minutes for the meeting to create WIPO), 1224; Report on the Work of Main Committee V (World Intellectual Property Organization) by Joseph Voyame, Rapporteur.

15 WIPO, "Report of the World Intellectual Property Organization to the Economic and Social Council of the United Nations at Its Fifty-Ninth Session," Analytical Summary for the year 1974, Geneva, April 30, 1975, 13.

16 Alan Story, "Burn Berne: Why the Leading Copyright Convention Must Be Repealed," *Houston Law Review* 40, no. 3 (2003): 763–801; Carlos Correa, *The WIPO Patent Agenda: The Risks for Developing Countries* (South Centre, 2002); Matthew Rimmer, "Patents for Humanity," *The World Intellectual Property Organization WIPO Journal* 3, no. 2 (2012): 196–221.

17 Inside WIPO, www.wipo. int/about-wipo/en/.

18 World Intellectual Property Organization, *What Is WIPO*, http:// www.wipo.int/about-wipo/en/what_is_ wipo.html (visited February 8, 2007).

19 World Intellectual Property Organization, Proposed Program and Budget for 2006/07, Presented by the Director General, http://www.wipo.int/ edocs/mdocs/govbody/en/wo_pbc_8/ wo_pbc_8_3_pub.pdf (visited February 8, 2007).

20 WIPO, *What Is Intellectual Property?*, 3.

21 WIPO's Strategic Goals, www. wipo.int/about-wipo/en/goals.html.

22 Asia Indigenous Peoples Pact. "IPs to Withdraw from Active Participation in World Intellectual Property Organization (WIPO) Inter Governmental Committee," *Asia Indigenous Peoples Pact*, February 23, 2012, http://www.aippnet.org/home/ daily-sharing/724-ipss-decide-to-

withdraw-from-active-participation- in-world-intellectual-property- organization-wipo-inter-governmental- committee.

23 Catherine Saez, "Discussions on Genetic Resources, Traditional Knowledge Resume at WIPO against Stormy Background," *Intellectual Property Watch*, February 11, 2016, http://www.ip-watch.org/2016/02/11/ discussions-on-genetic-resources- traditional-knowledge-resume-at-wipo- against-stormy-background/.

24 Peter K. Yu, "ACTA and Its Complex Politics," *The WIPO Journal* 3, no. 1 (2011): 1–16; Peter Yu, "Deja Vu in the International Intellectual Property Regime," in *Sage Handbook of Intellectual Property*, ed. Matthew David and Debora J. Halbert (Sage, 2014), 113–129.

25 Daniel S. Hamilton, "America's Mega-Regional Trade Diplomacy: Comparing TPP and TTIP," *The International Spectator* 49, no. 1 (March 2014): 86.

26 Michael A. Carrier, "SOPA, PIPA, ACTA, TPP: An Alphabet Soup of Innovation-Stifling Copyright Legislation and Agreements," *Northwestern Journal of Technology and Intellectual Property* 11 (2013): 21–163; Erik Kain, "If You Thought SOPA Was Bad, Just Wait until You Meet ACTA," *Forbes*, January 23, 2013, http://www.forbes.com/sites/ erikkain/2012/01/23/if-you-thought- sopa-was-bad-just-wait-until-you-meet- acta/; Erik Kain, "IP Protection Standards in TPP Represent the Downside of the Trans-Pacific Partnership," *Forbes*, January 25, 2012, http://www.forbes. com/sites/erikkain/2012/01/25/ip- protection-standards-in-tpp-represent- the-dark-side-of-the-trans-pacific- partnership/.

27 Roma Patel, "A Public Health Imperative: The Need for Meaningful Change in the Trans-Pacific Partnership's

Intellectual Property Chapter," *Minnesota Journal of Law, Science and Technology* 16 (Winter 2015): 503.

28 Ibid., 507.

29 David Lee, "Europe Takes to Streets over ACTA," *BBC News*, February 11, 2012, http://www.bbc.co.uk/news/technology-16999497.

30 David S. Levine, "Bring in the Nerds: Secrecy, National Security, and the Creation of International Intellectual Property Law," *Cardozo Arts and Entertainment Law Review* 30 (2012): 117.

31 Debora J. Halbert, "What If . . . WIPO Never Existed?" *CopySouth Research Group and Network*, September 7, 2009, http://copysouth.org/portal/node/10.

32 Chidi Oguamanam, "Farmers' Rights and the Intellectual Property Dynamic in Agriculture," in David and Halbert, *Sage Handbook of Intellectual Property*, 238–57.

11 | WHAT IS INTELLECTUAL PROPERTY?

Blayne Haggart

Introduction

It is hard to overstate the influence of intellectual property law on our lives. It affects the creation of, and our access to, high and low culture. It sets the prices of life-saving drugs. It ensures that design companies like Apple make billions even though they long ago outsourced any actual manufacturing to offshore companies (whose take from products like a $700 iPad is dwarfed by Apple's).[1] It can even determine whether farmers have the right to fix the physical tractors they bought and thought they owned.[2] Furthermore, all signs indicate that it will continue to increase in importance, becoming an important power vector in the global political economy.

And yet, intellectual property (IP) remains little understood by most individuals and policymakers. IP law has a well-deserved reputation for complexity and opacity. Centuries of domestic legislation and litigation, and international treaty-making have created an ever-expanding, daunting, interconnected legislative edifice, the effects of which are subject to disagreement even among the intellectual property lawyers responsible for its creation and maintenance. From the perspective of a regular citizen, the law often seems to operate in defiance of common sense. In the United Kingdom, for instance, it is still illegal to rip a legally purchased CD for your personal use.[3]

In part because of this complexity, intellectual property debates often deteriorate rapidly into debates about basic morality that have little to do with intellectual property's actual objectives. Accusations of "theft," "stealing" and "piracy" abound, muddying the policy waters and obscuring the fact that intellectual property rights are not supposed to promote an individual or group's interests, but those of society as a whole.

The conflicting interest groups and moralities involved in copyright policy debates can make it difficult for non-experts (and even some experts) to reach an informed judgment about what a reasonable IP regime should look like and do. Given the rising frequency with which we come across "intellectual property" in our everyday lives, citizens need to have at least as good an understanding of the purposes and effects of IP as we do of other policy matters. Most people may not understand, say, the intricacies of their country's tax code, but they likely understand its basic purposes and justifications, and roughly how it functions.

Despite IP law's opacity, intellectual property's stated purpose – to encourage the creation and dissemination of knowledge and culture – is relatively straightforward and easy to grasp. This chapter argues that intellectual property is most usefully thought of as a form of knowledge governance; that is, as rules that determine how society creates and disseminates knowledge. It is an historically contingent, market-based answer to the question of how to encourage both the protection and dissemination of knowledge. While historically IP policy has been driven by power politics and value-laden discourses, this chapter argues that the field of economics offers the most useful approach to considering the *society-wide* effects of intellectual property. That said, the evidence that intellectual property actually delivers on its knowledge-creation objective is shockingly flimsy for an institution that has survived for hundreds of years. Rather than being an evidence-based policy, the intellectual property regime as we know it is largely the outcome of bargains amongst interest groups, with relatively little concern given to the effects of IP law on society.

This chapter is structured as follows. First, it provides a brief overview of the characteristics of intellectual property, highlighting the protection–dissemination paradox that lies at its heart. The second section outlines the politics that drive IP policy. The third presents an argument for analyzing IP laws as public policy, through an empirically based economic lens that emphasizes IP's role in promoting a socially optimal level of knowledge and cultural creation. It then applies this framework to the case of Aaron Swartz's prosecution for hacking the JSTOR academic journal article database at MIT as an example. The chapter then offers some guidelines for how we can cut through the legal thicket and moral arguments, and engage in a productive dialogue on how to reform the laws that govern something so fundamental as knowledge itself. It concludes with some final thoughts.

Most of this chapter is focused on the US intellectual property debate because it is the driving force behind global IP reform. While all countries face similar issues, their experiences, and their IP politics, are all somewhat different. That said, the principles developed in this chapter are generally applicable.

What is intellectual property?

Intellectual property is the currently dominant form of regulation governing the creation and use of knowledge. While it originated in Europe, IP law has spread to become the dominant way that we regulate knowledge worldwide. Roughly speaking, the three main categories of IP are copyright (creative works such as books, music and film, but also computer software and things like hull designs), patents (industrial processes, such as drug formulas and Amazon's one-click shopping) and trademarks (identifying marks, such as McDonald's Golden Arches, but also the phrase "Let's get ready to rumble").[4] Intellectual property is designed to commodify abstract works so that they can be bought and sold in a market economy.

Intellectual property is a state-created form of protection that provides IP owners with limited rights to determine how this knowledge may be used, including the right to buy or sell the IP. It commodifies knowledge. These rights, or privileges, allow for things such as music and drug formulas to be bought and sold, and limit the ability of others to use, or copy, these otherwise abstract ideas. In a market economy, the concern is that because it often takes a great deal of time and resources to come up with an idea, but it is relatively trivial to copy it, without some form of protection, there will be a suboptimal level of creation and invention. Consequently, intellectual property is designed to provide creators with certain rights that will allow them (potentially) to profit from their creation.

The protection–dissemination paradox In popular debates, intellectual property is usually thought of exclusively in terms of the protections that it provides creators for their work. This view, however, misunderstands both the objectives of intellectual property law and the fundamental nature of knowledge. Intellectual property law – like all rules governing the creation and use of knowledge and culture – involves striking a balance between what Doern and Sharaput call its *protection* and *dissemination* functions.[5] As noted above, protection in a market economy is required to ensure that the IP owner (who, again, may not be the author/creator) is able to appropriate some economic return for their work.

Knowledge, to be socially useful, must be shared with others. This is the only way in which new knowledge and culture can be created; it is the only way, as economists are increasingly recognizing, that economic innovation can occur. Despite the Romantic notion of the individual author and inventor, knowledge and culture creation is always and everywhere a social process, the individual author a "conceit" of intellectual property law.[6] Knowledge is cumulative: "Every artist is a cannibal, every poet is a thief,"[7] or as Bono's intellectual precursor, Sir Isaac Newton once remarked, "If I have seen further, it is by standing on the shoulders of giants."

Intellectual property rules, by setting the terms of access to existing knowledge, necessarily shape the direction and content of future knowledge. Granting current intellectual property holders full control over their works – the position of many intellectual property-based industries and authors – would provide them with a veto over the future direction of economic and cultural change. Economically, such protection would allow firms to stave off competitors because they would set the terms on which newcomers would use existing knowledge to innovate and compete.

As a result, intellectual property law necessarily limits these rights in order to avoid just such monopolistic outcomes. Copyright and patents, for example, are limited in time – generally, life of the author plus 70 years in the United States for copyright, and 20 years for patents, so that this knowledge can (eventually) be disseminated more widely, and copied, improved upon by others, and transformed into new knowledge. IP law also includes many rules allowing for knowledge to be used without seeking permission or requiring payment. For example, copyright laws often allow the copying of copyrighted works for the purposes of reporting, research or criticism, while drug patents can often be overruled to deal with pandemics.[8] Because IP laws must encourage both protection and dissemination, these rules are not *exceptions* to IP rights, they are *fundamental* to a functioning IP regime and should be thought of as co-equal with IP's monopoly rights.

While IP debates tend to focus on creators and IP owners, in fact, the main purpose of intellectual property laws is *not* the allocation of rights to individuals or groups. Rather, it is to ensure that an appropriate amount of knowledge and culture is created for the use and enjoyment of *society as a whole*. This point is embedded in Article 1, Section 8, Clause 8 of the US Constitution, which provides Congress with the power "To promote the Progress of Science and useful Arts, by securing for limited Times to Authors and Inventors the exclusive Right to their respective Writings and Discoveries." Here, the exclusive rights of "Authors and Inventors" are clearly the means by which the end of increasing *socially beneficial* knowledge is to be secured. Because knowledge must be communicated in order to be useful, and because it is seen as undesirable to give current IP holders a monopoly over the future direction of knowledge, these rights are limited in both time and scope. In short, while current intellectual property discourse usually focuses on protecting creators, IP law is actually designed with *future* creators in mind, to ensure a sufficient supply of future creative works.

A similar point was made in a September 2016 Indian court ruling involving academic publishers suing a photocopying kiosk for unauthorized copying. It found that photocopying textbooks was allowed as "fair use" under Indian copyright law. As it noted:

> Copyright, especially in literary works, is thus not an inevitable, divine, or natural right that confers on authors the absolute ownership of their creations. It is designed rather to stimulate activity and progress in the arts for the intellectual enrichment of the public. Copyright is intended to increase and not to impede the harvest of knowledge. It is intended to motivate the creative activity of authors and inventors in order to benefit the public.[9]

Ideally, IP law should be about finding the optimal balance between protection and dissemination. Unfortunately, an optimal balance that works for all time can never be reached for the simple reason that intellectual property's protection and dissemination functions are fundamentally irreconcilable. Strengthening knowledge protection necessarily inhibits its dissemination. As a result, the balance between protection and dissemination must be politically negotiated, and is always contestable.

Power and (lack of) evidence: the drivers of intellectual property policy

To an outsider not indoctrinated in the nuances of intellectual property law, one of the most remarkable aspects of IP policy is the extent to which empirical evidence is absent from the policymaking process. With the possible exception of the War on Drugs, it is hard to think of another area of economic policy that has lasted for so long – centuries, in this case – with so little attention paid to the question of whether it is fulfilling its fundamental objective, which, in the case of intellectual property, is the promotion of "the Progress of Science and useful Arts." For example, when proposing and negotiating international agreements, governments typically provide analyses of the anticipated effects of policies such as lower tariff barriers and regulatory harmonization. However, although the strengthening of the protection dimension of intellectual property rights has been a prominent objective of international economic agreements for over 20 years, attempts at quantifying their effects is rarely, if ever made. While it is admittedly difficult to forecast the effect of IP changes on innovation, and thus economic growth, even simpler calculations, such as the inevitability of higher drug prices and restrictions of books moving out of copyright, are absent from analyses of recent agreements such as the Trans-Pacific Partnership (TPP) conducted by the World Bank.[10]

This neglect of intellectual property's effect on economic activity in analyses of trade agreements is not unusual.[11] Intellectual property also was not factored into the 2008 headline figure Canada and the European Union used to tout the benefits of the Canada-Europe Trade Agreement, their (currently in limbo) economic agreement.[12] Similar to the World Bank report, that document focused on tariff and non-tariff barriers, and liberalization of bilateral trade in services. Similarly, multiple official reviews of the United Kingdom's intellectual property system have "deplored the lack of [economic] evidence to support policy judgments."[13]

In the absence of a reliance on evidence, IP policy tends to be based on, and can be explained almost completely in terms of, interest-group politics and the relative political power of these groups. More specifically, the current global IP regime has been expanding in a largely one-way march toward tighter IP rights, including "(a) a significant *shrinkage of the legal domains of the commons of open source*;

(b) a related (but not fully overlapping) *extension of* the domain of *matters considered patentable*; and (c) a significant *extension of the depth and breadth* of patents themselves."[14] This 30-year expansion dates to US-based decisions in the 1970s.[15] Key IP industries, such as the pharmaceutical industry, convinced the US government that the solution to then-dominant concerns about the potential loss of economic hegemony lay in stronger IP protection. This argument has had lasting effects: the United States has treated the protection of intellectual property as a matter of national security since the mid-to-late 2000s.[16]

The United States has been the main state driver of the global expansion of ever-stronger intellectual property rights. As Sell and Drahos and Braithwaite document, this preference for stronger IP was institutionalized within its international trade policy, with the United States negotiating trade agreements that exchange access to the US market for its partners' implementation of domestic intellectual property reforms.[17] Internationally, the turning point was the US-driven adoption of the 1995 Agreement on Trade-Related Aspects of Intellectual Property Rights (TRIPS) as part of the World Trade Organization. TRIPS instituted for the first time an enforceable global floor for intellectual property rights, and a system that has been criticized for imposing a developed-country standard that is not necessarily appropriate for developing economies.[18] Just as most individuals are only now starting to understand what IP even is, very few of the countries that signed onto TRIPS fully understood the implications of the agreement.[19] TRIPS plays a key role in intellectual property's global political economy, serving as the (enforceable) normative framework within which intellectual property reforms are discussed worldwide. In addition to TRIPS, the United States plays a key role in exporting ever-stronger IP rights via bilateral and plurilateral trade agreements. Internationally, developed countries, particularly the United States and the European Union, continue to set the (ever-rising) IP standard for developed countries, both bilaterally and through the World Intellectual Property Organization (WIPO), the leading international intellectual property institution. As Drahos summarizes the situation, "Developing countries are encircled in the [IP] standard-setting process. TRIPS sets minimum standards. Bilaterally, the bar on intellectual property standards continues to be raised. When developing countries turn to WIPO for assistance, more often than not they are put on a TRIPS-plus path."[20]

Within this international framework, which includes the powerful effect of norms-setting by powerful states, TRIPS and WIPO, intellectual property's domestic politics feature a similar mix of interest-group politics and lack of politicization. Until very recently, IP law was the concern of only those interest groups directly affected by what was seen as an obscure area of commercial law. For example, in Mexico, a 2003 extension of the term of copyright protection to a world-leading life of the author plus 100 years attracted almost no debate and passed almost unanimously.[21] Similarly, in Canada IP was not historically a matter of public interest and was attended to only by interest groups.[22] The same pattern largely held in the United States since the negotiation of the 1909 *Copyright Act*, where copyright laws effectively were negotiated amongst interest groups (in the music, motion picture and publishing industries, for example), with Congress approving the resulting legislation. This process emerged in response to "the dilemma of updating and simplifying a body of law that seemed too complicated and arcane for legislative revision."[23] While for Congress, getting various interest groups to compromise on a law was treated as equivalent to representing the public interest, the public was not directly represented, with little-to-no direct attention as to whether the law would (or did) actually spur the creation of knowledge and culture. IP was, and continues to be, evaluated as an adversarial zero-sum game of winners and losers, rather than from the overall societal perspective.

One of the possible reasons for the absence of this societal perspective is the dominance of legal studies in the intellectual property policy arena, and the relative absence of economists in the policymaking process. While IP is economic policy – it provides the framework within which abstract concepts can be bought and sold – legal scholar Pamela Samuelson remarks that "as compared with other fields of economic regulation, particularly antitrust law, economics has had very little influence thus far in the intellectual property law and the policymaking process."[24] She argues – speaking specifically about copyright, although her insight is valid for intellectual property generally – that this lack of influence on the policymaking process is the result of "the tight nexus between the copyright industry and the policy-making community."[25]

Intellectual property, through the eyes of economics

In contrast to the adversarial approach inherent in current IP policymaking, economic analyses tend to start from analyses of the protection–dissemination balance's effect on the *social* provision of knowledge, that IP is a double-edged sword: it increases the rewards of innovation, but also "increases the cost of creation."[26] At best, economics can be said to be agnostic about IP's overall effect, in theory and practice. One reason for this skepticism is the constant focus on how IP's incentive/protection effect can be swamped by its potential to restrict competition and access to knowledge. Economic analyses begin with the fact that strong IP rights provide IP owners with a way to engage in "rent-seeking behaviour"[27] that allows them to shield themselves from competition and restrict future knowledge creation.[28]

Stronger intellectual property laws, in this view, *always* create monopolistic pressure, providing IP holders with disproportionate market power. The only question, then, is whether these monopoly rights can be justified by their end result. As Hurt and Schumann remark, if copyright (in this case) is theoretically inefficient, one must look to the actual effect of actually existing regimes to determine if "it is held to be a necessary supplement to the free market in promoting the best allocation of scarce resources according to the priorities of human wants."[29] They conclude: "we can say that the traditional assumption that copyrights enhance the general welfare is at least subject to attack on theoretical grounds; the subject certainly deserves more investigation and less self-righteous moral defence."[30] In short, it is not enough to say that IP provides creators with a reward; we must examine the trade-offs effect on the creation and dissemination of knowledge for society as a whole.

Economist Fritz Machlup's much-quoted conclusion from 1958 summarizes the state of analysis even today as a mix of theoretical and empirical skepticism and a lack of knowledge about IP's full effects:

> If we did not have a patent system, it would be irresponsible, on the basis of our present knowledge of its economic consequences, to recommend instituting one. But since we have had a patent system for a long time, it would be irresponsible, on the basis of our present knowledge, to recommend abolishing it.[31]

Even economist Kenneth Arrow's foundational 1962 article arguing that the negative monopoly rights in knowledge could theoretically be justified for incentivizing knowledge creation and dissemination ended by noting that "there is clear need for further study of alternative methods of compensation."[32] Forty years later, however, economists Ruth Towse and Rudi Holzhauer remarked that "we still cannot say with any conviction that in general IP law stimulates creativity or promotes innovation, though it may contribute to the process of communication between producers and consumers. That is no argument for not having it, but it should sound loud notes of caution about increasing it. We still know very little about its empirical effects."[33]

That said, economists are increasingly concluding that the evidence in support of intellectual property as a means to encourage economic development or the spread of knowledge is very weak. As Cimoli et al. conclude, "if there is a robust historical fact, it is the laxity or sheer absence of intellectual property rights in nearly all instances of successful catching up" by developing countries, and that patents' role as incentives come alongside "their potentially negative consequences for processes of knowledge and capability accumulation that are typical of latecomers to industrialization."[34] In other words, economic development comes not from strong IP protection, but from the freedom to copy.

Even if some degree of intellectual property protection may be beneficial, current IP regimes far exceed these levels and are causing actual harm by restricting economic development and innovation. The evidentiary record, at the very least, should give us pause as to the wisdom of strengthening IP law. For example, James Watt's zealous enforcement of his 1769 patent on the separate condenser, an invention that improved steam engine efficiency and laid the foundation for the Industrial Revolution, as well as a 1782 patent, actually stymied further innovation for decades. It was only after the patents expired that the resulting pent-up innovation allowed steam power to come "into its own as the driving force of the Industrial Revolution . . . The key innovation was the high-pressure steam engine – development of which had been blocked by Watt's strategic use of his patent."[35] Similar stories can be told for the automobile and the airplane.[36]

More recently, Giovanni Dosi and Joseph E. Stiglitz, whose pioneering work on the economics of information won him the 2001

Nobel Prize in Economics, remark that US IPR policy, promoted via international economic agreements and via the Agreement on Trade-Related Aspects of Intellectual Property Rights (TRIPS) have more to do with extracting economic rents for US pharmaceutical and entertainment industries than in promoting the creation and spread of knowledge.[37] In their meta-survey of the field, they find little conclusive evidence that the enormous increase in patent applications by US corporations between 1988 and 2000 have led to increases in the rate of innovation.[38] Instead, this period has been characterized by the emergence of patents as defensive tools, to "block rival use of components and acquire bargaining strength in cross-licensing negotiations,"[39] or to restrict competition.[40] They conclude:

> While the evidence that IPR *in general* promotes innovation is far from convincing, there is good evidence that there may be adverse effects, especially with poorly designed "tight" IPR regimes: access to life-saving medicines may be restricted and so too access to knowledge that is necessary for successful development, and even for follow-on innovation.[41]

The state of IP law and policymaking, then, is such that, even if the fundamental objectives for IP are sound – that it must be limited in scope, and it should promote the creation and dissemination of knowledge and culture – it is unclear whether IP law as it is actually constituted promotes these objectives, in theory or in practice. Furthermore, the trend in domestic US law and international agreements for the past several decades has been to reinforce the protection side of IP law, at a time when more and more economists are raising the alarm about the effects of this expansion on innovation.

Applying the framework: the case of JSTOR and Aaron Swartz

The US federal legal prosecution of Aaron Swartz for downloading millions of academic articles from JSTOR, an online archive, at the Massachusetts Institute of Technology (MIT) in 2010 and 2011, offers a useful, if tragic, example of the problems with the current IP regime. Born in 1986, Swartz was a computer prodigy and champion of open access. In 2008 he published the *Guerilla Open Access Manifesto*,[42] in which he argued that:

The world's entire scientific and cultural heritage, published over centuries in books and journals, is increasingly being digitized and locked up by a handful of private corporations. Want to read the papers featuring the most famous results of the sciences? You'll need to send enormous amounts to publishers like Reed Elsevier.

[Those with access to these databases] have a duty to share it with the world. And you have: trading passwords with colleagues, filling download requests for friends . . . It's called stealing or piracy, as if sharing a wealth of knowledge were the moral equivalent of plundering a ship and murdering its crew. But sharing isn't immoral – it's a moral imperative. Only those blinded by greed would refuse to let a friend make a copy.

Swartz was arrested on January 6, 2011, by MIT police and a US Secret Service Agent. He was eventually charged with felonies with a maximum sentence of 50 years of imprisonment and $1 million in fines.[43] However, Swartz committed suicide on January 11, 2013, before the case had run its course.

Even had Swartz never taken his own life, his prosecution illustrates both the strong interest in the US government in protecting intellectual property, and the extent to which intellectual property law as it is currently constituted is linked only nominally with its underlying statutory mission to promote scientific and cultural advancement. Universities generate knowledge, and the journal article is one of the main ways in which this knowledge is disseminated. Although these articles are protected by copyright, copyright is not required as an incentive to spur academics, who are expected to produce research as part of their salaried position, and in order to gain reputation within their disciplines, and to get tenure. Instead, academics typically assign their copyrights to the small number of academic publishers that control the majority of academic journals and exert oligopolistic control over the market. In 2013, the five largest publishers accounted "for more than 50% of all papers published in 2013," with concentration ranging from a low of 20% for the humanities to a high of 70% for the social sciences.[44] Even as digitization has decreased publishing costs, academic publishers have continually raised prices. This has led to a crisis in university funding: because academic libraries are effectively a captive audience of the publishers, needing to provide faculty with access to the latest knowledge, they have little choice but to pay whatever the publishers demand.[45] Price hikes have become so exorbitant that Harvard University has warned that it cannot afford to keep paying for these high-cost journals.[46] As Gould notes,

> This situation perpetuates global inequalities in scholarship and in many other spheres. In an age when electronic copies can be made for free – when the cost of distributing an article to one person is roughly the same as distributing it to a million people – such a state of affairs is scandalous.[47]

Prosecutors zealously pursued the Swartz case, as evidenced by the involvement of the Secret Service, the number and severity of the charges, and the statement from Carmen Ortiz, the Obama-appointed District Attorney responsible for the case, that "stealing is stealing, whether you use a computer command or a crowbar and whether you take documents, data, or dollars."[48] It is also in keeping the prevailing conventional wisdom, that IP protection is a good in and of itself, which drives US IP policy.

However, the deeper issue is: should Swartz have been prosecuted in the first place? Was society improved by his zealous prosecution, even leaving aside its potential contribution to his suicide? Or, less politely, is the law an ass? An economics-driven societal approach to this case provides a clearer picture of the principles at stake. The first question to ask is, who benefits most from Swartz's prosecution?[49] MIT and JSTOR decided not to pursue civil charges against Swartz. Academics do not depend on copyright as an incentive to write journal articles; their only possible incentive in this case would be to ensure that their works are published. However, as has already been noted, academic publishers charge far beyond a competitive market price for academics to access the work that they themselves have created. It is, instead, the copyright holders – the large publishing houses themselves – whose oligopolistic profit levels and business model depend on strong copyright protection

Second, and most importantly, if one focuses on copyright's underlying purpose – to promote the production and dissemination of knowledge for the good of society – the wisdom of both the zealousness of the prosecution and the underlying copyright law that gave rise to it – are called into question. From a social-good perspective, protection can only be justified to the extent that it serves as an incentive for creative production. In academia, copyright's incentive function is highly questionable, mirroring issues raised by Stiglitz, Boldrin and Levine, and others in other areas. On the dissemination side, making electronic articles available to more people is a public good that can lead to greater innovation and creation, at a lower cost.[50]

From this perspective, it is difficult to conclude that Aaron Swartz's prosecution contributed to the progress of science or the arts. Rather, its main beneficiaries are the publishing intermediaries who have inserted themselves into the knowledge-dissemination process and earned oligopolistic profits in the process.

Toward a saner intellectual property future

This chapter has argued that while the underlying principle of the modern IP system – the promotion of knowledge and cultural creation and its dissemination – is sound, intellectual property law as it currently exists is rarely held to this standard. Intellectual property policy tends to be driven by interest-based politics, with IP as a whole resting on much more tenuous empirical and theoretical foundations than is typically acknowledged.

As IP becomes more important in the global political economy, and to the everyday lives of people around the world, addressing the inequities and problems inherent in intellectual property will become an ever-more pressing issue. Fortunately, mass political engagement on these issues has already begun, including the SOPA and ACTA protests referenced at the beginning of this chapter. In Canada, to offer one other example, IP's politicization can be seen in the success of a handful of academics and business people in challenging the idea that the Trans-Pacific Partnership is a trade agreement, arguing instead that it should be judged primarily according to its intellectual property provisions.[51] This politicization creates the potential for intellectual property provisions focused on public, rather than partial, interests.

The issues discussed in this chapter strongly suggest that both the foundations of current IP law and future IP proposals should be rethought. At the very least, current IP protection levels are too high, stifling innovation and creativity, rather than encouraging them. For example, providing authors with copyright protection lasting the entirety of their life *plus* 50-to-100 years, as is currently done worldwide, is almost farcically absurd when thought of as an incentive – which is the fundamental constitutional justification for copyright. Nobody ever has decided to create something based on how much money that creation would earn 50 years *after they're dead*. And yet, life-plus protection is a foundational rule in the global copyright regime, even though it makes less than no sense as an incentive to creating and disseminating creative works, which is the constitutional justification for copyright and intellectual property generally.

Intellectual property law, and how we think about intellectual property, are crying out for revision. To that end, three guiding principles can help us think about how to create a more just intellectual property regime.[52]

First, all intellectual property laws and proposals should be judged according to their empirical *effects on the future creation and dissemination of knowledge and culture, not on how they affect specific interest groups.* In other words, policy analyses should be focused on IP law's societal effects, and its effect on future knowledge creation. This utilitarian approach is open to the critique that it ignores creators' inherent rights in what they create (also known as moral rights). However, this claim to a unique, commodified relationship of intellectual creators to their work is weakened considerably by the reality that pretty much every idea everywhere builds on the work of past thinkers. From this perspective, saying that any specific idea is "mine and that I deserve exclusive monopoly rights over it, for all time," becomes much less defensible, as it ignores the "rights" of both previous and future creators.

This approach is also open to the critique that it ignores creators' right to make a profit from their intellectual work, an issue tied up in the relative low remuneration of many artists. However, the purpose of intellectual property law has never been to guarantee a "fair" return to individuals or companies any more than private property law was designed to guarantee that workers will receive a fair wage. In both cases, inequities emerge not from the specific property regimes, but from the nature of a capitalist, market-based society, and are related to survival in a market economy as a whole. To that end, as discussed below, alternative forms of knowledge governance could potentially create the conditions for more just remuneration of creators. Furthermore, other policies, such as a guaranteed annual income, could mitigate the economic inequities emerging from IP law.

Second, evaluation of intellectual property laws should consider whose interests are being served. All economic policies create winners and losers. Although intellectual property rights tend to be defended by reference to the rights of authors and inventors, in practice, the vast majority of economically valuable intellectual property rights are held by transnational corporations. These intermediaries (between the creator and the public) do not necessarily share the same interests as creators or the public: as IP owners, they stand to gain the most from both IP itself and stronger IP protection in particular.[53] An intellectual property policy that benefits a pharmaceutical company will not necessarily be best for university researchers or cancer patients.

It is also important to note that maximizing the production and dissemination of knowledge and culture is only one possible objective of an intellectual property regime. Knowledge governance regimes (of which IP law is but one possible form) reflect the underlying values of a society. Given the dominance of a Western, individualistic, entrepreneurial, market-based society, it is no surprise that IP is designed to commodify knowledge. Other societies, however, have different values. The debate over how "traditional knowledge" – cultural and natural knowledge held by indigenous peoples – should be treated is an example of a conflict with an alternative way of thinking about and using knowledge, one that does not necessarily prioritize the market-oriented maximization of knowledge production.

Related to this point, in coming up with a more just system, one should be careful not to replicate the power imbalances that have led to the current system. This disparity is particularly strong between the Global North (primarily exporters of commodified knowledge) and the Global South (knowledge importers). Globally, the dominant IP reformist voices tend to be based in the Global North, and their reform ideas, while well-intentioned, tend to reflect a particular view of how knowledge should be regulated. For example, while the Creative Commons licensing regime, created by American lawyer Lawrence Lessig as a way to make it easier to share creative works, has been exported throughout the world, it remains based on an American view of copyright, and of a legalistic approach to knowledge governance. The danger here is that even this reformist view may not reflect the desires and needs of people and societies in the Global South. Similarly, relatively young companies like Google, for example, are increasingly making themselves heard in policy circles against established IP interests. While they have traditionally taken a more expansive approach to issues like copyright than, say, the music industry, their status as for-profit corporations means that their IP interests will often diverge from the public interest as described in this chapter. The danger here is that reformists may adopt the well-funded Google's definition of the appropriate protection/dissemination balance as their own. To avoid replicating power imbalances, dialogue, deliberation and a constant reference to empirical evidence is key.

Third, and most importantly, one should not assume that intellectual property protection is the best way to promote the creation and dissemination of knowledge. Intellectual property is not always needed to incentivize knowledge creation and dissemination. University-related scientific discovery for centuries has been based on the open-access model, in which it is customary to share results freely with colleagues. The property incentive in this work – to the extent it can be referred to as such – involves the right to claim credit for the work and to earn a reputation from it, not the right to restrict its use.[54] In contrast to such a model, in which researchers, paid for by universities or the public at large, are allowed to claim credit and make their research freely available, the IP model shows itself to be unduly restrictive and potentially hostile to the creation of new knowledge.

Even within the market system, many have proposed and evaluated alternative forms of compensation for encouraging innovation and knowledge creation. Back in 1966, Hurt and Schumann remarked that copyright "seems to be an inefficient device for simply rewarding authors. The grant of tax relief to successful authors or direct payment for unremunerative literary creation would probably be more convenient, and these alternative forms of reward are actually given today."[55] Boldrin and Levine argue that first-mover advantages are enough to encourage knowledge and culture creation,[56] while Dosi and Stiglitz argue that government-funded prizes or direct funding can encourage creation without the negative effects of monopolies.[57]

While each of these proposals, including the option of removing knowledge creation from the marketplace entirely, has their advantages and disadvantages, and while their effects will differ depending on the society and activity being considered, they all merit consideration when thinking about how best to create and share knowledge and culture.

Conclusion

While there is much that can (and should) be done to reform or replace intellectual property law, some of it quite radical,[58] one should not expect even the abolition of IP law to usher in an era of equity and fairness. Information is never "free": as noted near the outset of this chapter, the nature of knowledge itself means that it will always require rules restricting how it is used (for whom, by whom, for what purpose) and encouraging its dissemination. The balance between these two (theoretically irreconcilable) imperatives must always be politically negotiated. What remains, then, are the questions: What should these limits be, and whose interests will they serve? It would be a significant advance if we started asking these questions with some regularity and relied on evidence to reach our answers.

Notes

1 Jason Dedrick, Kenneth L. Kraemer and Greg Linden, "Who Profits from Innovation in Global Value Chains? A Study of the iPod and Notebook PCs," *Industrial and Corporate Change* 19 (2010), http://web.mit.edu/iso8/pdf/Dedrick_Kraemer_Linden.pdf.

2 Kyle Wiens, "We Can't Let John Deere Destroy the Very Idea of Ownership," *Wired.com*, April 21, 2015, https://www.wired.com/2015/04/dmca-ownership-john-deere/.

3 "Ripping Music and Films Illegal Again after High Court Overturns New Law," *BBC*, July 17, 2015, http://www.bbc.co.uk/newsbeat/article/33566933/ripping-music-and-films-illegal-again-after-high-court-overturns-new-law.

4 Which has made owner, boxing announcer Michael Buffer, more than $400 million. John Berman and Michael Milberger, "'Let's Get Ready to Rumble'

Worth $400M," *ABC News*, November 9, 2009. http://abcnews.go.com/GMA/Weekend/lets-ready-rumble-meet-man-catchphrase/story?id=9022704#.ULPPquOe_n4.

5 G. Bruce Doern and Markus Sharaput, *Canadian Intellectual Property: The Politics of Innovating Institutions and Interests* (University of Toronto Press, 2000).

6 Jessica Litman, "The Public Domain," *Emory Law Journal* 39 (1990): 965–1011, https://law.duke.edu/pd/papers/litman_background.pdf.

7 U2, "The Fly," *Achtung Baby* (Island Records, 1990).

8 The AIDS pandemic offers a sobering illustration of the importance of such flexibilities to deal with health crises, particularly in developing countries such as South Africa, India and Brazil. It also illustrates the potential

conflict between rights holders and the public interest; in South Africa, for example, PhRMA, a pharmaceutical association "was exposed for its role in planning a secret campaign against the reforms of the South African patent law . . . [which] was aimed to introduce various public health flexibilities in the South African patent law" (K.M. Gopakumar, "Twenty Years of TRIPS Agreement and Access to Medicine: A Development Perspective," *Indian Journal of International Law* 55, no. 3 (2015): 367–404. doi:10.1007/s40901-016-0022-7).

9 Cited in Mike Masnick, "Indian Court Says 'Copyright Is Not an Inevitable, Divine, or Natural Right' and Photocopying Textbooks Is Fair Use," *Techdirt.com*, September 19, 2016, https://www.techdirt.com/articles/20160917/00432335547/indian-court-says-copyright-is-not-inevitable-divine-natural-right-photocopying-textbooks-is-fair-use.shtml.

10 World Bank, "Potential Macroeconomic Implications of the Trans-Pacific Partnership," *Global Economic Prospects*, World Bank Group (January 2016), 219–255, http://pubdocs.worldbank.org/en/847071452034669879/Global-Economic-Prospects-January-2016-Implications-Trans-Pacific-Partnership-Agreement.pdf.

11 See, for example, Peter A. Petri and Michael G. Plummer, "The Economic Effects of the Trans-Pacific Partnership: New Estimates," Peterson Institute for International Economics, Working Paper 16-2 (2016), https://piie.com/publications/wp/wp16-2.pdf; Jeronim Capaldo and Alex Izurieta with Jomo Kwame Sundaram, "Trading Down: Unemployment, Inequality and Other Risks of the Trans-Pacific Partnership Agreement," Global Development and Environment Institute Working Paper No. 16-01 (2016). http://ase.tufts.edu/gdae/Pubs/wp/16-01Capaldo-IzurietaTPP.pdf.

12 European Commission and Government of Canada, "Assessing the Costs and Benefits of a Closer EU-Canada Economic Partnership" (2008), http://trade.ec.europa.eu/doclib/docs/2008/october/tradoc_141032.pdf.

13 Ian Hargreaves, "Digital Opportunity: A Review of Intellectual Property and Growth." Independent report for the government of the United Kingdom (2011), 6, http://webarchive.nationalarchives.gov.uk/20140603093549/http:/www.ipo.gov.uk/ipreview-finalreport.pdf.

14 Giovanni Dosi and Joseph E. Stiglitz, "The Role of Intellectual Property Rights in the Development Process, with Some Lessons from Developed Countries: An Introduction," in *Intellectual Property Rights: Legal and Economic Challenges for Development*, ed. Mario Cimoli, Giovanni Dosi, Keith E. Maskus, Ruth L. Okediji, Jerome H. Reichman and Joseph E. Stiglitz (Oxford University Press, 2014), 16.

15 Peter Drahos with John Braithwaite, *Information Feudalism: Who Owns the Knowledge Economy?* (Earthscan, 2002).

16 Debora Halbert, "Intellectual Property Theft and National Security: Agendas and Assumptions," *The Information Society* 32, no. 4 (2016): 256–268.

17 Susan K. Sell, *Private Power, Public Law: The Globalization of Intellectual Property Rights*, (Cambridge University Press, 2003); Drahos and Braithwaite, *Information Feudalism*.

18 Mario Cimoli, Giovanni Dosi, Roberto Mazzoleni and Bhaven N. Sampat, "Innovation, Technical Change, and Patents in the Development Process: A Long-term View," in Cimoli et al., *Intellectual Property Rights*, 57–88.

19 Drahos and Braithwaite, *Information Feudalism*, 192.

20 Peter Drahos, "Developing Countries and International Intellectual Property Standard-setting," *The Journal of World Intellectual Property* 5 (2002): 788–789.

21 Blayne Haggart, "Birth of a Movement: The Anti-Counterfeiting Trade Agreement and the Politicization of Mexican Copyright," *Policy & Internet* 6, no. 1 (2014): 73.

22 Doern and Sharaput, *Canadian Intellectual Property*.

23 Jessica Litman, *Digital Copyright* (Prometheus Books, 2006), 36.

24 Pamela Samuelson, "Should Economics Play a Role in Copyright Law and Policy?" *University of Ottawa Law and Technology Journal* 1 (2003–2004), 1, http://ssrn.com/abstract=764704.

25 Ibid., 4.

26 Michele Boldrin and David K. Levine, *Against Intellectual Monopoly* (Cambridge University Press, 2008), 10–11.

27 Rent-seeking refers to the appropriation of economic gains without providing any benefit to others or society, as when a firm seeks ways to drive out its competition so that it can then charge higher prices.

28 Ibid., 3.

29 R. Hurt and R.M. Schumann, "The Economic Rationale of Copyright," *American Economic Review* 56, no. 1–2 (March 1966): 425–426.

30 Ibid., 432.

31 Cited in Dosi and Stiglitz, "The Role of Intellectual Property Rights," 15.

32 Kenneth Arrow, "Economic Welfare and the Allocation of Resources for Invention," in *The Rate and Direction of Inventive Activity: Economic and Social Factors* (Princeton University Press, 1962), 624, also available at http://www.litagion.org/pubs/papers/2006/P1856.pdf.

33 Ruth Towse and Rudi Holzhauer, "Introduction," in *The Economics of Intellectual Property*, vol. 1, ed. Ruth Towse and Rudi Holzhauer (Edward Elgar, 2002), xxxxi.

34 Cimoli et al., "Innovation, Technical Change, and Patents in the Development Process," 58.

35 Boldrin and Levine, *Against Intellectual Monopoly*, 1–2.

36 Ibid., 264.

37 Dosi and Stiglitz, "The Role of Intellectual Property Rights," 4.

38 Ibid., 18–22.

39 Ibid., 21.

40 Ibid., 24.

41 Ibid., 8.

42 Aaron Swartz, "Guerilla Open Access Manifesto," 2008, https://archive.org/stream/GuerillaOpenAccessManifesto/Goamjuly2008_djvu.txt.

43 Tim Cushing, "US Government Ups Felony Count in JSTOR/Aaron Swartz Case from Four to Thirteen," *TEchdirt.com*, September 18, 2012, https://www.techdirt.com/articles/20120917/17393320412/us-government-ups-felony-count-jstoraaron-swartz-case-four-to-thirteen.shtml.

44 Vincen Larivière, Stefanie Haustein and Philippe Mongeon, "The Oligopoly of Academic Publishers in the Digital Era," *PLOS One*, June 15, 2015, http://dx.doi.org/10.1371/journal.pone.0127502.

45 Ibid.

46 Ian Sample, "Harvard University Says It Can't Afford Journal Publishers' Prices," *The Guardian*, April 25, 2012, https://www.theguardian.com/science/2012/apr/24/harvard-university-journal-publishers-prices.

47 Rebecca Gould, "Aaron Swartz's Legacy," *Academe* 100, no. 1 (2014): 19–23.

48 Maria Bustillos, "Was Aaron

Swartz Stealing?" *The Awl*, August 3, 2011, https://theawl.com/was-aaron-swartz-stealing-5182be68ob5f#.ex49lc39v.

49 Susan Strange, *States and Markets*, 2nd ed. (Continuum, 1994), 234.

50 Swartz, it should be noted, did not distribute the downloaded articles.

51 For example, Jim Balsillie, "For Canadian Innovators, Will TPP Mean Protection – or Colonialism?" *Globe and Mail*, January 30, 2016; Dan Breznitz, "Trans-Pacific Partnership Is a Wonderful Idea – for China," *Globe and Mail*, December 26, 2015, http://www.theglobeandmail.com/report-on-business/rob-commentary/trans-pacific-partnership-is-a-wonderful-idea-for-china/article27939142/.

52 This section draws in part on Blayne Haggart, "Copyfight: Global Redistribution in the Digital Age," in *Structural Redistribution for Global Democracy*, ed. Jan Aart Scholte and Lorenzo Fioramonti (Lanham, MD: Rowman and Littlefield, 2016).

53 Benkler makes this point with respect to copyright, but it holds for IP in general. Yochai Benkler, "A Political Economy of the Public Domain: Markets in Information Goods Versus the Marketplace of Ideas," in *Expanding the Boundaries of Intellectual Property: Innovation Policy for the Knowledge Society*, ed. Rochelle Cooper Dreyfuss, Diane Leenheer Zimmerman and Harry First (Oxford University Press, 2001), 279–284.

54 Brad Delong, "Outline of: Joel Mokyr: A Culture of Growth: The Origins of the Modern Economy," *Bradford-delong.com*, September 14, 2016, http://www.bradford-delong.com/2016/09/outline-of-joel-mokyr-a-culture-of-growth-the-origins-of-the-modern-economy.html.

55 Hurt and Schumann, "The Economic Rationale of Copyright," 424.

56 Boldrin and Levine, *Against Intellectual Monopoly*.

57 Dosi and Stiglitz, "The Role of Intellectual Property Rights."

58 See, for example, Story for a compelling argument for developing countries to disengage from the Berne Convention, the foundational international copyright treaty: Alan Story, "Burn Berne: Why the Leading International Copyright Convention Must Be Repealed," *Houston Law Review* 40, no. 3 (2003): 763–801.

Mat Callahan

The figure of the pirate looms large in the history and politics of Intellectual Property. From the first copyright legislation to the latest trade negotiations, piracy has been invoked as a singular, unmitigated evil; the nihilist scourge against which all civilization must stand united. While it may be obvious that this invocation of piracy is rhetorical hyperbole and piracy, in this instance, is only a metaphor, the accusation nonetheless succeeds in obscuring the substantive issues involved in both IP and actual maritime piracy. The charge of "piracy," furthermore, serves to silence criticism of the law and government that polices the territory (the sea or the printing press or the internet) upon which the pirate emerges. No doubt, as metaphor, piracy can be turned around and applied to those making the charge in the first place. Thus, Vandana Shiva's famous 1997 book *Bio-Piracy: The Plunder of Nature and Knowledge*, uses the term to describe the practices of the world's largest corporations. Indeed, the term biopiracy is now employed by governments (e.g. Peru, South Africa, India) to define the purpose of defensive national policy, its use so widespread as to have become a generic description of what the Global North has done to the Global South since colonization. Polemical deployment of the metaphor was clearly the intent of the Pirate Bay file-sharing site and the reasons Pirate Parties have arisen, drawing their popularity, in part, from a wellspring of youthful disdain for the staged solemnity governments use to mask official hypocrisy. But piracy becomes more curious when "good, old-fashioned" maritime piracy simultaneously reappears, as it did off the coast of East Africa in 2005. When real pirates are attacking real ships it is inevitable that a comparison will be made between such activity and that of teenagers sharing music. Nevertheless, the dubiousness of the charge of piracy does not lie simply in the misuse of a name, like calling a cat a dog. Rather, the timeliness of its deployment must be critically examined within the broader historical context. The latter includes, of course, the definition of the word pirate, i.e. *sea robber*, in the English language, but also its frequent application at the historical conjuncture of European colonization, the waves of enclosure within Europe itself and the promulgation of the first intellectual property regimes (both copyright and patent). The coincidences are not accidents; the modern state is built on this bedrock of colonial conquest, the slave trade, the enclosure of common lands and the policing of all forms of expression – be they literary, scientific or political.

But why the pirate? Why not the bandit, bootlegger, counterfeiter or con artist? Why invoke this quasi-romantic figure that somehow attracts as it repels? Recent scholarship has clarified both the first uses of the term in reference to copyright and patent and its multiple, even contradictory, uses over the subsequent 300 years. Adrian Johns and Kavita Philip, for example, have each explored piracy as, on the one hand, crucial to the legitimation of states, and, on the other hand, to the invention of the author. Johns' deeply researched study, *Piracy: The Intellectual Property Wars from Gutenberg to Gates* (2009)[1] shows how with the advent of print, piracy was first deployed, its metaphorical usage validated by reference to principles established in St. Augustine's *The City of God*. Philip's essay, "What Is a Technological Author? The Pirate Function and Intellectual Property" (2005),[2] shows how the pirate function necessarily flows from unequal power relations. Also referencing Augustine, Philip takes a further step by quoting Brecht's song, "Pirate Jenny," with its message of avenging injustice. These references highlight piracy's role as both practice and image. How, on the one hand, maritime piracy arises not merely as base criminality but as a challenge to the state's legitimacy, while on the other, the term piracy can be used to defy authority as well as an indictment of industry practices, as in "biopiracy."

Augustine is worth quoting in full since he puts in stark relief what is at stake:

Remove justice, and what are kingdoms but gangs of criminals on a large scale? What are criminal gangs but petty kingdoms? A gang is a group of men under the command of a leader, bound by a compact of association, in which the plunder is divided according to an agreed convention. If this villainy wins so many recruits from the ranks of the demoralized that it acquires territory, establishes a base, captures cities and subdues peoples, it then openly arrogates to itself the title of kingdom, which is conferred on it in the eyes of the world, not by the renouncing of aggression but by the attainment of impunity.

For it was a witty and a truthful rejoinder which was given by a captured pirate to Alexander the Great. The king asked the fellow, "What is your idea, in infesting the sea?" And the pirate answered, with uninhibited insolence, "The same as yours, in infesting the earth! But because I do it with a tiny craft, I'm called a pirate: because you have a mighty navy, you're called an emperor."[3]

Augustine's perspective is illuminating. From Cortez's conquest of Mexico to the final defeat of the United States in Vietnam, the long arc of European colonization was one vast piratical enterprise. All the attempts to legitimize it were ultimately unsuccessful, culminating in the wave of decolonization that swept the world following World War II, leading through the Chinese to the Cuban to the Vietnamese revolutions, to the worldwide revolutionary upsurge known simply as *1968*. It is no coincidence, then, that what Johns calls the "Intellectual Property Defense Industry" began to form in the 1970s, bringing together trade associations, police and military intelligence experts to join with legislators along a new battlefront.[4] This was not only to recover ground lost to worldwide insurgency, it was to address the even more fundamental issue of systemic crisis.

The mid-1970s marked both the high water mark of revolutionary struggle and the beginning of the first major crisis of capitalism since the Great Depression. Many economists and historians see the crash of 2008 as originating in the crisis of 1971–1973. The parallels are consistent since it was on October 13, 2008, and in the shadow of financial collapse, that George Bush signed into law a Joint Strategic Plan for worldwide anti-piracy policing.[5] Given the shocking and awful results of the War on Terror and that other great success, the War on Drugs, one might be forgiven a large dose of skepticism about this latest move, bringing to mind Gore Vidal's famous "war on dandruff" comparison. Indeed, for many people this was just another example of government posturing.[6]

The reason, however, to take seriously a discussion of piracy is not because of an image, be it defiant or demonic, nor is it to engage in linguistic sleight of hand or oratorical gymnastics. The reason is the very one Augustine calls attention to and the real grievances and resistance that reside in acts called piracy by defenders of the status quo. Not only is the pirate's rejoinder to Alexander echoed in social movements pitting people against states and industries that dominate the world, but, absent justice, there is no way states and industries can ever attain the legitimacy they need to maintain their authority. Indeed, even in the case of maritime piracy – which might appear to be mere violent theft – the defense presented in court by Somali pirates was precisely that their actions were justified by crimes committed against their country, a subject we'll revisit further on. Furthermore, as Johns suggests in the conclusion of his book we may now be witnessing the end of intellectual property as technological and social forces render its maintenance impossible. The end of intellectual property may in turn be part and parcel of the terminal crisis of capitalism, the outcome of which remains to be determined. It is this eventuality, more than piracy, as such, which leads us to consider alternatives – some already appearing in practices which today are being criminalized. Sharing is the prime example.

If it is a commonplace that law presupposes crime – witness the "Thou shalt nots" of the Ten Commandments – it should be recalled that law also presupposes two other constitutive elements: the commons and labor. The commons, or commonwealth, are a necessary condition for any claim to legal authority. Labor is necessary for the production and reproduction of life. Absent justice, however, the only rule that applies to either commons or labor is might makes right, whereby, as Augustine put it, "the renouncing of aggression" is supplanted by "the attainment of impunity." And, as we shall see, this is precisely why piracy, both virtual and maritime, has reemerged today.

What is piracy?

As the foregoing has shown, any discussion of piracy in the twenty-first century has to confront the fact that the term, "piracy," is clouded with ambiguity, not because it lacks a precise definition, but because that definition has been deliberately obscured. McGill

University professor Jonathan Sterne expressed the dilemma in an interview in *Pitchfork Magazine* (2012):

> piracy is not a real thing. In fact, it's a crazy term because it combines people in their rooms downloading music with armed thieves in boats off the coast of eastern Africa. So really we're talking about an industry that wants to limit copying as much as possible and control the means of purchase, use, and recirculation in problematic ways.[7]

Sterne, whose book (*MP3: The Meaning of a Format*) is a study of the technology central to the downloading and sharing of music, goes further to explain the physical processes behind the fog of "crazy" terminology:

> The mp3 took off after an Australian hacker cracked a piece of encoding software that the Fraunhofer Institute, which owns a lot of the patents for the mp3, created. It gets re-released for free, and people start using the software to rip mp3s from their CDs. Within a year or two, because they're so common, companies like Microsoft and Apple are signing deals with Fraunhofer, and by the time Napster takes off, anyone with a computer could use software to rip a CD to mp3.

Yet, as Sterne hastens to add, these developments cannot be understood in isolation.

> That's part of the story, but there's a much more important part. When we think about music piracy or unauthorized copying, we normally think about it in terms of a record industry and an end user. But I actually think there's a more important relationship involving the conduit industries, which are as much media industries as the recording industry. These people benefit tremendously from file-sharing. My favorite example of this comes from 2001, when Sony Music (the record label) joins a suit against Napster put forward by the Recording Industry Association of America at the same time Sony (the consumer electronics manufacturer) releases a CD player that can play mp3s. Where do you think those mp3s come from?[8]

This example illustrates how interested parties, i.e. the music, film and publishing industries, orchestrated a campaign based on the usage of a term, "piracy," to sew moral panic and justify repressive measures such as invading people's homes, confiscating personal property, threatening jail terms and imposing fines. Yet the term "piracy" is, in this instance, only a metaphor. It has no statutory validity. In fact, such usage is explicitly excluded from the Law of the Sea governing and adjudicating maritime piracy.

Legal definition of piracy

Piracy is defined by dictionaries and by international law as robbery at sea. More specifically, it must involve at least two vessels. According to the *Max Planck Encyclopedia of Law*:

> Piracy by the law of nations, in its jurisdictional aspects, is *sui generis*. Though statutes may provide for its punishment, it is an offence against the law of nations; and as the scene of the pirate's operations is the high seas, which it is not the right or the duty of any nation to police, he is denied the protection of the flag he may carry, and is treated as an outlaw, as the enemy of mankind – *hostis humani generis* – whom any nation may in the interest of all capture and punish.[9]

Lest there be any ambiguity, this article explicitly states:

> The notion of "pirate radio stations," reflected in Art. 109 UN Convention on the Law of the Sea whereby jurisdiction is given to States to suppress these on the high seas, is not a true example of piracy (→ Pirate Broadcasting). Still less is the notion of "piracy" justified as applied to the unlawful sale and use of copyrighted material such as music, films, and books.[10]

Even though the term "piratical" was applied to literary practices as early as the seventeenth century, its statutory expression is: *copyright infringement* or *counterfeiting*. This differed from actual piracy in two crucial ways: universality and criminality. The Law of the Sea is, by definition, universal. Copyright law has, to this day, differed from country to country and in some cases did not exist at all. The same is true for patent and as Erich Schiff explained in his widely quoted

1971 study, the Netherlands and Switzerland, in particular, made considerable commercial and technical gains precisely because they were not thereby constrained.[11] Furthermore, application of the law is necessarily debatable. In other words, what constitutes copyright or patent infringement is settled on a case by case basis in civil court. In the vast majority of cases this involves litigation, not criminal charges, and is settled by financial awards (*Apple vs. Samsung*, for example). The application of the term "piracy" today seeks to make sharers of music or other cultural products "hostis humani generis," that is, enemies of mankind. It is to close the gap between two uses of the same word, making the different actions they name equivalent and those engaged in either "whom any nation may in the interest of all capture and punish." This justifies any nation pursuing a pirate anywhere, even if this involves invading a territory to apprehend the pirate. Numerous recent cases (Richard O'Dwyer, Kim Dotcom, Rapidshare)[12] have amply demonstrated that this is precisely what the US government is attempting to do. The United States has not launched invasions of the UK or New Zealand but it has attempted to force these governments to extradite the "pirates" to the territorial United States where they can be prosecuted according to US law.

Legally, however, the United States is on shaky ground because, as shown above, international law explicitly excludes from the definition of piracy such activities as pirate radio, pirating of copyright, patented or trademarked materials or, for that matter, any other activity not codified in the legal definition of piracy. In order to amend legislation and secure legal sanction the United States (and allied governments) need to establish an equivalence in law between piracy as it was traditionally defined and those acts that have hitherto been mainly subject to civil litigation, not criminal prosecution. This is the significance of the recent attempts (and defeats) of such legislation as SOPA, PIPA and ACTA.[13] As this is being written new attempts are underway: the Trans-Pacific Partnership (TPP) and the Transatlantic Trade and Investment Partnership (TTIP). As Julian Assange stated upon WikiLeaks' release of the relevant documents:

> The US administration is aggressively pushing the TPP through the US legislative process on the sly. If instituted, the TPP's intellectual property regime would trample over individual rights and free expression, as well as ride roughshod over the

intellectual and creative commons. If you read, write, publish, think, listen, dance, sing or invent; if you farm or consume food; if you're ill now or might one day be ill, the TPP has you in its crosshairs.[14]

This objective furthermore explains the sowing of moral panic by, among others, representatives of the music industry. Sociologists have, at least since 1973, used the term "moral panic" to describe a phenomenon wherein "moral entrepreneurs" spread fear among the populace that a grave threat to society is posed by those identified as "folk devils."[15] Witch hunts are the classic example but so are present day campaigns that transform genuine concerns into mass hysteria. Moral panic perfectly describes use of the term "piracy" as applied to cultural products. Moral entrepreneurs – such as the Recording Industry Association of America (RIAA) or the International Federation of the Phonograph Industry (IFPI) – whipped up an irrational and groundless frenzy directed against the folk devils, in this case young people "stealing" music. Commenting on the process, economist G. Narasimha Raghavan wrote,

> A semantic analysis of the word "piracy," very often attributed to copyright infringers, does not attempt to capture the reality of breach, but rather attempts to inflict a pessimistic shade to the act, reminiscent of anarchic hooliganism . . . No economic logic exists behind the statistics on piracy, and its superfluous coverage in the media is only an act to secure "unwarranted authenticity" and support.[16]

To further emphasize the political, as opposed to narrowly economic, nature of this campaign, Kavita Philip notes:

> Anti-piracy discourses now frequently intersect with anti-terrorist security discourses, where both pirates and terrorists function as threats to free markets and civilized nations. Media sociologist Nitin Govil argues that the relationship between intellectual property piracy and terrorism has been naturalized by policy makers, international police, and popular culture since 9/11: "For example, British detectives claim that Pakistani DVDs account for 40% of anti-piracy confiscations in the UK, and

that profits from pirated versions of *Love, Actually* and *Master and Commander* funnel back to the coffers of Pakistan-based Al Qaeda operatives."[17]

The success of moral panics, however, resides not only in sowing confusion but in diverting public attention from their perpetrators' actual objectives. Other chapters of this book examine in detail how particular industries, such as music, agri-business and pharmaceuticals, have unfolded strategies to increase profit and control at the very moment they are claiming to be victims of piracy. Chapter 8 in the current volume, "Meet the New Boss, Same as the Old Boss," compares the music industry's claims of imminent demise with its actual, highly profitable, restructuring, while Chapter 6, "Owning up to Owning Traditional Knowledge of Medicinal Plants," looks at current conflicts arising between farmers, indigenous peoples and whole countries against giant agri-business and pharmaceutical firms protected by US and European IP law. But in a broader sense, the objective was and remains to divert attention from a campaign underway since the 1970s for the defense and expansion of intellectual property regimes, the enclosure of the internet *and* terrestrial commons (e.g. seeds), and suppression of any challenge to corporate rule. As stated previously, Adrian Johns calls this the "Intellectual Property Defense Industry." "At a global level, it surveils the digital world and probes virtual homesteads; at a local, it impinges on physical households, workplaces, and farms." The industry, moreover, tells us, "What we 'know' about piracy – its rates, locations, costs, and profits – is usually what this industry sees and transmits to us. What we do not know about it – principally its cultural bases and implications – is what it does not see."[18] The resemblance to Orwell's "Thought Police" is striking.

This still leaves troubling questions about the nature and significance of rampant international practices. Could it be that "piracy" is just another name for black market or underground economy? What, moreover, do such "economies" tell us about the state of the world economy as a whole?

The black market

Research in this field was established long before the advent of the internet and the scope and influence of such economies are well documented. For example, it is reported that the black market or "informal economy" accounts for 1.8 billion jobs and 1.8 trillion dollars in revenue worldwide.[19] Under the heading "black market" are drug trafficking, arms trafficking, prostitution, tobacco and alcohol smuggling as well as the sale of "counterfeit" goods from drugs to electronics (both hardware and software). Current use of the term "piracy" seems to be referring to something else. But is it, really? At least since the 1970s, with the advent of cassette tapes, music was "pirated" throughout countries of the Global South. From Jamaica to India, most music (and later film) was sold through networks of street vendors and home production facilities. To a large extent this continues today, albeit in forms modified by digital technology, the use of cellular phones and the internet. The point here is not to make an exhaustive study of all manifestations of such black market or informal economies but to draw attention to one aspect of the division between the Global North and South, on the one hand, and to pin down the elusive term "piracy" in its multiple and contradictory uses, on the other.

It need hardly be said that all the criminal activities normally associated with the black market are punishable by long established laws making no reference to piracy. Furthermore, these activities continue to expand, in some cases comprising not just the underground economy but the only functioning economy. For example, Nigeria.

Brian Larkin in his "Degraded Images, Distorted Sounds: Nigerian Video and the Infrastructure of Piracy," states:

> But in Nigeria, the second economy has grown to such a scale
> that no one really knows how to represent it. No one is sure how
> large the GDP is; no one can calculate the balance of payments
> or even the size of Nigeria's population (Bayart, Ellis, and Hibou
> 1999; Hecht and Simone 1994). Strong forces are at work to
> make sure that revenue streams from major industries, like oil,
> are obligingly opaque. Jean-François Bayart, Stephen Ellis,
> and Béatrice Hibou (1999) have argued that illegal activities in
> Nigeria (such as fraud, corruption, and the import and export of
> illegal oil, drugs, and videos) have grown to such a degree that
> they now form part of the routine operations of the state rather
> than a pathology outside of it. Nigerians have become famous
> within Africa and beyond for migrating as workers, importers,

exporters, smugglers, drug carriers, and fraudsters. While the federal state continues to take part in the formalized ritual of the official economy, many Nigerians see a widening gap between it and the everyday reality of how Nigeria functions.[20]

Larkin concludes, "Piracy and the wider infrastructure of reproduction it has generated reveal the organization of contemporary Nigerian society. They show how the parallel economy has migrated onto center stage, overlapping and interpenetrating with the official economy, mixing legal and illegal regimes, uniting social actors, and organizing common networks."[21]

The "underground" or "black market" economy raises other questions beyond material scarcity or abundance. In India, for example, legal scholar and activist Lawrence Liang of the Alternative Law Forum has exposed the legal and practical inconsistencies at the heart of IP Law and its enforcement (or unenforceability?), especially in the Global South. Liang's position is summarized by Kavita Philip,

In opposition to Indian bureaucrats and entrepreneurs who call anxiously for a stronger enforcement of the Intellectual Property Regimes (IPRs) of Multinational Corporations (MNCs), Liang celebrates the possibilities of copying and sharing, the leaks in modernity, or what he calls the "porous legalities" of postcolonial "stolen modernities." These leaks in modernity happen in banal and everyday instances of ripping off, in which populations outside the law sidestep the processes by which they are supposed to define themselves as bourgeois legal subjects. In the absence of ownership and respect for property, they can only be assigned a position outside bourgeois legality. Their authorial function lies not in the creation of localizable content but of dispersed, shared meaning, through the activities of an electronic commons. A shared imagination emerges via the activities of producing, circulating, and consuming appropriated digital texts. The possibilities of being a subject in this sphere are detached from the requirement of unique authorship—the bourgeois author recedes; the appropriative function is foregrounded.[22]

While the profits lost to major corporations are considerable, circumstances such as these reveal there is more at stake than money.

Indeed, attention is inevitably drawn to the legitimacy of authority, the means by which power is exercised or resisted and how subjects construct themselves in opposition, not obedience, to law. It is not surprising that throughout history and throughout the world, bandits, bushrangers and bank robbers, as well as pirates, have in many cases defended their activities on apparent contradictions between the law and justice. This furthermore explains the persistence in popular legend of figures such as Robin Hood, Ned Kelly, Pretty Boy Floyd and Phoolan Devi.

But there is more to piracy than popular legend might suggest. From the fifteenth century to the present, piracy has singular significance *historically*, in the construction of the modern state. This is evident, not only militarily, as in the wars fought between contending European powers, (one nation's pirate was another nation's privateer) but in methods, legal and political, taken to establish the state as an effective entity.[23] This, in turn, derives from the terrain on which the pirate emerges and the obstacles this terrain presents to governance. On the one hand, this is the sea, on the other, it is the idea – expressed via the printing press and, now, the internet.

It follows that what lends piracy its uniqueness is also a defining characteristic of capitalism: globalization. Peter Linebaugh and Markus Rediker write in *The Many-Headed Hydra*:

> Adam Smith (1723–1790), the first comprehensive theorist of capitalism, and Karl Marx (1818–1883), its profoundest critic, agreed in their approach to globalization. Both understood its maritime origins, arguing that the discovery of the sea routes to the Americas and the East Indies marked a new stage in human history. And both understood its social consequences, the fact that the expansion of commodity production (Smith called it the extent of the market, Marx the social division of labor) resettled the globe and transformed the experience of work.[24]

This, furthermore, reveals the links between maritime piracy and colonial conquest, on the one hand, and piracy and invention of the author, on the other – the *sea* and the *idea* presenting the same difficulty of occupancy or *possession* for interested parties be they private enterprises or governments.[25]

While this explains how and why the term for sea robber was appropriated by defenders of copyright, it nonetheless leads to another, more significant question arising, not from the designation piracy, itself, but from the purpose such designation is to serve. In other words, what *is* authority if not the power to authorize, authenticate and certify; to constitute not only piracy but authorship and ownership as well?

Who's pirating who?

In 2012, a German court convicted ten Somali men of kidnapping and conducting an attack on maritime traffic. What came to light in this trial is that illegal fishing and dumping of toxic wastes in the waters of Somalia had ruined the local economy.[26] Since the 1980s the Italian mafia, under contract to various European states, has been dumping nuclear and other toxic waste off the coast of Somalia. "European companies found it to be very cheap to get rid of the waste, costing as little as $2.50 a tonne, where waste disposal costs in Europe are closer to $1000 per tonne."[27] Simultaneously, illegal fishing was expanding out of control. According to various reports, this led to the acts considered piracy by the German court. "Through interception with speedboats, Somali fishermen tried to either dissuade the dumpers and trawlers or levy a 'tax' on them as compensation" wrote Wikipedia.[28] "It's almost like a resource swap, Somalis collect up to $100 million a year from pirate ransoms off their coasts and the Europeans and Asians poach around $300 million a year in fish from Somali waters," wrote piracy expert Peter Lehr.[29] Even mainstream news outlets ask, "Off the lawless coast of Somalia, questions of who is pirating who" (*Chicago Tribune*).[30]

In a recent summary of the conditions that led to the outbreak, the Oceans Beyond Piracy group wrote:

> Across many interviews, respondents paint a remarkably consistent picture. The piracy phenomenon began as an armed response to illegal fishing. This "popular uprising" was subsequently hijacked by criminal gangs interested strictly in profit, who attacked other, unrelated vessels. Nonetheless, so long as illegal fishing persists and curtails already-scarce economic opportunities, particularly employment for coastal youths, the potential for piracy will

remain. International navies have been effective at treating
the symptoms, by making pirate operations untenable, but
can be maintained only at great cost and do nothing to address
the underlying condition. Somali piracy has been suppressed,
not solved. Ominously, so long as this remains the case, a
resurgence of piracy off the coast of Somalia cannot be
ruled out – and indeed is seen as an inevitability by many
locals.[31]

"Who is pirating who?" is more than a rhetorical question. It
is of course at the heart of Vandana Shiva's aforementioned claim
regarding biopiracy and it is posed repeatedly by a wide range
of opponents of current IP regimes. But "Who is pirating who?"
implies as well that piracy and criminality of any kind are the
product of a certain set of historical conditions. While it may be
obvious that poverty, corruption and war are such conditions, what
then are the prospects for eliminating them? And furthermore,
where does IP and resistance to IP fit into the larger struggle for
peace and justice?

This larger context should be kept in mind whenever wealthy
celebrities – especially musicians – come before the public protesting
their victimhood and demanding greater government protection.
We are asked to support the prosecution of teenagers sharing files
while ignoring the claims of indigenous communities that their
methods of cultivation and the resulting medicinal and nourishing
plants are being taken and patented by Syngenta, Monsanto, Bayer
and other giant corporations without the prior informed consent of
these communities. We are further asked to ignore the persecution
of Julian Assange, Chelsea Manning and Edward Snowden, who are
not, incidentally, accused of piracy but of espionage and treason!
As glaring as such contradictions are, they are nevertheless, just
cautionary remarks. "Who is pirating who?" leads to far more
fundamental questions.

Ironically, the Intellectual Property Defense Industry may
ultimately contribute to the end of IP as we know it. Its propaganda
and oppressive tactics have certainly intensified rather than alleviated
its own crisis. Furthermore, the struggle that has arisen on behalf of
the commons – as a concept and as a physical location – may lead to
an even greater social transformation than one confined to IP.

In the case of IP, Adrian Johns suggests:

> Such turning points have happened before – about once every
> century, in fact, since the end of the Middle Ages. The last major
> one occurred at the height of the industrial age, and catalyzed the
> invention of intellectual property. Before that, another took place
> in the Enlightenment, when it led to the emergence of the first
> modern copyright system and the first modern patents regime.
> And before that, there was the creation of piracy in the 1660s–
> 1680s. By extrapolation, we are already overdue to experience
> another revolution of the same magnitude. If it does happen in
> the near future, it may well bring down the curtain on what will
> then, in retrospect, come to be seen as a coherent epoch of about
> 150 years: the era of intellectual property.[32]

Johns furnishes much compelling evidence from conflicts within
the academic and scientific communities to deepening distrust on
the part of legal scholars and some legislators as to the practical
benefits, not to mention legality, of ever-expanding IP regimes. One
should read the book for more but suffice it to say that while his
speculation as to what might replace IP are open to debate, Johns'
exhaustive study of the subject strongly suggests that IP as we know
it is doomed.

This, then, begs the question of how IP is imbricated in the crisis
facing capitalism. According to one noted critic, Slavoj Žižek, our
contemporary crisis is delineated along certain fault lines. For Žižek,
"The only *true* question today is: do we endorse the predominant
naturalization of capitalism, or does today's global capitalism contain
antagonisms strong enough to prevent its indefinite reproduction?"[33]
In response, Žižek identifies four specific antagonisms: (1) the threat
to the environment – "looming . . . ecological catastrophe"; (2) the
"inappropriateness" of the accelerating and intensifying privatization
of intellectual property; (3) the "socio-ethical implications of new
techno-scientific developments" – i.e. the inappropriateness of the
privatization of "internal nature" – human genes, seeds, cloning
and so forth; (4) "new forms of social apartheid" – the "antagonism
between the included and the excluded."[34] For Žižek, the first three
of these "antagonisms" represent different forms of the commons.
In one instance, the commons of external nature; in another, the

"commons of culture"; and in the third, the commons of "internal nature." As such, for Žižek, the commons represents the crucial battleground in the struggle to curtail the incessant reproduction of global capitalism. Moreover, the fourth "antagonism" indicated by Žižek – "new forms of social apartheid" – relates to who Žižek perceives as the effective victims of the privatization of the commons. The excluded are more than those marginalized, minority voices conventionally labeled as the excluded. They (we) are, in fact, the great majority of humankind.

Whether one views Žižek's framing as comprehensive or not, highlighting the role of IP and its proliferation through multi-faceted manifestations of crisis is instructive. It corresponds, as well, to the growing awareness that this once arcane subject, formerly the province of legal experts, businessmen and legislators, is literally a matter of life and death for millions, and a harbinger of struggles to come.

What unites these struggles is neither romantic imagery nor theatrical posturing but demands for justice and equality. History is replete with examples of laws being overturned, governments being overthrown and those formerly deemed outlaws being vindicated as upholders of right. In the case of the creation and expression of ideas, the demand is for a commons possessed by no one and open to everyone. A commons, moreover, that is not a subterfuge enabling ideologues of the market to reassert private ownership, but is, to use the language of IP, the public domain. In other words, the home and *guarantor* of humanity's noblest aspirations and renewal.

Therein lies the great potential of sharing – and why the term has already been co-opted, i.e. "sharing economy," to prevent that potential from being realized. Trivialized and demonized by defenders of privilege, sharing holds a key for unlocking the doors of a prison. Not only is there great utility in the free exchange of knowledge but there is a far wider horizon in sharing effort and ideas than in hoarding great piles of lifeless objects.

Perhaps the best current example of such sharing is Sci-hub.[35]

Knowledge to all is freedom of thought

The story is simple and undramatic: a young student researcher in a poor country cannot afford access to papers she needs to complete her studies. She uses her computer skills to access said papers by circumventing publishers' paywalls. She realizes, simultaneously, that her needs are shared by millions worldwide and the effort she is making for herself could just as well be made to serve humanity in general. Thus she creates the website, Sci-hub, and within a couple of years there are 60 million papers available for free to anyone, anywhere. Furthermore, scientists and researchers continue to contribute to, as well as access, this ever-expanding library. Of course, she is labeled a pirate and is sued by Elsevier, one of the largest academic publishers in the world. (Elsevier won the case but results are inconclusive due to jurisdictional issues – Sci-hub is, effectively, nowhere and everywhere?!)[36]

The young researcher is Alexandra Elbakyan from Kazakhstan. She has openly declared the purpose of Sci-hub as: "knowledge to all, no copyright and open access." Elbakyan makes clear, moreover, that: "If Elsevier manages to shut down our projects or force them into the darknet, that will demonstrate an important idea: that the public does not have the right to knowledge."[37]

Other chapters of this book discuss Access to Knowledge and Open Access movements in greater detail but as relates to the question of piracy, Sci-hub's existence and unqualified success marks a limit beyond which the term just seems silly. The appropriate response – and one doubtless shared by millions of researchers – is "so what?" Are we free to think or are we not. If we are free to think we must have "food for thought," in short, knowledge. If we are not free, then we are less than slaves. We are animals with no thinking capacity beyond physical survival.

The consequences are as obvious as they are inevitable. Elsevier can win its case, but it has lost its legitimacy. It is the perpetrator of fraud. A fraud, moreover, that denies not only what is right, but what human beings need to be human.

Notes

1 Adrian Johns, *Piracy: The Intellectual Property Wars from Gutenberg to Gates* (University of Chicago Press, 2009).

2 Kavita Philip, "What Is a Technological Author? The Pirate Function and Intellectual Property," *Postcolonial Studies* 8, no. 2 (2005): 199–218.

3 St. Augustine, *Concerning the City of God against the Pagans*, trans. Henry Bettenson, Book IV, part 4 (Penguin, 1972), 620–621.

4 "The intellectual property defense industry began to take its current form in the 1970s. It emerged from what were originally dispersed ventures in particular trades and in-house operations in discrete businesses. As it consolidated, it drew on people, devices, and practices that

often originated in police or military circles – ex-officers, surveillance techniques, encryption – to form a distinct enterprise with branches in digital, pharmaceutical, agricultural, and other domains. By the mid-1980s it was multinational. Trade associations had by then established divisions for antipirate policing in Asia, Africa, Europe, and the Americas. The MPAA, for example, maintained what it called 'Film Security Offices' not only in Los Angeles, New York, and London, but also in Paris, Hong Kong, and South Africa. Coordinating such offices was a Joint Anti-Piracy Intelligence Group (JAPIG), founded in 1984 as an intellectual property counterpart to Interpol. JAPIG was capable of tracking cargo vessels across the oceans and tapping local customs agents to intercept them when they made landfall. In the 1990s, such bodies became players alongside governments, the United Nations, and Interpol in overseeing globalization. The World Health Organization's International Medical Products Anti-Counterfeiting Taskforce, launched in Rome in 2006, was a late but extremely important addition to their ranks. By this point a huge and multifaceted enterprise, antipiracy policing combines the interests and reach of states, corporations, multinationals, and world bodies" (Johns, *Piracy*, 498–499).

5 Ibid., 500.

6 There is an evident relationship of inverse proportion between increases in organized criminal activity and the defeat of organized political opposition. When revolution is on the ascendant, motives and targets change. "Lawlessness" is directed at freeing the oppressed and expropriating the expropriators not mere self-aggrandizement and personal profit. Counterrevolution inevitably brings in

its train all the sordid manifestations of mafia, drug cartel and gang violence, as is clearly evident today. When, for example, the Zapatista's took the world stage to protest NAFTA in 1994, accusations of piracy were nowhere to be heard. When protestors, inspired to a large extent by a new generation of hackers and digital rebels, gathered in Seattle and took down the WTO, the charge of piracy could not be made. But the coincidence of the war on drugs, war on terror or war on piracy with what are unambiguously political struggles is not accidental. These "wars" are all staged to reinforce police and military power under the guise of the public interest at exactly that moment when political struggle is gathering strength.

7 Interview with Eric Harvey: http://pitchfork.com/features/paper-trail/8913-jonathan-sterne/.

8 Jonathan Sterne, ibid.

9 Ivan Shearer, "Piracy," *Max Planck Encyclopedia of Public International Law*, October 2010, 1.

10 Ibid.

11 Eric Schiff, *Industrialization without National Patents: The Netherlands, 1869–1912; Switzerland, 1850–1907* (Princeton Legacy Library, 1971).

12 These three cases are notorious and have been explored in countless articles and essays. For ease of reference, three web links are given here: www.theguardian.com/uk/2012/nov/28/wikipedia-extradiction-law-review-odwyer; www.stuff.co.nz/national/7540788o/kim-dotcom-loses-extradition-case-files-immediate-appeal; http://arstechnica.com/business/2010/12/watch-out-big-content-rapidshare-has-hired-a-lobbying-firm/.

13 The Stop Online Piracy Act, the Protect Intellectual Property Act, the Anti-Counterfeiting Trade Agreement.

14 www.theguardian.com/media/2013/ nov/13/wikileaks-trans-pacific-partnership-chapter-secret?CMP=fb_us.

15 Stanley Cohen, *Folk Devils and Moral Panics* (Paladin, 1973).

16 G. Narasimha Raghavan, 16 March 2008, www.mainstreamweekly.net/ article585.html.

17 Philip, "What Is a Technological Author?" 205–206. Quoted material: Nitin Govil, "War in the Age of Pirate Reproduction," *Sarai Reader* 4 (2004), at www.sarai.net/journal/reader4.html.

18 Johns, *Piracy*, 499–500.

19 Havocscope Global Black Market Information, www.havocscope.com/.

20 Bruce Larkin, "Degraded Images, Distorted Sounds: Nigerian Video and the Infrastructure of Piracy," *Public Culture* 16, no. 2 (2004): 298.

21 Ibid., 314.

22 Philip, "What Is a Technological Author?" 240–241.

23 A prime example is the following: "To define and punish Piracies and Felonies committed on the high Seas, and Offenses against the Law of Nations" (Article 1, Section 8, clause 10 of the US Constitution). Interestingly, this follows almost immediately after the famous clause regarding copyright and patent, Article 1, Section 8, clause 8.

24 Peter Linebaugh and Markus Rediker, *The Many-Headed Hydra* (Beacon Press, 2000), 327.

25 The term "occupancy" has special importance given its use by, among others, Grotius in his formulation of the *Mare Liberum* (Freedom of the Seas) argument. Grotius argued that the sea, like air, could not be occupied by anyone and therefore could not be claimed by any nation as its exclusive domain. See: Ellen Meiksins Wood, *Liberty and Property* (Verso, 2012), 124.

26 www.spiegel.de/international/ germany/hamburg-court-hands-down-somali-pirate-sentences-a-862350.html.

27 Najad Abdullahi, "Toxic Waste behind Somali Piracy", originally published October 11, 2008, now available at: www. informationclearinghouse.info/ article22428.htm.

28 http://en.wikipedia.org/wiki/ Piracy_in_Somalia#Waste_dumping.

29 Johann Hari, "You Are Being Lied to about Pirates," *The Independent*, January 5, 2009.

30 Paul Salopek, "Off the Lawless Coast of Somalia, Questions of Who Is Pirating Who," *Chicago Tribune*, October 10, 2008.

31 http://oceansbeyondpiracy.org/ publications/somali-perspectives-piracy-and-illegal-fishing.

32 Johns, *Piracy*, 508.

33 Slavoj Žižek, *First As Tragedy, Then As Farce* (Verso, 2009), 90–91.

34 Ibid., 90–91.

35 See: https://sci-hub.ac/.

36 See: https://torrentfreak. com/elsevier-cracks-down-on-pirated-scientific-articles-150609/; also see: https://en.wikipedia.org/wiki/Sci-Hub.

37 https://torrentfreak.com/sci-hub-tears-down-academias-illegal-copyright-paywalls-150627/.

13 | SUMMARY AND CONCLUDING REMARKS

Mat Callahan and Jim Rogers

A core preoccupation of this book is to think the "unthinkable" – that intellectual property rights regimes do not serve the public interest, and do not provide the best, let alone the only frameworks for compensating artistic or scientific endeavor.

What is at the heart of this problem, and what has driven this book project, is that people *seem* simply unwilling to think about such alternatives. Here, one of the current authors argues this from experience. For example, in June 2014 Mat Callahan participated in a panel at the Left Forum conference in New York on this subject, and ostensibly most of the people there were leftists. Yet, the same division that we see in society at large was right there. On one side were proponents of the open source movement, people who enthusiastically advocate freedom of access (such as the Pirate Party and others). On the other, were journalists and musicians expressing serious concerns about how they were going to survive. This perfectly characterizes the polarization that has happened and that fails to realize the scope of possibilities that can exist for the management and administration of creative and scientific resources, and a related system of reward or compensation. This is, in reality, a divide and conquer strategy, and who wins? The major copyright owners! Those same corporate intermediaries that have grown to dominate, for example, the music and broader media industries over the decades and who continue to enjoy an oligopolistic stranglehold on these domains.

So, this book first and foremost offers scrutiny and analysis of intellectual property in its various forms and guises. Drawing upon a range of case studies from around the globe, the preceding chapters have each critiqued aspects of copyright, trademark and patent in specific ways. All of the chapters have one obvious trait in common – that each of them in turn reject and challenge what has become conventional, common-sense thinking around the efficacy of intellectual property rights in terms of incentivizing the generation of knowledge and culture and producing a greater social good.

Moreover, as we have seen, some authors have pushed far beyond the domain of critique to offer solid suggestions for radical and innovative reforms, alternatives to orthodox IP regimes, pointing to potentials and opportunities arising from the repudiation of such conventional systems in favor of approaches to the management and administration of resources that prioritize the welfare of the many over profits of the few. These proposals present themselves as valid and workable alternatives to the market-based economy (or, in some cases, modifications of it) in creative works that copyright, trademark and patent law enables. Such alternatives involve the public interest, which militates against and is more important than any concept of the individual author, inventor, composer or artist, or, indeed, the individual right.

Here, we summarize those key alternatives advanced in the course of the book which, in some instances, call for radical reform of the intellectual property rights system, but in others, propose an outright abandoning of this system and the creating of a new paradigm.

The history of intellectual property rights must be re-written

As intellectual property rights are not generally analyzed and evaluated in a historical context, we saw Colin Darch outline the necessity for a critical historical perspective to be brought to bear on this domain. Moreover, demonstrating how those histories that do exist often have severe limitations, Darch advocates a major revision of how we understand accounts of the evolution of IPRs as to critically inform our reasoning regarding their role, function and whose interests and agendas they actually serve in contemporary society. In demonstrating how its origins are to be found in a diverse range of traditions and contexts (encompassing different religions and civilizations), he posits that intellectual property cannot be considered as a coherent concept. He stresses the urgency for a plurality of perspectives and experiences to be acknowledged and considered, extending far beyond the confines of those economists and legal scholars whose narrow, homogenous accounts have assumed prominence as the primary shapers of how we view and comprehend the trajectory and value of such proprietary systems in our lives.

To this end, the work is already underway with, as Darch outlines, studies and accounts emerging across a range of different disciplines which combine to offer a more nuanced critique that acknowledges the complexities of the IPR sphere. This includes work which engages with "changing and contested theories of knowledge at various historical conjunctures; the emergence of the author as creator; a growing understanding of the collective nature of inspiration and invention; the impact of technologies of production and reproduction; and the significance of systems of distribution."

Traditional knowledge must be safeguarded

Models for the preservation of traditional knowledge informed Josef Brinckmann's intervention. Drawing upon specific state initiatives from Peru (the National Commission Against Biopiracy) and India (Traditional Knowledge Digital Library) designed to protect traditional knowledge fundamental to health and food security, Brinckmann advances the case for keeping such traditional knowledge outside the IP system. Such initiatives present particular types of property protection regimes that differ fundamentally from the orthodox Western conception of individual property ownership.

In Peru, a combination of governmental bodies, NGOs, research and business institutions constitute the NCAB which acts as an advisory body to safeguard the Peruvian state against biopiracy. Since 2002, the Peruvian National Institute for the Defense of Free Competition and Protection of Intellectual Property (INDECOPI) manages and administers a registry for the preservation of collective knowledge regarding biodiversity. Brinckmann explains how exploitation of this knowledge by corporate interests is protected against by law (Peruvian Law No. 27811) in that it cannot be used without the "informed consent" of indigenous groups, and provisions are made for such groups to license the rights to their knowledge in return for set minimum compensation.

Since 2001, a similar registry – this time for medicines and health care – has existed in India under the aegis of the TKDL.

A tiered approach to copyright is fundamental to enhancing education

Proposals and ideas associated with the Access to Knowledge movement formed the focus of Caroline B. Ncube's contribution.

For her, the "foundation premise" is thus: "[H]ow can copyright law be crafted to be supportive of state obligations to respect, protect and fulfill the right to education?" In her overview and critique of developments and initiatives advanced by the A2K movement, Ncube's suggestions for change come in the form of a radical restructuring of the existing copyright order into a tiered system, which, in the case at hand, would prioritize educational materials relevant to basic education.

Her approach is informed by a critical and comprehensive evaluation of a range of existing studies and recommendations, and Ncube proceeds to outline suggestions for tiered systems, and existing examples that illustrate such tiers. On one hand she points to specific instances of current "tailored copyright" in the United States.[1] More pertinently, she outlines how Skladany's two-tier proposal would establish a system whereby a person could procure non-renewable protection for a particular work for a period of between ten-to-twenty years; or alternatively for a period of one year, renewable indefinitely upon the payment of renewal fees provided the work achieves a set minimum revenue threshold.[2] While such developments would require the fundamental reconfiguring of the Berne Convention (or abandoning it entirely), this would result in numerous advantages and payoffs for society at large. Crucially, both tiers would result in a significant shortening of copyright protections as currently guaranteed under Berne thus allowing works to pass more quickly into the public domain and, it would eliminate orphan works (thus enhancing access to materials for schools that cannot currently avail of orphan works licensing schemes).

Moreover, Ncube flags the disparity that exists between current copyright law and widely established user norms and practices, where activities that constitute copyright infringement in many territories are commonly deemed to be morally and socially acceptable. Ncube also puts forward reasons as to why the evolution of tiered copyright protection carries benefits for producers of content/works. She points to the failure of existing copyright law to recognize and respect the interests and motivations of a "creator" in producing a work. As it stands, Berne Convention rules apply to all works, even where no reward or protection is sought by the creator.

A world without copyright promises new possibilities for music and the arts

As the evidence presented by Jim Rogers demonstrates, the business of music has, over recent decades, increasingly centered on the exploitation of intellectual property rights (primarily copyright, but also trademark) in a proliferating range of contexts. As his studies illustrate, while developments in the realm of digital technologies are commonly held to have produced severe adverse effects on the fortunes of the music sector by rendering copyright unenforceable, its role and value has never been more relevant, enabling the industry's biggest actors to sustain themselves through times of great technological change as well as a period of global economic turmoil. Copyright remains widely accepted as the primary (or even only) system of reward for musical creativity and innovation. Considering the concentration of power across the music industry, and the apparent polarization of wealth that sees a tiny minority of artists and rights owners account for the bulk of royalties from recording rights and performing rights alike, Mat Callahan advanced a more equitable system for rewarding creativity.

Here, we saw him outline the fundamental reasons why copyright is unfair. It creates an artificial category – "the author" – that separates the individual writer of a work from all of the people to whom they are indebted, including not only their teachers and the people who inspired them musically, but their audiences, their fellow musicians and other parties (engineers and instrument builders, for example) who help shape the creative process. As such, copyright does not *allow* credit to be given to all the sources of an actual musical composition, in some cases even preventing credit from being given to the actual author, if that author is not the copyright's owner. Indeed, in theory and practice, copyright law proves that credit and ownership are not equivalent. Rather, they are contradictory. But if credit and ownership are *disassociated*, credit being no more than the honest recognition of the contributions made to creative processes, it would undermine the basis for the endless proliferation of lawsuits while freeing creative people from the fear of such litigation. This would enable the satisfaction of one of the two concerns foremost in most music-maker's minds: appropriate credit. The second is just compensation.

Imagine a scenario where musicians and composers were not compensated from the sale or licensing of recordings, but rather from public funds. Such a system could be managed and administered via such organizations as the current performing rights societies (for example, SUISA or other non-profit royalty collection societies), or by juries composed of music-makers themselves, along with educators and even representatives of the general public. Such a combination of skill, judgement and socially-determined priorities would be far better than "markets" for determining the quality or importance of a musical work or music as an ongoing social need. If, moreover, music (or art in general) is viewed, not as a disposable commodity, but as a necessary nutrient for people and society, it would be accorded support similar to health care or education.

Such an approach to rewarding musical creativity could ensure that artists are compensated in amounts similar to those of their audiences. For example, if an artist's audience is made up of teachers, health-care providers, manual workers, farmers, etc., a rough average of combined incomes can be calculated to determine the level at which artists should be compensated when their work meets a particular set of criteria. This set of criteria could in turn be established on the basis of current schemes in operation in most European countries for the dissemination of budgets/grants in the realms of education, the arts and sciences. To a limited extent, these structures already exist, but in most countries apply only to classical music and, in some cases, jazz.

Such structures could, if they were applied in the same manner as public libraries, public schools and those other institutions that are funded by the public through taxpayers' money be applied and dispersed to musicians and composers based on their labor and the resulting works. Such a system would deliver a much more equitable solution to the issue of reimbursing music-makers instead of a very small number getting the lion's share of all pots.

Proposals for a more equitable balancing of the public good against private interests

In detailing and critiquing the roles and agendas of opposition movements across the domains of free software and open source, a key contribution of Paul McKimmy's chapter in the current volume is that it very clearly captures and articulates the perspectives of a growing number of people in the Global North, in the high-tech domain and within European–North American jurisprudence.

Ultimately, the author stresses the need for these movements to form sites of resistance and voices of dissent against the prevailing intellectual property industry lobby groups who hold sway in the corridors of political power. McKimmy ultimately proposes a series of six legislative actions aimed primarily at a more equitable balancing of the public good against private interests.

First, he advocates the enactment of Aaron's Law – i.e. revising the Computer Fraud and Abuse Act, as to address the issues of disproportionate penalties, ambiguous terminology and prosecutorial overreach. Second, McKimmy calls for a significant rethinking of campaign finance and other "money-in-politics" issues as to allow for a plurality of voices to be heard at the political table and restrict the scope of corporate power to be a dominant influence on policy-making circles. Third, he promotes reform in terms of copyright duration as to prevent copyright owners "locking it away for generations." Fourth, McKimmy advocates legal protections for developers against prosecution for patent violation by legislating that developing, distributing or running a program on generally used computing hardware does not constitute patent infringement. Fifth, he calls for the abolition of the Digital Millennium Copyright Act and the de-criminalization of Digital Rights Management (DRM circumvention). Sixth, McKimmy puts forward a proposal for open source software mandates for publicly funded institutions. As he indicates, such efforts already exist, but require both public support and protection from corporate lobbies.

A new WIPO order

While, on one level, critiquing the effects of the World Intellectual Property Organization (WIPO) on the developing world, we saw Debora Halbert offer an ambitious and optimistic vision of what the WIPO could be if it engaged with its sister United Nations institutions (such as UNESCO, WHO, UNIDO, UNCTAD). Such a re-working of WIPO would enable a fairer, more democratic shaping of the institution in the interests of its broader membership as opposed to affording primacy to the dominant industrial states.

At the core of this approach is the argument that intellectual property should be fundamentally coupled with (and its advancement dependent upon) "the goals of development and technology transfer." In short, Halbert unpacks how WIPO could work in conjunction with those other UN agencies to provide clearinghouses for copyrights and patents across a diverse spectrum of realms that they represent and administer to (including education, health, agriculture, engineering, etc.).

Halbert takes in turn each respective agency and illustrates how this would work in practice. For example, a WIPO–UNESCO partnership could greatly enhance access to scientific knowledge and vital educational texts for people in developing countries by virtue of the establishment of a clearinghouse for textbooks and scientific discoveries. Such a proposed partnership, Halbert argues, should prioritize open access textbooks across the range of academic disciplines, rather than foregrounding the rights of the copyright owners, so as to, in the first instance, enhance literacy levels in the developing world, and beyond that, grant it access to fundamental tools for development.

A parallel clearinghouse initiative with UNCTAD would readily allow developing nations access to agricultural technologies and knowledge fundamental to addressing issues of food security. In such an imagined environment, "the global south could leapfrog the environmentally destructive technologies of the industrial world and instead embrace new forms of energy generation, water purification, food production and more that would substantially improve the lives of those living in poverty today." Similarly, a WIPO–UNIDO collaboration could release the engineering knowledge and wisdom required to deliver, for example, the technological innovation fundamental to fostering the development of infrastructure across the breadth of social and economic spheres. Equally, a joint WIPO–WHO initiative would enable the developing world access to necessary medicines by, in the first instance, ensuring fair and equitable licensing agreements with patent-owning pharmaceutical corporations and accommodating local production and distribution of the most vital drugs.

"What if?" is the recurring question throughout. Such a potential future direction for WIPO thus envisages it as a crucial support structure designed to enhance the core performance of other UN agencies in aiding development. Such a reconfiguring of priorities away from the framing of standard international IP laws which favor the world's wealthiest trading nations would, as Halbert contends, "first work to create the conditions for development and then allow the laws that will govern IP to emerge out of the process itself."

A radical refocusing of IPR policy analyses

Blayne Haggart highlighted those underlying statutory principles that do exist, yet are the subject of constant challenge by multiple litigants. Analyzing specific legal challenges of recent years (most notably the case of Aaron Swartz, JSTOR and other scientific publishers), in essence, we have seen him argue that the very foundations of intellectual property law need to be rethought, and advance a series of possible remedies which would, necessarily, lead to the abolition or radical modification of IP law in general. These come in the form of three guiding principles that can serve to deliver a fairer, more equitable intellectual property regime.

The first guiding principle states that policy analyses of IPRs (their role and efficacy) should be informed primarily by IP law's societal effects and its implications for the generation of knowledge and culture in the future. As such, policy makers should not concern themselves with the perceived author or creator, but rather make decisions on the basis of the greatest benefit to the greatest number. As every idea grows out of existing ideas and builds on a body of existing knowledge, the argument that "creator's rights" need to be defended, cannot itself be defended.

Related to this comes Haggart's second proposed guiding principle for reform – that amending and revising IP law demands that policy makers consider that the primary beneficiaries of IP systems are not the perceived figures of the artist or author, but rather non-creative corporate intermediaries who do not share the same interests as either "creators" or the public. Other, non-market approaches to the management and administration of proprietary rights (such as the treatment afforded to "traditional knowledge" in other cultures) needs to be considered in policy circles.

Finally, Haggart's third guiding principle for devising IP reform simply emphasizes that we should not assume that IP protections provide the most beneficial approach to incentivizing and promoting creativity and the generation of knowledge. Promoting the open access model as a more efficient and encouraging approach to scientific discovery within the academy, Haggart also draws upon earlier proposals around direct public funding and tax relief as ideas that could be incorporated into systems of promotion and reward.

Concluding thoughts

The spheres of conflict selected for scrutiny in this book resonate with some of our most fundamental needs and rights as human beings. Article 25 of the *Universal Declaration of Human Rights* tells us that "Everyone has the right to a standard of living adequate for the health and well-being of himself and of his family, including food." Article 26 advances that "Everyone has the right to education. Education shall be free, at least in the elementary and fundamental stages." Article 27 states that "Everyone has the right freely to participate in the cultural life of the community, to enjoy the arts and to share in scientific advancement and its benefits."

Drawing upon scholars from a relatively broad spectrum of disciplinary fields (and from the contexts of the Global South and Global North alike), the various contributions herein ultimately combine to offer a set of distinctive alternatives to how we might approach, manage and administer resources of knowledge, culture, information as natural resources in the interest of the great majority of people. The pertinent issues have been approached from historical, philosophical, socio-economic and political angles and arising from the analysis and debate has come a call for fundamental changes rather than superficial fixes to current conceptualizations and implementation of intellectual property.

Notes

1 John Tehranian, "Infringement Nation: Copyright Reform and the Law/Norm Gap," *Utah Law Review* (2007): 537–550; Lydia Pallas Loren, "The Pope's Copyright? Aligning Incentives with Reality by Using Creative Motivation to Shape Copyright Protection," *Louisiana Law Review* 69 (2008): 1–41.

2 Martin Skladany, "Unchaining Richelieu's Monster: A Tiered Revenue-Based Copyright Regime," *Stanford Technology Law Review* 16, no. 1 (2012): 131–159.

ABOUT THE EDITORS AND CONTRIBUTORS

Editors

Mat Callahan is a musician and author. He founded seminal world-beat band Looters, the artists' collective Komotion International, and produced the revival of James Connolly's "Songs of Freedom." He's authored four books, *Sex, Death and the Angry Young Man*, *Testimony*, *The Trouble with Music* and *The Explosion of Deferred Dreams*.

Jim Rogers is a lecturer in communications at the School of Communications, Dublin City University, Ireland. His research interests center on the political economy of the media. His first book, *The Death and Life of the Music Industry in the Digital Age*, was published in 2013. Beyond this, his research has been published in a host of international peer-review journals and various edited collections.

Contributors

Josef A. Brinckmann is a research fellow at Traditional Medicinals (Sebastopol), and has also served as an international consultant for medicinal plants at ITC/UNCTAD/WTO (Geneva) 2001–2016. An elected member of the USP Dietary Supplements and Herbal Medicines Expert Committee, he is also an advisory board member at the American Botanical Council, member of the IUCN Species Survival Commission Medicinal Plant Specialist Group, and FairWild Foundation board member.

Colin Darch retired in 2013 after a 46-year career as a librarian, documentalist, journalist and academic, working in universities and research institutes in Ethiopia, Tanzania, Mozambique, Zimbabwe, Brazil and South Africa. He has a PhD in economic and social analysis from the University of Bradford, and lives in Cape Town.

Blayne Haggart is associate professor of political science at Brock University in St Catharines, Ontario, Canada. He holds a PhD in political science from Carleton University in Ottawa, Ontario. His book,

Copyfight: The Global Politics of Digital Copyright Reform, was published in 2014.

Debora J. Halbert is the associate vice chancellor for academic affairs and professor of political science at the University of Hawai'i at Mānoa. She is the author of *Intellectual Property in the Information Age: The Politics of Expanding Rights* (1999), *Resisting Intellectual Property* (2005) and *The State of Copyright* (2014).

Bob Jolliffe is a computer programmer, engineer, teacher and learner who lives in Dublin, Ireland. He works for the global Health Information Systems Project based in the University of Oslo, promoting health information systems strengthening across the world using free open source software (FOSS) and open standards. In South Africa he was actively involved in the formulation and implementation of government FOSS policy.

Paul McKimmy is a faculty member in the University of Hawai'i-Mānoa department of Learning Design and Technology. As director of technology and distance programs for the College of Education, he herds the cats in instructional support, technical services and distance learning design teams. He gets excited about learning technical skills, leveraging open source software and maintaining a mild caffeine buzz.

Caroline B. Ncube is a professor in the Faculty of Law at the University of Cape Town. She researches and writes in intellectual property law with a special interest in copyright law from a public interest perspective.

Michael Perelman is a professor of economics at California State University, Chico. He is the author of 21 books, most recently, *Railroading Economics* and *The Invisible Handcuffs*.

INDEX

Wellington's Waterloo Allies